Envelopes

Bankers and pockets

Bankers have the flap on the long edge.
Pockets have the flap on the short edge.
Bankers can be filled mechanically.

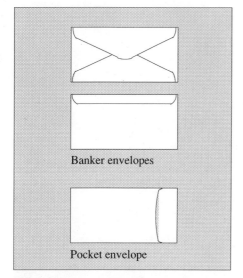

Banker envelopes

Pocket envelope

Window and aperture envelopes

The document inside is folded (usually
with the help of fold marks) so that the
address can be read through the window. The address is keyed within a
guide frame so that it is correctly
positioned.

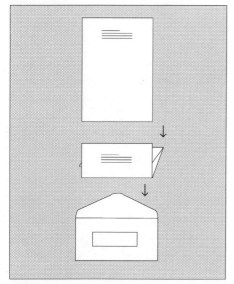

Address labels

Address labels are used for large
numbers of envelopes or when the
envelopes are too large for the printer
or typewriter.

ISO envelopes

The International Organization for
Standardization (ISO) recommends two
ranges of envelopes:
- C – designed for ISO A size enclosures
- B – designed for C range envelopes
  with their enclosures.
  The ISO also recommends DL and
  B6/C4 envelopes.

The illustration below shows the
relationship between A size paper and
ISO-recommended DL and B6/C4
envelopes.

Imperial envelopes

'Imperial' envelopes are still in use in
some offices. The most popular sizes
are 3 $\frac{1}{2}$" $\times$ 5 $\frac{3}{4}$" (90 $\times$ 145 mm) and
4" $\times$ 9" (100 $\times$ 230 mm).

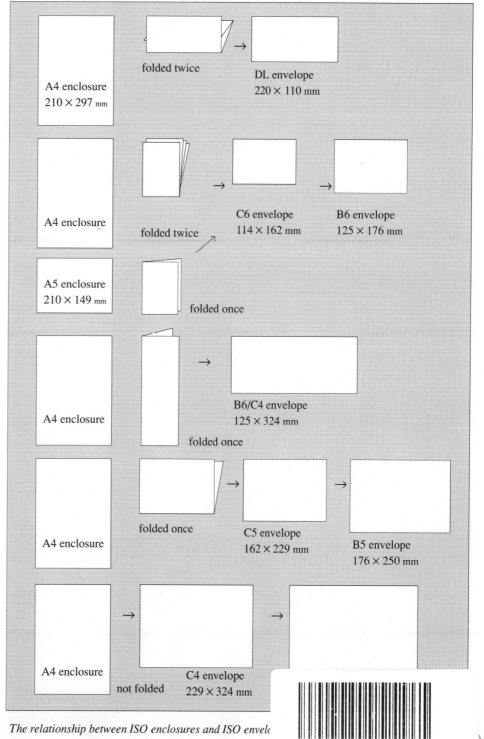

The relationship between ISO enclosures and ISO envel[...]

GW00598036

KDP

Keyboarding and Document Production

Adapted by

| ALAN WHITCOMB |

| BARBARA BOWEN |

Acknowledgments

The publisher wishes to thank the many teachers who reviewed the manuscripts
and made helpful comments and suggestions: in particular

- Mrs Judith Barnes of Hornsby TAFE, New South Wales, and others who trialled Module 1
- Mrs Joan Logan of Royal Melbourne Institute of Technology for review of and comments on parts of the book
- Lorraine Martin Business College, Brisbane, for advice on Module 1
- Mrs Dorothy Jackson of Holmesglen College of TAFE, Melbourne, for her comments.

They would also like to thank

- the Accident Compensation Commission, Wellington, New Zealand for permission to draw on material for exercises illustrated in Unit 1.1
- Verbatim Australia Pty Ltd for photographs used for exercises illustrated in Unit 1.1
- Canon Australia Pty Ltd and Olivetti Australia Pty Ltd for manuals and photographs supplied
- IBM Australia for sales brochures supplied
- the Anti-Cancer Council of Australia and the Environment Protection Authority, Victoria for material used in exercises throughout the book
- the Energy Information Centre for permission to use material from brochures for several passages in Appendix 1.

First published as *Keyboarding and Document Production Full Course* by Thomas Nelson Australia 1990.

First UK edition published in 1993 by:
Stanley Thornes (Publishers) Ltd
Old Station Drive
Leckhampton
CHELTENHAM
GL53 ODN
England

A catalogue record for this book is available from the British Library
ISBN 0 7487 1523 1

Printed and bound by Wing King Tong, Hong Kong

For the teacher

Keyboarding and Document Production is of a comprehensive course in keyboarding, formatting and document processing that will meet the needs of students in the 1990s.

Although much emphasis is given to word processing in *KDP*, a student using an electronic typewriter will not be disadvantaged. In fact the text recognises that a competent keyboard operator should be able to use both a word processor and an electronic typewriter.

KDP is comprehensive and authoritative. Teachers will find it a useful reference and a reliable guide to current practice, as well as an invaluable teaching resource.

Among its many features are:

- its rational but flexible structure
- its thorough approach to all aspects of the science of keyboarding and document production
- its unique methodology and clear teaching style
- the provision of exercises to extend the more able student
- the quality and quantity of content
- the integration of word processing into the production process.

Structure

For the most part the course is not lesson planned; apart from *Module 1: The keyboard*, the teacher need not work through the units in the order in which they appear. However, many teachers will find that the order of presentation suits their course and will choose, more or less, to follow the sequence given. If they do this, their students will not encounter techniques they have not been taught and there will be systematic reinforcement as the book progresses.

The book is programmed. Each of the ten modules presents a related series of topics, graded in difficulty, and each unit within a module concentrates on a single topic.

Business correspondence, the most important aspect of keyboarding and document processing, is covered in two stages. Level 1 (Module 4) is introduced after the keyboard, basic formatting, punctuation and style. Module 4 teaches the fully blocked style with open punctuation. Level 2 (Module 8) advances the student to the full range of enumeration styles within letters and memoranda (already introduced in Module 7) and to continuation pages. The semi-blocked style with closed punctuation is deferred to the end of Module 8, allowing teachers to present and *fully reinforce* the most widely accepted style before exposing students to a less popular alternative.

Other modules are devoted to tabular work, and travel and business forms.

Appendices 1 and 2 comprise 'straight copy' passages and production test material.

Methodology

KDP presents all aspects of document production from elementary to intermediate. Techniques are taught step by step. The course emphasises current practice but recognises that there is sometimes more than one way to format a job.

Introduction of alphabetic keys:

Apart from the home keys, which appear in the first keyboard unit, the alphabetic keys are introduced according to their frequency in the English language. Thus words, phrases and sentences can be included early.

In determining the keyboard sequence, following the West* principle, there has been a conscious effort to avoid repetitive letter combinations. Instead, the student is immediately exposed to all the common digraphs that can be taught at a particular stage. For example, *n*, the most common consonant in English, is systematically paired with every key taught so far. Subsequent drills include a wide range of words containing *n*. So far as possible, words are not repeated.

Introduction of numeric keys:

The teacher is given the choice of teaching the alphabetic and numeric keys concurrently or separately.

Introduction of new techniques:

The approach to teaching a new technique is to follow up a simple, brief explanation of the theory with an exercise that gives the student as much guidance as possible on how to tackle the job. The 'copy' is not usually an exact representation of the finished document but a clear draft accompanied by a reduced-size module for the student to emulate. Short of providing the actual finished document to copy (which in effect offers only copy typing), the student is given maximum help on such introductory exercises. Similar jobs follow, unaccompanied by models and graded in difficulty. They are designed to encourage student initiative.

Proofreading and communication skills:

A keyboard operator needs to have good communication and proofreading skills. Tasks emphasising these skills appear throughout.

Quality and quantity of content:

To a large extent a business is judged by its correspondence. Every letter or report it sends is an advertisement. The importance of a high standard of document production cannot therefore be over-stressed.

KDP sets a high standard. It offers examples of well-produced correspondence and other document and provides exercises that emphasise the keyboard operator's role in correcting spelling, punctuation and stylistic errors to arrive at a 'usable document'. The content of exercises is as authentic as can be managed in a textbook and no effort has been spared to offer variety and interest.

*L J West, Acquisition of Typewriting Skills, 2nd edn, Macmillan 1983

Contents

Reference section
For the teacher ... iii
Acknowledgements ... ii

Envelopes ... Facing inside front cover
Glossary of computer and word processor terms ... vi
List of common long-hand abbreviations ... viii
Formal methods of address ... ix
Overseas address styles ... x

Module 1 The keyboard
Unit 1.1 Preparing to key ... 1
Unit 1.2 A S D F J K L; ... 9
Unit 1.3 E N 3 ... 10
Checkpoint A Margins and paper sizes ... 11
Unit 1.4 T I 5 8 ... 12
Unit 1.5 R H 4 ... 13
Unit 1.6 Shift keys Full stop ... 14
Checkpoint B Vertical centring ... 15
Unit 1.7 O C 9 ... 16
Checkpoint C Proofreading Speed tests ... 17
Unit 1.8 U G 7 ... 18
Unit 1.9 W M 2 ... 19
Checkpoint D Proofreading marks 1 Word processing functions ... 20
Unit 1.10 B Y 6 ... 21
Unit 1.11 P V 0 ... 22
Checkpoint E Proofreading marks 2 Handwritten copy ... 23
Unit 1.12 Q Comma , ... 25
Unit 1.13 X Colon Shift lock ... 26
Unit 1.14 Z Question mark ... 27
Checkpoint F Proofreading marks 3 ... 28
Unit 1.15 Hyphen/dash Backspace and underscore Exclamation mark ... 29
Unit 1.16 Quotation marks Apostrophe ... 30
Checkpoint G Proofreading marks 4 Italic and bold type ... 31
Unit 1.17 Numeric keys 3 5 8 4 ... 33
Unit 1.18 Numeric keys 9 7 2 6 ... 34
Unit 1.19 Numeric keys 0 1 ... 35
Unit 1.20 Numeric keypad ... 36
Unit 1.21 Parenthese Solidus (slash or stroke) Dollar sign Pound sign ... 37
Unit 1.22 Ampersand Asterisk 'At' sign Per cent sign ... 38
Unit 1.23 Mathematical symbols ... 39
Unit 1.24 Speed tests ... 40

Module 2 Formatting 1 Basic principles
Unit 2.1 Tab keys Formatting The tabulator Blocked and indented paragraphs ... 43
Unit 2.2 Planning and setting margins Planning margins Paper sizes and type pitch Calculating equal left and right margins Setting margins Automatic return Word division at line endings Margin release key Justified and unjustified right margin Splitting paragraphs ... 47
Unit 2.3 Word division When to use word division Word division with automatic return Hyphens: hard and soft Hard space Rules for word division ... 50
Unit 2.4 Centring between margins Automatic centring Centring manually ... 53

Module 3 Punctuation and style
Unit 3.1 Punctuation 1 Full stop Ellipsis Question mark Exclamation mark ... 55
Unit 3.2 Punctuation 2 Comma Semicolon Colon ... 57
Unit 3.3 Punctuation 3 Apostrophe Underscoring Quotation marks ... 59
Unit 3.4 Punctuation 4 Hyphen Dash Parentheses Square brackets Solidus ... 61
Unit 3.5 Style 1 Figures or words? Thousands marker Decimal point BC and AD Figure spans Dates Street numbers Per cent ... 63
Unit 3.6 Style 2 Currency Metric measurements Hours, minutes and seconds ... 65
Unit 3.7 Style 3 Abbreviations Contractions Plurals ... 67
Unit 3.8 Style 4 Capital letters ... 69
Unit 3.9 Style 5 Roman numerals ... 71
Unit 3.10 Style 6 Methods of address ... 73

Module 4 Business correspondence 1
Unit 4.1 Memoranda 1 Standard memoranda on plain paper Features of a blocked memorandum with open punctuation ... 75
Unit 4.2 Memoranda 2 Standard memoranda on headed paper ... 77
Unit 4.3 Addressing envelopes, labels and cards Standard address format How to key the address Attention line 'Personal' and 'confidential' ... 79
Unit 4.4 Overseas addresses ... 81
Unit 4.5 Business letters 1 Personal business letters Fully blocked style with open punctuation Features of a personal business letter Selecting line length ... 82
Unit 4.6 Business letters 2 Simple business letter Presenting letters for signature Features of a simple business letter Mail merge ... 85
Unit 4.7 Business letters 3 Subject heading ... 88
Unit 4.8 Business letters 4 Attention line ... 90
Unit 4.9 Business letters 5 Confidential/personal notation Postscript ... 92
Unit 4.10 Business letters 6 Enclosure notation ... 94
Unit 4.11 Carbon copies No carbon required (NCR) paper ... 96
Unit 4.12 Business letters 7 Hard copies Electronic filing systems Disclosed copy notation Blind copy notation Highlighting/ticking copy notations Envelopes for copies of letters ... 97

Module 5 Formatting 2 Paragraphs and headings
Unit 5.1 Block indented paragraphs ... 100
Unit 5.2 Hanging paragraphs ... 102
Unit 5.3 Side (shoulder) Paragraph headings ... 104
Unit 5.4 Marginal headings at left ... 106
Unit 5.5 Numeric enumeration ... 108
Unit 5.6 Sub-enumeration ... 110
Unit 5.7 Decimal enumeration ... 112

Module 6 Formatting 3 Spaced capitals, block centring, margin alignment, leader dots
Unit 6.1 Spaced capitals ... 114
Unit 6.2 Block centring ... 116
Unit 6.3 Right margin alignment (justification) ... 118
Unit 6.4 Leader dots ... 120

Module 7 Formatting 4 Tabular work
Unit 7.1 Formatting columns ... 123
Unit 7.2 Blocking headings over columns ... 125
Unit 7.3 Centring column headings over columns ... 126
Unit 7.4 Centring columns below column headings ... 128

Unit 7.5 More complex tables – centring columns and
   column headings of varying lengths   129
Unit 7.6 Formatting columns within existing margins
   (blocked paragraphs)   130
Unit 7.7 Multiple-line column headings   131
Unit 7.8 Figures in columns Thousands marker
   Decimal points/decimal tab Numeric punctuation   132
Unit 7.9 Money columns   133
Unit 7.10 Money columns with totals Double underscoring   134
Unit 7.11 Tables with horizontal rules   135
Unit 7.12 Ruled tables with open sides Footnotes   136
Unit 7.13 Ruled tables with closed sides (boxed tables)   138
Unit 7.14 Tables with sub-divided column headings   140
Unit 7.15 Tables with vertical column headings   142

Module 8 Business correspondence 2
Unit 8.1 Business letters 8 Numeric enumeration   144
Unit 8.2 Business letters 9 Sub-enumeration
   Continuation page   146
Unit 8.3 Memoranda 3 Decimal enumeration   147
Unit 8.4 Business letters 10 Circular letter with tear-off
   slip   150

Unit 8.5 Business letters 11 Standard letters   151
Unit 8.6 Business letters 12 Semi-blocked style
   with closed punctuation   154

Module 9 Business forms
Unit 9.1 Purchase orders   156
Unit 9.2 Invoices   158
Unit 9.3 Keying on forms   160
Unit 9.4 Form design   161

Module 10 Meeting and travel documents
Unit 10.1 Notice of meeting   163
Unit 10.2 Agenda   164
Unit 10.3 Minutes   166
Unit 10.4 Itinerary   168

Appendix 1 Speed tests   171
Level 1   172
Level 2   177
Level 3   181

Appendix 2 Production assignments   189
Blank stationery   196

Reference

Glossary of computer and word processor terms

Access The process of obtaining data from or placing data into storage in a computer

Archive To store files on tape or floppy disk

Author The person originating a document (also *originator*)

Back-up To store a duplicate copy separately as a safeguard

Bi-directional printing The printing of lines from both left to right and right to left

Bit The smallest unit of information used with a computer. It can have two values, eg 'true' and 'false' or 1 and 0

Boot To put a computer into operation

Buffer Memory space in a printer that stores characters for printing

Byte A group of bits. It is the most common unit of computer storage, equivalent to one character (see **Kilobyte, Megabyte** and **Memory**)

Central processing unit (CPU) The computer itself – it coordinates the entire system by fetching, decoding and executing instructions

Character string A group of characters or words that may be used in the search and replace function (also *string*)

Command An instruction to the system to carry out a specific function, eg centring or bolding

Control space See **Hard space**

CPU See **Central processing unit**

Crash Malfunction in a system causing loss of data or memory

Cursor A movable marker on a video display screen that indicates the point at which text will be entered or changed

Cut and paste To remove material from text and insert it somewhere else

Daisy-wheel printer A printer where the characters are positioned on the ends of spokes attached to a wheel hub. Produces letter-quality print-out.

Data Facts and figures. Not to be confused with information

Data base An organised body of data that is systematically recorded, retrieved and updated

Dedicated Limited to one set of functions or operations

Default options The present values that control a computer program's operation and that prevail unless changed by the user

Desktop publishing system (DTP) A system dedicated to producing printouts of a standard fit to be published. It incorporates a graphics program

Dictionary See **Spell check**

Directory A list of files stored in memory or on disk. It usually gives details of each file such as date created, amount of space used and space left on disk (also *index*)

Disk A flat, circular medium coated to accept magnetic storage of information. It may either be fixed or removable. A hard disk (or *fixed disk*) is generally built into the computer. It can hold more information than a floppy disk. A floppy disk (or *diskette*) is thin and flexible and can be inserted or removed. Floppies can be 3 5/8 5 1/4 or 8 inches in diameter.

Disk drive The electro-magnetic device that houses, spins, reads and stores information on a disk

Diskette Floppy disk

Disk operating system (DOS) Software that manages the storage and retrieval of information on disk

Document Any amount of text or data recorded as a unit with an identifying name. In WP, a file is usually a single document, a group of related documents or a portion of a long document (also *file*)

Document assembly See **Merge**

DOS See **Disk operating system**

Dot matrix printer Prints characters as clusters of small dots. The quality of the copy depends on the number of dots per square inch

Downtime The period of time when a system is not operating because of hardware or software breakdowns

DTP See **Desktop publishing**

Electronic mail Messages or documents transmitted electronically between two or more users. Supplements or replaces conventional mail or memoranda in large organisations

Erase To remove a document from memory

Facsimile (fax) A scanning device that transmits by the telephone system printed material or figures, one page at a time, for reproduction at the destination point

Field Part of a record containing specific information. Often used in the generation of standard/form letters

File See **Document**, also **Save**

Find See **Search (and replace)**

Footer or **Footing** Reference line at the bottom of each page in a document

Forced See **Hard**

Format To prepare a floppy disk for use in a particular system (also *initialise*)

Format line See **Ruler**

Form feeder A mechanism that feeds stacks of single-sheet paper into a printer

Forms tractor A mechanism with cogged wheels that feeds perforated paper into a printer (also *tractor feed*)

Global search (and replace) The same as **Search (and replace)**, except the function finds (and replaces) all occurrences throughout the document

Glossary Memory space set aside, usually on a disk, for words, phrases or format instructions that are used frequently (also *standard paragraphs*)

Hard Describes functions such as spaces or hyphens where word spaces or hyphens must be printed out in a particular form specified by the operator (also *code, command, control, forced, protected,* or *required*)

Hard copy Paper copy of a document or file (also *printout or output*)

Hard disk See **Disk**

Hard hyphen A hyphen required to appear in a printout, regardless of whether it occurs at the end of a line (also *code, command, control, protected* or *required hyphen*)

Hard page break A page break determined by the operator and not inserted automatically (also *forced or required page break*)

Hard space A word space inserted so that certain groups of words or numbers, such as dates, are not automatically broken at the end of a line (also *code, command, control, non-break, protected or required space*)

Hardware The electro-mechanical components of a computer

Header Reference line at the top of each page in a document

Highlight Used in WP to indicate a change in text output appearance, eg bolding

Hot zone The last few character spaces in a line where the line break is automatically determined when a word space or a hyphen occurs (also *H-zone, soft zone, zone width*)

Housekeeping Periodically going through the contents of disks, deleting files that are no longer needed

H-zone See **Hot zone**

Index See **Directory**

Information line See **Status line**

Initialise See **Format**

Input To enter data into a system

Insert To add new text or data to an existing file

Integrated software The incorporation of software such as WP, spreadsheets, data bases and graphics

Interface To connect two or more systems or devices by means of a cable, modem, chips etc

Justify To align left, right or both margins in text

K, KB or Kbyte See **Kilobyte**

Kilobyte See **Byte, Megabyte** and **Memory**. Refers to the memory capability of a computer – 1024 bytes, which is frequently rounded to 1000 bytes. Abbreviated to K, KB or KByte

Laser printer See **Letter-quality printer**. A high-resolution dot matrix printer which produces print-quality output

Letter-quality printer See **Daisy-wheel printer** and **Laser printer**. Produces printing that is indistinguishable from that typed on an electronic typewriter

Library See **Spell Check**

M, MB or MByte See **Megabyte**

Mainframe computer See **Microcomputer** and **Minicomputer**. A category for the largest computers

Marker A non-printing character indicating new lines, paragraphs, tabs, text to be copied, moved or deleted etc

Megabyte See **Byte, Kilobyte** and **Memory**. A measurement of the memory capability of a computer – 1 048 576 bytes, frequently rounded to 1 000 000 bytes. Abbreviated to M, MB or MByte

Memory See **Byte**, **Kilobyte** and **Megabyte**. A storage area for information, usually on silicon chips or on disks. Memory is measured in bytes.

Menu A list of possible actions presented to the user by data or WP software

Merge To combine data from two or more sources. See **Standard paragraphs**

Microcomputer See **Mainframe computer** and **Minicomputer**. A category for the smallest computers

Minicomputer See **Mainframe computer** and **Microcomputer**. A category of computers that are smaller than mainframe computers, but larger than microcomputers

Modem A device that enables data to be transmitted between computers across telephone lines (short for modulator/demodulator)

Monitor See **Screen**

Mouse A device used to manipulate the cursor and select specific applications

Move Shift text or data from one position to another, either within a file or from file to file

Non-break space See **Hard space**

OCR See **Optical character reader**

Off-line A terminal or other component in a system not in communication with the CPU

On-line A terminal or other component in a system in communication with the CPU

Operating system Software that manages a computers resources and schedules its operations

Optical character reader (OCR) A photo-sensitive machine that scans and reproduces a printed letter, number of symbol in computer-readable form (also *scanner*)

Originator See **Author**

Output The result of a computer operation. It can be a paper printout or appear on screen

Page break A code indicating the point at which a new page will start when the document is printed

Pagination The division of a document into pages prior to printout

Panning Moving text across the screen

Password A code or set of characters that identify a user

Personal computer (PC) See **Microcomputer**

Printout See **Hard copy** and **Output**

Program A set of instructions that a computer follows. See **Software**

Prompt A message point from the system or computer program requiring some user response

Proportional spacing The spacing of characters in proportion to their width rather than making each letter occupy the same amount of space; *also* varying word spacing in a line so that text can be justified

Protected space See **Hard space**

Ragged Describes lines of text that are aligned on the left but vary on the right according to their length. Also called *unjustified*

Random access memory (RAM) Silicon chips that store and recall data in any order or sequence. The size of a WP's RAM is a measure of its power

Recall Retrieve a document or data from memory or disk (also *retrieve*)

Required space See **Hard space**

Response time The time it takes for a computer or other device to do what is asked of it

Retrieve See **Recall**

Ruler A line, usually at the top of the screen, showing left and right margins and tab stops in a document (also *format line*)

Save To transfer a document from temporary to permanent memory on disk (also *file* or *store*)

Scanner See **Optical character reader**

Screen Also called a *monitor* or *visual display unit (VDU)*

Scroll To move text up, down or horizontally on a screen

Search (and replace) The function that finds an occurrence of a particular character string and replaces it with another. See **Global search (and replace)**

Sheet feeder An attachment to a printer for holding a stack of paper, feeding it into a printer and retrieving it one sheet at a time

Soft copy Copy of information or data displayed on screen

Software See **Hardware** and **Program**. The instructions that a computer follows. Software is intangible, but it resides or is stored on something tangible, eg a silicon chip, disk etc

Soft zone See **Hot zone**

Sort To arrange information in a meaningful pattern, eg numerically or alphabetically

Spell check A software program for proofreading and verifying spelling (also *dictionary*, *library*, *spelling checker*, *spelling verification*)

Spreadsheet An electronic worksheet containing data in various columns and rows, which can perform automatic calculations

Stand–alone system A category of WPs that are self–contained and require no additional equipment

Standard paragraphs See **Glossary** and **Merge**. Paragraphs created as separate documents, stored and merged as required with other information

Status line Provides information on the format of a document or file. Usually appears at the top of the screen (also *information line*)

Stop code (SC) A code or mark indicating the point where information is to be inserted

String See **Character string**

System disk A hard or floppy disk used to store software (in particular, operating system software) rather than text

Terminal Computer equipment consisting of keyboard and screen

Tractor feed See **Forms tractor**

Variable Any piece of data that can be replaced by another if required, eg a label for a line in an address in form letters

Visual display unit (VDU) Screen or terminal

Windows The facility of dividing the screen into different sections to hold or view related information

Word wrap *See* **Wraparound**

WP Word processor, word processing

Wraparound The automatic movement of a word to the next line when it will not fit at the end of the previous line (also *word wrap*)

List of common
longhand abbreviations

Longhand abbreviations are used in handwriting, but the words must be keyed in full. Care should be taken to spell the words accurately.

accom	accommodation	info	information
a/c(s)	account(s)	mfr(s)	manufacturer(s)
ack	acknowledge	misc	miscellaneous
advert(s)	advertisement(s)	necy	necessary
altho'	although	opp(s)	opportunity/ies
amt	amount	org	organisation
appt(s)	appointment(s)	p/t	part time
approx	approximate/ly	poss	possible
asap	as soon as possible	rec	receive
bel	believes	recd	received
bus	business	recom	recommend
cat(s)	catalogue(s)	ref(s)	reference(s)
cttee(s)	committee(s)	refd	referred
co(s)	company/ies	resp	responsible
cont, contd	continued	sec(s)	secretary/ies
def	definite/ly	sep	separate
dev	develop	sh	shall
dr	dear	shd	should
encl	enclose	sig(s)	signature(s)
ex	exercise	suff	sufficient
exp(s)	expense(s)	temp	temporary
exp	experience	thro'	through
f/t	full time	wh	which
gov(s), govt(s)	government(s)	wd	would
gntee(s)	guarantee(s)	w	with
hrs	hours	wl	will
immed	immediate/ly	yr(s)	year(s)
incon	inconvenient/ence	yrs	yours

days of the week (eg Mon, Sun)
months of the year (eg Jan, Feb)
words in addresses (eg Ave, St)
complimentary closes (eg ffly)

Commonly used standard abbreviations such as NB, etc, eg, and & in company names should be retained. However, '&' when used in text must be expanded

Formal methods of address

FORM OF ADDRESS	SALUTATION
Private individuals	
Mr/Ms/Miss/Mrs/Dr M Smith	Dear Mr/Mrs/Miss/Mrs/Dr Smith
Peter Crockford, Esq	Dear Mr Crockford
Mr & Mrs J Ryan	Dear Mr & Mrs Ryan
Mr J & Mrs S Casey	Dear Mr & Mrs Casey
Mr L & Dr B Khee	Dear Mr & Dr Khee
Dr C & Mrs J Arndt	Dear Dr & Mrs Arndt
Dr T & W Webb	Dear Drs Webb
Messrs E & K Cooper	Dear Gentlemen
Mesdames H & G Steiner	Dear Ladies
Ms F & D Morgan	Dear Ladies (Ms is both singular and plural)
Misses S & R Romeo	Dear Ladies
Mr G Leek & Mr D Bell	Dear Gentlemen
Ms N Aaron & Ms S Beck	Dear Ladies
Ms T Ward & Mr G Vero	Dear Ms Ward & Mr Vero
Mr P Hicks & Mrs D Ellis	Dear Mr Hicks & Mrs Ellis
Honours	
Dame Anne Brown	Dear Dame Anne
Sir Mark Russo	Dear Sir Mark
Mrs Ellen Marks OBE	Dear Mrs Marks
Medical	
Medical practitioner:	
Dr Margaret Wells	Dear Dr Wells
Surgeon:	
Mr James Simsek FRCS	Dear Mr Simsek
Miss/Ms/Mrs Irene Wells FRCS	Dear Miss/Ms/Mrs Wells
Academic	
Chancellor of a university:	
The Chancellor of the University of...	Dear Chancellor
Vice-chancellor of a university:	
The Vice-Chancellor University of...	Dear Vice–Chancellor
Professor:	
Professor Mark/Margaret Brown	Dear Sir/Madam
Business	
Company:	
The Manager/Secretary/Accountant Smithson & Co Ltd	Dear Sir or Madam or Dear Manager/Secretary/ Accountant
Organisation/society:	
The Secretary/President etc	Dear Sir or Madam or Dear Secretary/President
Judiciary	
Chief Justice, High Court:	
The (Right) Hon Justice Lim	
Justice, High Court:	Dear Chief Justice
The (Right) Hon Justice Bell	
Chief Judge of other courts:	Dear Judge
The Hon Mr Justice Gibb (male)	
The Hon Justice Gibb (female)	Dear Chief Judge
Judge of other courts:	
The Hon Mr Justice Pitt (male)	
The Hon Justiice Pitt (female)*	Dear Judge
Chief Judge, District Court:	
His/Her Honour Judge W B Cole	Dear Chief Judge
Judge, District or County Court:	
His/Her Honour Judge A Patel	Dear Judge

FORM OF ADDRESS	SALUTATION
The Royal Family	
Her Majesty the Queen:	
The Queen's Most Excellent Majesty	May it please your Majesty
Prince:	
If a Duke, His Royal Highness the Duke of...	Sir
If not a Duke His Royal Highness Prince (Christian name)	
Princess:	
If a Duchess, Her Royal Highness the Duchess of...	Madam
If not a Duchess, Her Royal Highness the Princess (Christian name)	
Peerage	
Duke:	
His Grace the Duke of...	
Duchess:	My Lord Duke
Her Grace the Duchess of...	
Marquess:	Madam
The Most Hon the Marquess of ...	
Marchioness:	My Lord Marquess
The Most Hon the Marchioness of...	
Earl:	Madam
The Right Hon the Earl of...	
Countess:	My Lord
The Right Hon the Countess of...	
Viscount:	Madam
The Right Hon the Viscount...	
Viscountess:	My Lord
The Right Hon the Viscountess...	
Baron:	Madam
The Right Hon Lord...	
Baroness:	My Lord
The Right Hon the Baroness...	
	Madam
Baronets and Knights	
Baronet:	
Sir (Christian name and surname) Bart	Sir
Baronet's wife:	
Lady (surname)	Madam
Knight Bachelor:	
Sir (Christian name and surname)	Sir
The Church	
Archbishop:	
His Grace the Archbisop of...	
Cardinal:	My Lord Archbishop
His Eminence Cardinal... or if also an Archbishop, His eminence the Cardinal Archbishop of...	My Lord Cardinal
Bishop:	
The Right Reverend the Lord Bishop of...	
Dean:	My Lord Bishop
The Venerable Archdeacon of...	
Clergy:	Venerable Sir
The Reverend (Christian name and surname)	Dear Sir
Political	
Prime Minister:	
The Right Hon J Major MP	Dear Prime Minister
Member of Parliament:	
(Christian name and surname) MP	Dear Sir/Madam

When addressing mail to overseas countries:

- It is essential to include the postcode or zip code.
- Make sure that the address shows the country of destination.
- Because the article will be processed in the UK before it is sent overseas, it is advisable to key the name of the country of destination in English.
- This is a selection only, as it is not practicable to cover the address style of every country in the world.

Australia

MR NEIL BURNS
4 CROSS STREET
ADELAIDE SA 5000

- The last line of the address consists of the city or town, state or territory (abbreviated) and postcode in that order.
- In the example above 'SA' stands for South Australia.
- Two spaces are left before and after the first part of the postcode.

French-speaking countries

HENRI GASTON
EDITIONS AQUITAINE SA
12 RUE ST GERMAIN
F-75006 PARIS CEDEX 01
FRANCE

- It is acceptable in France not to use a title, as in the example above. Otherwise, use M (Monsieur) for a male addressee and Mme (Madam = 'Mrs') or Mlle (Made- moiselle = 'Miss') for a female addressee.
- SA represents 'Limited'.

German-speaking countries

HERR J STRAUSS
STIEGLITZ AG
JOHANNESSTRASSE 3A
A/1101 WIEN
AUSTRIA

- Use Herr ('Mr'), Frau ('Mrs') and Fraulein ('Miss').
- The German word for 'street' (Strasse) is frequently combined with the street name to form one word (eg Scherrstrasse).
- The street name precedes the street number.
- AG represents 'Limited'.

Holland (The Netherlands)

MW. A. L. DE JONG
G ACHTERBERG NV
WATERTORENWEG 180
3010 AB ROTTERDAM
THE NETHERLANDS

- Use the initials rather than the full given name of the addressee.
- Use De Heer for a male addressee and Mevrouw (Mevr. = 'Mrs') or Mejuffrouw (Mej. = 'Miss') for a female addressee. Mw. is an accepted abbreviation for both Mevrouw and Mejuffrouw. It is also acceptable to use 'Mr', 'Mrs' and 'Miss'.
- The street name precedes the street number.

Hong Kong

MR P C CHANG
CATHAY JADE CO
20/F CHRISTIE BUILDING
18 JOHNSTON ROAD
WANCHAI
HONG KONG

Italy (including Italian-speaking Switzerland)

SIG. G BORDIERI
BORDIERI SRL
VIA ANCAINI 3
I-06082 ASSISI (PG)
ITALY

- Use Signor (Sig.) for a male addressee, Signora (Sig.ra = 'Mrs') or Signorina (Sig.na = 'Miss') for a female addressee.
- The street name precedes the street number.
- The Italian word for 'Street' is Via.
- SRL means 'Limited'.

Japan

SHIZAWA YOKO
2-8-9 GOHONGI MEGURO-KU
TOKYO JAPAN

- In Japanese names the addressee's family or surname precedes the given name, although the Western practice of putting the given name first is becoming common.
- Do not use the title 'Mr', 'Ms', 'Mrs' or 'Miss'.

Singapore (Chinese)

LIEW FU LAN
CHANG YOK PTE LTD
22# 04-100 SPRING STREET
TAMPINES
SINGAPORE 1852

- In Chinese names, the addressee's family name precedes the given name.
- Do not use the title 'Mr', 'Ms', 'Mrs' or 'Miss'.
- Pte Ltd is equivalent to Limited.

Spanish-speaking countries

SENORA M FERNANDEZ
ULTRAMAR SA
JOSEFA VALCARCEL 27
E-2807 MADRID
SPAIN

- Use Senor for a male addressee and Senora or Senorita for a female addressee.
- The street name precedes the street number.
- SA means 'Limited'.

Taiwan

YANG FU LAN
LEE ELECTRONICS CO, LTD
3RD FL, 38 BEACH ROAD
TAIPEI
TAIWAN, ROC

- In Chinese names, the surname precedes the given names.
- 'ROC' stands for 'Republic of China'. Taiwan does not recognise the People's Republic of China.

Thailand

SURASAK WONGSANIT
12 SOI ARISAMPHAN 6
THANONYOTHIN 4
BANGKOK 10400
THAILAND

- In Thailand, the given name precedes the surname.
- Do not use 'Mr', 'Mrs' or 'Miss'.

United States of America

MS ELEANOR LONGUE
8392 WINCHESTER DRIVE APT H
CHARLESTON SC 29418-3926
USA

- The state name is always abbreviated. In the example above 'SC' stands for South Carolina.
- Use 'USA' or 'United States of America' rather than 'America'.

Module 1   The Keyboard

Performance goals

At the end of Module 1 you should be able to:

- operate the alphabetic, punctuation, numeric and symbol keys by 'touch'
- operate the space bar, return, shift, shift lock and back-space keys by 'touch'
- operate the basic function keys
- operate the numeric keypad (unless the keypad is deferred to a later stage of the course)
- create, store, retrieve, perform simple editing functions and print documents (if your system allows)
- distinguish between hard and floppy disks and take appropriate care of floppy disks
- use correct keyboarding techniques
- key from hard and handwritten copy with confidence, accuracy and speed
- proofread and mark corrections on hard and handwritten copy
- set left margin
- centre text horizontally and vertically on the page.

Preparing to key

1 Arranging your work station

- Clear the desk of unwanted paper, books and other materials.

- Align the front edge of the keyboard with the front edge of the desk (if appropriate to the system in use).
- Position this book at the right or left of the keyboard (whichever is more comfortable), preferably upright as shown in the diagram on this page.

2 Keyboarding posture

Keyboarding is physically as well as mentally demanding, especially in the early learning stages. You will find it is less stressful if you adopt the comfortable posture shown below.

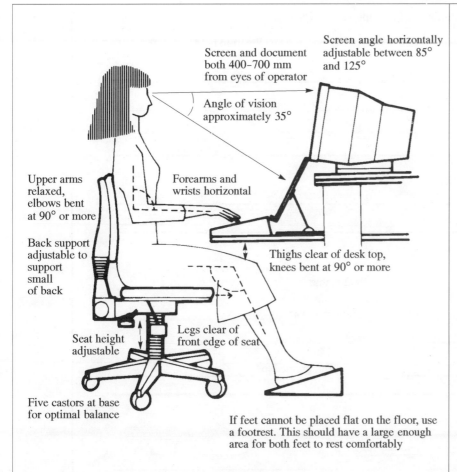

Screen and document both 400–700 mm from eyes of operator

Screen angle horizontally adjustable between 85° and 125°

Angle of vision approximately 35°

Upper arms relaxed, elbows bent at 90° or more

Forearms and wrists horizontal

Back support adjustable to support small of back

Thighs clear of desk top, knees bent at 90° or more

Legs clear of front edge of seat

Seat height adjustable

Five castors at base for optimal balance

If feet cannot be placed flat on the floor, use a footrest. This should have a large enough area for both feet to rest comfortably

Avoid twisting. Here are two alternative ways to arrange your keyboard, screen and document

Screen and keyboard directly in front of operator; document to one side for occasional reference

Document and keyboard directly in front of operator; screen to one side for occasional reference

Correct position at the keyboard

J M KENT & CO
EMPLOYMENT APPLICATION

APPLICATION FOR THE POSITION OF: _____

SURNAME: _____ GIVEN NAMES: _____

ADDRESS: _____

POSTCODE: _____ TELEPHONE NO: _____

DATE OF BIRTH: _____

EDUCATION/QUALIFICATIONS

SECONDARY: School _____ Years _____

Highest qualification gained _____

TERTIARY: Institution _____ Years _____

Highest qualification gained _____

PREVIOUS EMPLOYMENT (put most recent employment first)

Year/s	Employer	Position held

DUTIES PERFORMED
_____
_____

REFERENCES

1 Name _____   2 Name _____

  Address _____   Address _____

  _____   _____

  Telephone No _____   Telephone No _____

Signature: _____

Date: _____

3　Tone up

The simple exercises on this page will help you to avoid stiffness and injury.

Try all the exercises and select those that you feel are the most beneficial.

If any exercise causes you pain or discomfort, do not persist with it.

When you work at one task for long periods at a time, it is important that you take frequent breaks and do something quite different for a few minutes. Exercises and stretches are a good way to loosen up, either during these breaks or at the beginning of the session.

HANDS AND ARMS

These exercises will help you avoid any stiffness or injury to your hands and arms.

1　With your forearms on a table in front of you, turn your palms up and then down.

2　With your fingers straight, spread first your forefingers and middle fingers apart, then bring them together again. Do this with all your fingers in turn.

3　Touch each finger to your thumb in turn. Repeat, sliding each fingertip to the base of the thumb.

4　Bend your wrist down to 90° with the fingers straight and make a fist.

NECK AND SHOULDERS

Tension in the neck and shoulders can cause fatigue and headaches. Here are two stretches to help keep your neck and shoulders relaxed.

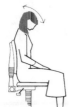

5　Start with your head upright and relaxed. Lower your chin, then return. Pause. Tilt your head back, then return. Do not attempt full neck circles, as this can injure the joints of the neck.

6　Start with the shoulders still and head forward. Bend your head towards your left shoulder, then return. Repeat on the other side.

EYES

When you use a keyboard, your eyes are focused on a screen and/or a sheet of paper, both of which are within one metre of you. The glare of a screen is also tiring after a long period. You should give your eyes a rest regularly, simply by glancing away from your task and looking into the middle distance for a moment or two.

7　If you have a window, this will be ideal. Make sure, however, that your screen is not so close to the window that it will reflect glare back into your eyes.

8　Posters, photo murals, wall hangings or tapestries will give relief to your eyes if there is no window in your room.

STRETCH

Just getting up, walking around and stretching will remove any stiffness and tension from prolonged sitting down. Do these exercises *slowly* until you feel a mild stretching sensation.

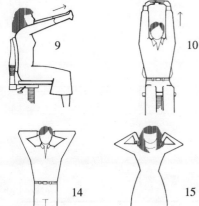

Repeat stretches 11 and 12 on the left side.

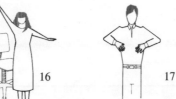

13　Stretch your forearm by putting your palm flat on the chair and gently straightening your arm.

Tone up

TOY SUPPLIERS CO LTD
18 Carlton Street
LONDON W13 8SZ

PO Box 65
LONDON W13 8SZ

Fax (071) 644 5655
Telephone (071) 644 5641

Invoice No: 2230

Date:

Order No: 451

Delivery:
Terms: net 30 days

Quantity	Description	Rate	Total

4 Getting started

Become familiar with the equipment and system you are using by studying the operator's manual or asking your teacher. *Paragraphs 5–8 apply to computers and word processors. If you are using a typewriter, go straight to paragraph 9.*

5 Computers 💻

a Your teacher will explain how to
  • boot the system (if appropriate)
  • format (or initialise) a working disk
  • load the software for the system you are using (if appropriate). Different steps are followed according to whether you are using a hard disk system or a floppy disk system
  • insert your working disk
  • name and create a document
  • store (save) a document (the process is automatic on some systems)
  • exit the system
  • retrieve a document
  • print a document.

A *document* is any piece of text that you create: a memorandum, letter or report; a menu; a paragraph; even a set of keyboard drills.

The flashing light on your screen (in the form of a block, underscore or other graphic) is the *cursor*. It marks the place on the screen where the next character you key will appear.

Word processors have an *automatic return* feature. If a word will not fit at the end of a line, the whole word is automatically moved to the next line. The return key (see paragraph 16) is only used at the end of a paragraph. While you are learning the keyboard, however, it is recommended that you do not make use of this feature. Therefore do not set a right margin. At the end of each line use the return key to move to the next line.

b Documents are stored on two kinds of disk.
  • The *hard* (or *fixed*) *disk* is built into the machine and cannot be removed.
  • The *floppy disk* is removable. Floppy disks are very delicate and must be treated with care. See the illustration *Dos and don'ts with floppy disks* on page 4 for instructions on handling these very important parts of your system.

c Your word processing program has a number of *default settings* which show on the *status* or *information line* at either the top or bottom of your screen. The status line provides information on the format of a document. Default settings are the settings that apply if you do not make your own selection. Your teacher will explain how to re-set
  • line spacing
  • pitch
  • margin settings.

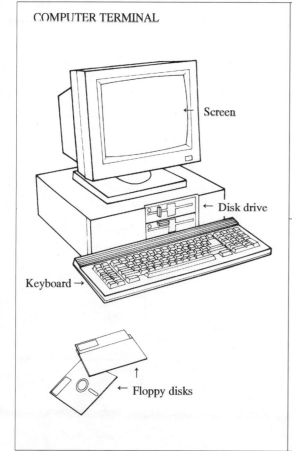

COMPUTER TERMINAL
Screen
Disk drive
Keyboard →
← Floppy disks

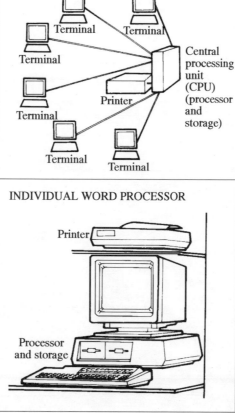

MULTI-USER WORD PROCESSOR
Terminal
Terminal
Terminal
Terminal
Printer
Terminal
Terminal
Central processing unit (CPU) (processor and storage)

INDIVIDUAL WORD PROCESSOR
Printer
Processor and storage

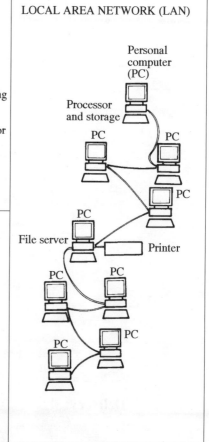

LOCAL AREA NETWORK (LAN)
Personal computer (PC)
Processor and storage
PC
PC
PC
PC
File server
Printer
PC
PC
PC
PC

A word processing system

Purchase Order No 451

B JENKINS & CO
228 Burwood Road
SWINDON SN2 4AS

Telephone (0793) 642 7800

Telex JENKTOY
Fax (0793) 642 1034

Date:

Please supply the following goods:

Quantity	Item	Rate	Total

Delivery:

6 Selecting line spacing

Select single line spacing now.

7 Selecting pitch

The *pitch* (size of type) you can print text in depends on the type of printer you have and the number of fonts, cartridges or daisy wheels that are available for your particular printer. You can print out in

- 10 pitch (also known as pica) – 10 spaces to 25.4 mm horizontally
- 12 pitch (also known as elite) – 12 spaces to 25.4 mm horizontally or
- 15 pitch – 15 spaces to 25.4 mm horizontally. (15 pitch is not in common use.)

See the examples of type sizes at the foot of this page. You should select the pitch to suit your printer.

8 Setting margins

The default margin settings usually suit the pitch for which your printer is pro- grammed. Later in this book you will change your margins to suit different tasks. Leave your margins on the default settings at present.

Now go straight to paragraph 14.

9 Electronic typewriters

Locate and identify the parts of your machine illustrated on page 5.

Align the *paper edge guide* with the start of the *pitch/margin scale*.

10 Inserting the paper

Your machine may have an *automatic paper feed*. If it has and you are not already familiar with it, consult your operator's manual. If your machine does not have the automatic paper feed facility, insert the paper as follows.

- Set the paper edge guide at 0 on the pitch/margin scale.
- Take a sheet of A5 paper in your left hand and place the long edge against the paper edge guide behind the *platen/cylinder*. (The term for a sheet presented short side up is 'portrait'. If it were turned sideways, it would be termed 'landscape'.)

Dos

Mark with felt-tipped pen only | Use corner to pick up disk | Keep disk in its protective cover

Don'ts

Don't bend disk | Don't write on disk except with felt-tipped pen | Don't touch disk surface

Don't expose disk to heat | Don't expose disk to magnetic fields | Don't attempt to clean disk

Dos and don'ts with floppy disks

Insert the disk gently into the disk drive slot, with the label upwards and the exposed part away from you, until it clicks. | When the disk is in place, close the latch. The disk drive will not operate if this is not done. | The activity light indicates that the disk drive is active. *Do not remove the disk, or do anything else to it, while this light is on.*

Inserting a floppy disk in the disk drive

- Using the *index/paper up key* or the *right platen knob*, turn the paper into the machine until the top edge comes into sight above the *aligning scale*.
- Raise the *paper bail* with your left hand and, using the index key or right platen knob, continue to turn the paper into the machine until it is about 25 mm above the aligning scale. Position the paper bail so that it holds the paper against the platen.
- If the paper is not straight, raise the paper bail again, pull the *paper release lever* forward, straighten the paper manually, and push the paper release lever back.
- Position the paper bail so that it holds the paper against the platen again.

There are six lines of single-spaced type to 25.4 mm, regardless of pitch.

10 characters
This is a row of 10-pitch type.

12 characters
This is a row of 12-pitch type.

15 characters
This is a row of 15-pitch type.

25.4 mm (1 inch)

Examples of 10, 12 and 15 pitch type

Staff who wish to take advantage of this facility should speak to Morenza Silver.

The company is all too consious of the dangers of cycling on busy roads, and to encourage the wearing of safety helmets, staff who are allocated a place in the bicycle rack will be offered a safety helmet at the companys expense.

lc.yi
eric

A4 portrait • LL: 60 • SS • centre vertically and horizontally

CAR PARKING ALLOCATION

Please place 'No' column in numerical order 1-6

Names	Department	Registration No	No
P Arias	Sales	ADF 397	5
A Hasan	Sales	TRS 192	6
L Fielding	Communications	RXL 301	2
R Selley	Operations	CLU 896	1
A Sharrock	Sales	NQT 768	4
S Tregise	Sales	PDR 608	3

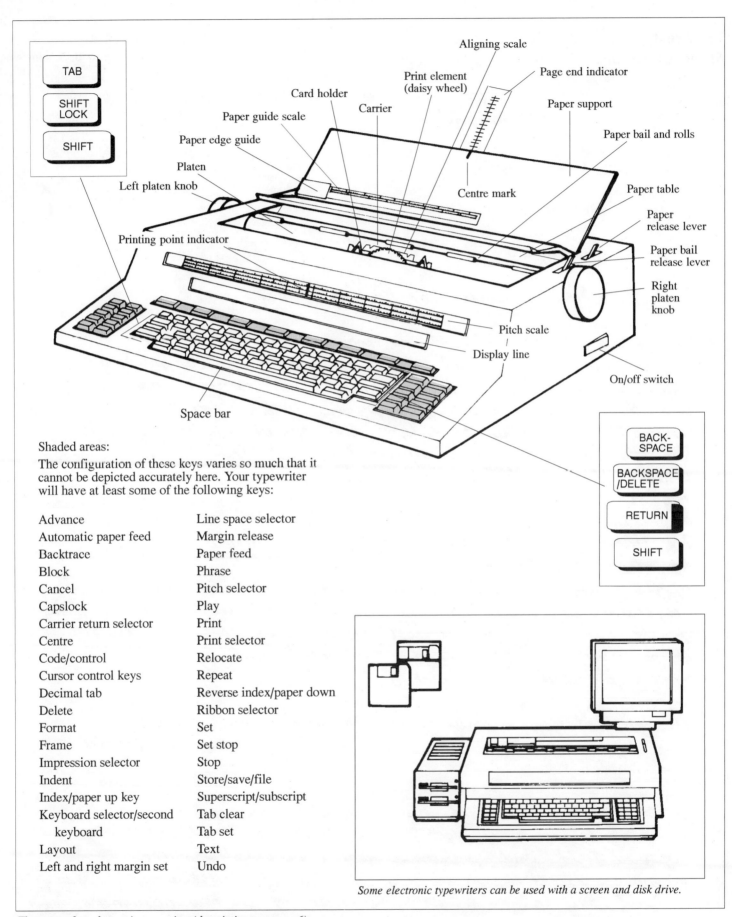

TAB

SHIFT LOCK

SHIFT

Aligning scale

Print element (daisy wheel)

Card holder

Carrier

Page end indicator

Paper support

Paper bail and rolls

Paper guide scale

Paper edge guide

Platen

Left platen knob

Printing point indicator

Centre mark

Paper table

Paper release lever

Paper bail release lever

Right platen knob

Pitch scale

Display line

On/off switch

Space bar

BACK-SPACE

BACKSPACE /DELETE

RETURN

SHIFT

Shaded areas:

The configuration of these keys varies so much that it cannot be depicted accurately here. Your typewriter will have at least some of the following keys:

Advance	Line space selector
Automatic paper feed	Margin release
Backtrace	Paper feed
Block	Phrase
Cancel	Pitch selector
Capslock	Play
Carrier return selector	Print
Centre	Print selector
Code/control	Relocate
Cursor control keys	Repeat
Decimal tab	Reverse index/paper down
Delete	Ribbon selector
Format	Set
Frame	Set stop
Impression selector	Stop
Indent	Store/save/file
Index/paper up key	Superscript/subscript
Keyboard selector/second keyboard	Tab clear
	Tab set
Layout	Text
Left and right margin set	Undo

Some electronic typewriters can be used with a screen and disk drive.

The parts of an electronic typewriter (descriptions on page 6)

Memorandum

To :   All Staff

From :   Leonard Cameron

Date :   Today's

Subject :   New Premises: Car Parking   caps

T/S

One of the consequences of our move to the new office building in march next year is that staff car parking facilities will be strictly limited I am sorry to have to say that council regulations applying to the premises will require the company to reduce the number of parking bays from the 10 we enjoy at present to ⑥. This is an unavoidable developement which the company deeply regrets.

The [table attached] shows how the six parking bays will be alocated. Priority has been given to the vehicles of the company's sales representatives. Private parking bays are available at ~~several~~ locations in the vicinity ~~many~~ stet of the building, but the cost of all day parking is likely to be very high.NP [Fortunatly the new building is well served by public transport.

                railway
The ~~train~~ station is only a few minute's walk away and there are tram stops close by. Their are also several bus routes.

Some members of staff have expressed an interest in cycling to work if we provide a racks that offers security against theft and protection from the weather. The company is therefor willing to install a secure, covered bicyde rack at the rear of the new building. run on to next para

Description of electronic typewriter parts

These are general descriptions only. For information specific to your machine, consult your operator's manual.

Acoustic/noise shield (attachment: not shown) muffles typewriter noise.

Advance key, on typewriters with a screen, advances the cursor around the screen.

Aligning scale is used to align the top edge of the paper as it is fed around the platen.

Anti-glare shield (attachment: not shown) reduces reflected glare from the acoustic shield.

Auto-just selector - see **Carrier return selector**.

Automatic paper feed feeds the paper to the first typing line.

Backspace moves the carrier back one space.

Backspace/delete key moves the carrier back one space, at the same time deleting the character in that position.

Backtrace moves the carrier back to any point of text within the correction memory.

Block function key performs various block operations.

Cancel key deletes a typed character and clears a stored phrase.

Capslock allows the operator to key upper-case letters continuously but leaves numerals in lower case.

Card/envelope holder holds cards, labels and envelopes against the platen.

Carrier/carriage carries the print element and ribbon across the paper.

Carrier return selector/auto-just selector selects manual or automatic return mode, and/or automatic justification.

Centre key centres text automatically. It can also right-align text.

Centre mark shows the horizontal centre of the paper when it is aligned with the paper edge guide.

Code/control key performs special automatic functions in conjunction with other keys.

Copy control lever (inside typewriter: not shown) moves the carrier unit forward or back to accommodate multiple copies or paper of varying thicknesses.

Correcting tape (inside typewriter: not shown) is a sticky ribbon used with correctable carbon ribbon to 'lift off' unwanted typed characters.

Correction key - see **Delete/cancel/correction** key.

Cursor control keys move the cursor in the display line right or left.

Cylinder - see **Platen**.

Daisy wheel/printwheel is a changeable print element featuring a specific typestyle.

Decimal tab/dec tab aligns columns of numbers at the decimal point, at a pre-set tab position.

Delete/cancel/correction key erases unwanted characters.

Display line displays text which is currently being keyed.

File - see **Store/save/file**.

Format function key sets and stores line and page formats.

Frame makes frames for tables, etc.

Function keys are used for special functions, including Block, Code/control, Format, Frame, Phrase, Play, Print, Set, Set stop, Stop, Store/save/file, Text and Undo.

Impression selector determines the impact of the print element according to paper thickness, ribbon type and whether carbon copies are being made.

Indent key sets temporary left margins and also centres blocks of text with equal left and right margin indents.

Index/paper up feeds the paper one line at a time.

Keyboard selector/second keyboard enables the operator to key obscure symbols and characters and accents which are uncommon in the English language.

Layout key sets column layouts without calculation or measurement on the part of the operator.

Line-of-writing scale - see **Pitch/margin/line-of-writing scale**.

Line space selector selects the required line spacing.

Margin release key allows the carrier to move beyond the current margins.

Margin scale - see **Pitch/margin/line-of-writing scale**.

Margin set keys set the left and right margins.

Non-impact print element (not shown) is a feature of some typewriters. No impression is made on the paper and printing is fast and very quiet.

Page end indicator shows, when the top edge of a standard sheet aligns with it, how many lines are left at the bottom of the paper.

Paper bail and rolls hold the paper against the platen.

Paper bail release lever lifts the paper bail off the platen.

Paper down - see **Reverse index**.

Paper edge guide is used to align the left edge of the paper. It can be moved to accommodate different paper sizes.

Paper feed - see **Automatic paper feed**.

Paper guide scale is used to set the paper edge guide position.

Paper release lever frees the paper from the platen roller so that it can be removed or realigned.

Paper support holds the paper upright.

Paper table supports the paper as it comes out of the typewriter.

Paper up - see **Index/paper up**.

Phrase key stores, prints and clears phrases.

Pitch/margin/line-of-writing scale, with the moving **printing point indicator**, shows the current carrier position according to the pitch selected.

Pitch selector sets character pitch to match the pitch of the print element used.

Platen/cylinder is the large rubber cylinder that carries the paper.

Platen knobs are used to feed paper into the machine manually. On some typewriters the left platen knob, if pressed in, frees the platen so that the paper can be fed to a precise position. This feature is called the **variable line spacer**.

Play function, on a typewriter with a screen, retrieves a document from memory and 'plays' it back on the display.

Print function key prints text.

Print element may be a daisy wheel (as shown) or non-impact print element.

Print selector selects normal or bold print and/or underscoring.

Printing point indicator - see **Pitch/margin/line-of-writing scale**.

Printwheel - see **Daisy wheel**.

Relocate key returns the carrier to its original position after a correction has been made.

Repeat key repeats the last typed character.

Return/new line key returns the carrier to the left margin, at the same time feeding the paper.

Reverse index/paper down reverse feeds the paper.

Ribbon cartridge (inside typewriter: not shown) contains the ribbon, usually correctable carbon. The ribbon can be carbon or fabric, correctable or uncorrectable and in different colours.

Ribbon selector chooses the setting corresponding to the type of ribbon to be used.

Save - see **Store/save/file**.

Second keyboard - see **Keyboard selector**.

Set key sets automatic functions.

Set stop sets various functions and stops or restarts printing of a stored phrase.

Shift keys enable the operator to key upper-case characters. They also release the shift lock.

Shift lock sets continuous upper case.

Space bar inserts a space or moves the carrier to the right.

Stop function stops or restarts printing of a stored phrase.

Store/save/file function key allows text to be stored in memory.

Superscript/subscript allows superscripts and subscripts to be typed without manually adjusting the paper.

Tab/tabulator key moves the carrier to the next tab stop.

Tab set sets tab stops.

Tab clear clears tabs and decimal tabs.

Text function key uses memory functions to perform various text operations.

Undo key cancels previous key operations, such as deletions made in error.

Variable line spacer – see **Platen knobs**.

STRESS

Everyone experiences stress to some degree, whether at home or at work. At times when stress is experienced the body, through the adrenal glands, releases the hormone adrenalin which makes the heart beat faster. This is an automatic body response and is not necessarily harmful.

The right amount of stress is necessary to help raise a person's level of performance and it can be enjoyable and exhilarating. Just as an athlete requires stress to reach a high level of performance and win a race, a worker needs stress to complete a difficult and challenging job.

However, too much stress can be harmful. If we build up a store of tensions and do not release them, the adrenalin can build up in our bodies and cause illnesses such as high blood pressure, ulcers, heart attack and headaches.

Symptoms of stress can be physical, such as a flushed face, cold hands or feet, clenched jaw, muscle tension and a pounding heart. They may be emotional - a keyed-up feeling, general irritability or fatigue. They may be behavioural and affect everyday behaviour, resulting in overall depression.

To overcome the effects of too much stress, the first thing to do is to identify the stress factors themselves to see what your response to them is. Are you over-reacting? Can you alter these circumstances? You may be able to alter those aspects of your life that cause undue stress.

Here are some things that can be done to reduce stress. Develop the habit of listening to relaxing music. Allow plenty of time for meals - eat slowly and chew well. Practise relaxation and/or meditation by listening to tapes or even attending classes. Cultivate a hobby that is creative rather than competitive. Work methodically and finish one task before commencing another.

11 Selecting line spacing

Using the *line space selector*, you can choose single, one-and-a-half or double line spacing. Some machines also offer three-quarter line spacing, which is used with 15-pitch type (see paragraph 12 below). Six lines of single-spaced type measure approximately 25 mm.

Find out how to select line spacing on your typewriter.

Select single line spacing now.

This is an example of single line spacing.
This is an example of one-and-a-half line spacing.
This is an example of double line spacing.
This is an example of triple line spacing.

Examples of line spacing

12 Selecting pitch

A typewriter can be set to print in
- 10 pitch (also known as pica) type – 10 spaces to 25.4 mm horizontally
- 12 pitch (also known as elite) type – 12 spaces to 25.4 mm horizontally or
- 15 pitch – 15 spaces to 25.4 mm horizontally. (15 pitch is not in common use.)

These settings are represented on the *pitch scale*.

Locate the *pitch selector* and select the pitch to suit the daisy wheel that you have in your machine.

13 Setting margins

Some electronic typewriters have pre-set margins. These margins apply if you do not set your own.

For the exercises in Units 1.2 and 1.3, use the pre-set margins if this facility is on your system. If your typewriter has no pre-set margins, set the left margin at 20 (10 pitch) or 29 (12 pitch) now. Set the right margin stop at the extreme right.

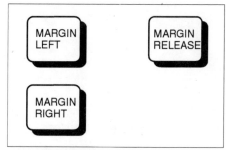

Margin set and margin release keys

Your electronic typewriter may have an *automatic return* feature. If a word will not fit at the end of a line, the whole word is automatically moved to the next line. While you are learning the keyboard, however, it is recommended that you do not make use of this feature. Instead, use the return key (see paragraph 16) at the end of each line.

14 The home keys

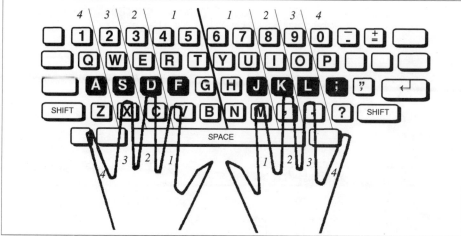

The home keys

The *home keys* are your 'base'. When they are not reaching to other keys, your fingers remain over the home keys. After striking another key, return the finger to its base.

Try placing your fingers over the home keys to get used to their position. Place the fingers of your left hand over **ASDF** and the fingers of your right hand over **JKL;**. Your fingers should be slightly curved and just clear of the home keys. The lower part of your hands should not rest on the edge of the keyboard.

Your goal is to 'touch operate' – to key with your eyes on the copy rather than on your fingers or the keyboard.

15 Correct keying technique

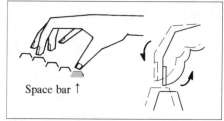

Correct keying technique

- As you key with your fingers, your hands, arms and wrists should be almost motionless.
- Tap the keys sharply but lightly with the fingertips. No force is required.
- Do not hold down your finger on a key. This will result in the character being repeated several times on the paper or screen.

16 Beginning a new line

To begin a new line manually (ie independently of the automatic return feature, if your system has one), the *cursor* (on a computer) or the *carrier* (on a typewriter) must be positioned at the start of the new line by striking
- the *return key* (on a typewriter keyboard)
- the *return/enter/new line key* (on a computer keyboard).

This key will from now on be referred to as the *return key*.

Keeping the **J** finger in position over its home key, reach to the return key with the little finger of your right hand.

accomplishing tasks- ie break down a large job into smaller componants and then take small 'bites' at them until the job is complete.

Your study may also uncover some timewasters. The attached chart lists the top 6 time wasters identified in a recent survey.

A4 portrait • LL: 60 • SS • centre vertically and horizontally

SECRETARIES' TOP SIX TIME WASTERS

TIME WASTERS	USA	EUROPE	AUSTRALIA
Telephone interruptions	1	3	2
Lack of planning	2	2	1
Attempting too much	3	4	3
Disorganised Boss	4	6	5
Socializing	5	5	6
Lack of communication	6	1	4

Tap the key lightly and return all the fingers to their home position.

Return/enter/new line key

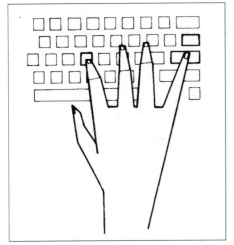

The reach to the return/enter key

Now practise the reach to the return key a few times.

17 Space bar technique

Space between letters by tapping the *space bar* lightly with your right thumb, keeping the **JKL;** fingers over their home keys. Tapping the space bar once moves the printing point one space to the right. The space bar is sensitive and will continue spacing if you keep your thumb on it.

Now practise using the space bar a few times.

18 Cursor control keys (computers only)

The four *cursor control keys* are used to move the cursor left, right, up or down one or more spaces.

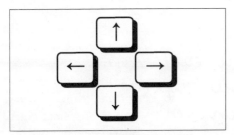

Cursor control keys

19 Backspace key (typewriters only)

When the *backspace key* is struck, the printing point moves back one character. Operate the key with the finger closest to it (usually the left or right little finger).

Backspace key

20 Backspace/delete key (computers and typewriters)

Backspace/delete key (computers)

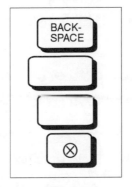

Typewriter configuration with backspace/delete key in addition to backspace key

Computers and electronic typewriters have a *backspace/delete key*, which moves the printing point back one space, simultaneously deleting the character in that position. On electronic typewriters the backspace/delete key is in addition to the backspace key.

Practise using the backspace and backspace/delete keys.

21 End of session procedure: computers

1 Save your work if necessary.
2 Your teacher may want you to print out a hard copy of each piece of work.
3 Remove your working disk, replace it in its envelope and store it securely.
4 Switch off the power on all components as necessary (computer, screen and printer).
5 Clear your work station.

22 End of session procedure: typewriters

1 Take the paper in your left hand.
2 If your typewriter has an automatic paper feed, use it; otherwise pull the paper release lever towards you.
3 Remove the paper. If you have no automatic paper feed, return the paper release lever to its normal position.
4 Switch off the power.
5 Cover the machine.
6 Clear your work station.

⌐Time Management⌐ Centre & underscore

The first step towards effective time management, is to prepare an analysis of your duties in the form of a work analyis sheet. Over a period of, say, two weeks record each task as you perform it and write down the time you took to complete the job. To simplify your work annalysis you might set up a simple basic coding system eg, you sp out could use 'F' for filing, 'MT' for machine transcription and 'PM' for preparing for meetings.

At the end of the period, study your analysis sheet to find out wether you are using time to your best advantage. You may find, for instance, that the first part of the day, is not the best time for filing because that is when your work is interupted most. Having carried out the analysis, rearrange your duties so that you can work more efficiently. Some tasks, such as ∧filing of papers, could be eliminated   unnecessary altogether. You may be able to delagate part of your work to a junior. ᴺᴾ[Set priorities by planning the order of your work and by completing any special or urgent tasks, such as telephone calls.

A basic part of efficency is seeing that each job is finished by completing any follow up actions. Use the 'swiss cheese' approach to

ASDFJKL;
(the home keys)

The highlighted line above the first exercise contains abbreviated instructions.

- It indicates line length (LL).
- It recommends that you use the default or pre-set margins on your system. If your system does not have this facility, set a left margin (LM) of 20 (10 pitch) or 29 (12 pitch) and set the right margin at the extreme right.
- It instructs you to select single line spacing (SS).

Computers
Access your word processing program.

Electronic typewriters
Paper: use A4 portrait or A5 landscape.
Use the automatic paper feed or start keying six single line spaces (25 mm) from the top of the paper.

Review

- arranging your work station (page 1)
- keyboarding posture (page 1)
- correct keying technique (page 7)
- space bar technique (page 8)
- beginning a new line (page 7).

Tone-up exercises

Do some exercises from page 2 before and after each keyboarding session.

Spacing after a semicolon

Leave one space after a semicolon in a sentence or phrase. See lines 13–20. In these exercises, if a semicolon occurs at the end of a line, return without spacing.

End of session procedure

End every session with the procedure described on page 8.

Practise the home keys

1 Place your fingers on the home keys:
  - fingers of the left hand on **ASDF**
  - fingers of the right hand on **JKL;**.
2 Key each line twice:
  - the first time watching your fingers as you locate the keys. Say each key to yourself
  - the second time watching the copy, keying as accurately as possible.
3 Strike the *space bar* with a quick, inward movement of the right thumb.
4 Copy the typescript line for line. Do not key the line numbers.
5 If you make a mistake, continue keying. It is natural to make mistakes at first.
6 Strike the *return* key at the end of each line to start a new line.
7 After each set of two lines, strike the return key twice to leave one blank line.

> LL: 43 • default (pre-set) margins *or* LM 20 (10) 29 (12) • SS

↓Space once

```
1  f ff j jj ff jj d dd k kk dd kk ff jj dd kk
2  s ss l ll ss ll a aa ; ;; aa ;; ss ll aa ;;
```

Consolidate the home keys

```
3  fj fj dk dk sl sl a; a; fdsa jkl; asdf ;lkj
4  jf jf kd kd ls ls ;a ;a asdf ;lkj fdsa jkl;
5  a; a; sl sl dk dk fj fj ;lkj asdf jkl; fdsa
6  ;a ;a ls ls kd kd jf jf jkl; fdsa ;lkj asdf
```

Build words

```
7  a as ask asks; a ad add adds; a al alf alfa
8  s sa sad sal salk; d da dad dads; f fa fads
9  ;f fl fla flas flask flasks; j ja jak jaks;
10 la las lass lad lads; sal sala salad salads
11 jaf jaff jaffa jaffas; fal fall falls; alas
12 al dads asks salk adds salads flasks jaffas
```

Practise phrases

One space after a semicolon ↓

```
13 add jaffas; dad asks a lass; ada asks a lad
14 a lad falls; as all flasks fall; a dad asks
15 alf adds a salad; alas a jaffa; a sad lass;
16 a sad fall; a lass asks a lad; all ask jak;
17 as a fad; a lad asks jak; dad adds a jaffa;
18 jaffa salads; ada asks lads; as all flasks;
19 jak adds all alfalfa; alas all flasks fall;
20 all alfa; salads fall; sad ada adds jaffas;
```

PREPARING FOR WORK

A desire to learn is the best preparation for work. Like anything worth while, job skills require determination and hard work, backed up by regular practice. Once acquired, your skills are never forgotten and they will form a keystone to your future success.

You will take the first step towards your future success by completing your course of study. Once their initial interest in the course wears off, some college students 'switch off'. They cannot see the relevance of what they are learning and long to be actually working. What they fail to realise, however, is that success at work depends first on gaining certain basic skills; and they can only be acquired in a formal course of study. Among other things, your course has been designed to help you to become a proficient keyboard operator and document processor, but you will only succeed if you are prepared to work.

When you start a new job, you will not instantly be a competent employee. You will need time to understand properly what is required of you. Learn all you can about the organisation, including its products and history, by reading the literature that is available to you. Don't hesitate to ask questions or to seek advice while you are settling in. During the settling-in period, you will find that your basic skills will stand you in good stead.

EN3

Review

- arranging your work station (page 1)
- keyboarding posture (page 1)
- correct keying technique (page 7).

Reaching from the home row

In Units 1.3 to 1.23 adopt the following plan to learn the reach from the home row to every new key.

1 Find the new key on the keyboard chart at the head of each unit.

2 Find the new key on your own keyboard.

3 Note the finger to use for the new key.

4 Place the fingers of both hands in their home key positions. Curve your fingers.

5 Reach from the home key position to the new key and back again several times:
- keeping your fingers curved
- keeping the fingers that you are not using on the home keys.

6 Key each line at least twice with your eyes on the copy:
- the first time saying the keys to yourself
- the second time keying at a slightly faster rate.

Numeric (figure) keys

This unit introduces you to your first numeric key. It is recommended that you learn the numeric keys alongside the alphabetic keys, but if your teacher chooses to delay introducing them until all the alphabetic keys are learnt, skip the highlighted lines.

The numeric keys as a whole are covered in Units 1.17 to 1.19. The numeric keypad is dealt with in Unit 1.20.

Follow the end of session procedure.

LL: 45 • default (pre-set) margins *or* LM 20 (10) 29 (12) • SS

Refresher: warm up on lines 1–3

1 asdf ;lkj fdsa jkl; asdf ;lkj dad asks al jad
2 jf kd ls ;a fj dk sl a; all a lad asks; jaffa
3 a sad lass; flak falls; jaffa salads; add ada

Reach to E with D finger

4 dee ded eee ded dde ded eed; dee eee dde eed;
5 ea es ef ek el ae se fe je ke le ea es ek el;
6 ease seal sell deal deaf dell feed feel keel;
7 else kale jell ales flee desk leak sale flake

Reach to N with J finger

8 jnn jnj nnn jnj jjn jnj nnj; jnn nnn jjn nnj;
9 jnj ne na ns nd nk nl n; en an sn dn fn kn ln
10 need neal nell send sand alan dank dean seen;
11 jane keen kane lean lane flan fend fens knee;

Reach to 3 with D finger

12 d3d d3 d33 d33d; d3d d3 d33 d33d; d3d d3 d33d
13 3 desks; 33 deans; 333 deals; 3 deeds; 3 dads
14 3 elks; 33 needs; 333 seals; 3 lanes; 33 fans
15 sell 3; send 33; lend 333; deal 333; lease 33

New words

16 anna sank sean jeff leaf land dale lank fade;
17 fleas ankle; easel jeans; faded asked; addle;
18 fended needed kneads; leases jandals sandals;

Figure review

19 jake sees 333; alan asks 333; jane needs 333;
20 33 kanaks sell 333 desks; sell jess 33 jeans;

Build skill on phrases

21 a leaf fell; jake and jane asked ken and neal
22 alan lane; dan lake sends jed and jeff a flan
23 adele feels keen; nell dean sells eel salads;
24 lena needs faded jeans; dan lane feeds fleas;
25 feed jane and jess dale flake and addled ale;

Appendix 2   *Production assignments*

Contents

Introduction
Test 1   Warm-up — Report — Time Management
Test 2   Warm-up — Memo — Car parking

Introduction

These passages will test your ability to follow written instructions, interpret proofreading symbols and format hand-written material.

Timing

- A preliminary reading time of 5 minutes is allowed.
- Warm-up passages are not part of the test itself. There is no fixed time limit on warm-ups, but they should take a minimum of 5 minutes.

- The tests themselves should be completed in 20 minutes.

Warm-up passages

The warm-up passages give the student a chance to become familiar with the handwriting of the test.

Production tests

These production tests assume a keying speed of approximately 25–30 wpm; the table is to be keyed or printed out on a separate page and has a single line of column headings and horizontal ruling only.

General instructions

- Line length should be 60 ch aract-ers.
- Key in single spacing unless you are instructed otherwise.
- You may use a dictionary.

- A preliminary reading time of 5 minutes is allowed, during which time you may make notes.
- The duration of the test is 20 minutes.
- You may use a dictionary during the t est.
- A line length of 60 keystrokes is required.
- Key the warm-up passage before you start the test; a minimum time of 5 minutes is allowed for this.
- Make all the corrections indicated by the proofreading marks.
- Find and correct spelling and punctuation errors in the test passages.
- Key the table on a separate sheet from the body of the test.
- Centre all work vertically and horizontally on the page.
- Neat, typewritten correction of errors is permitted.

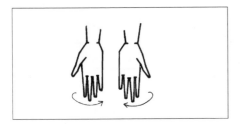
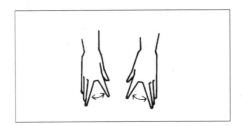
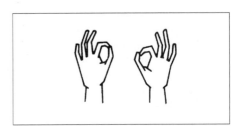
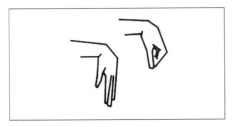

Checkpoint A

Equal left and right margins

In Units 1.2 and 1.3 you either used the default or pre-set margins on your computer or electronic typewriter or set the left margins only. On many systems default or pre-set margins are selected to give equal left and right margins on a line length of 60 or 65 spaces in 10 pitch. Work has a more pleasing appearance if it is balanced by equal margins.

Paper size and type pitch

Both A4 paper (portrait) and A5 (landscape) are 210 mm wide. This represents 82 spaces in 10-pitch type and 100 spaces in 12-pitch type.

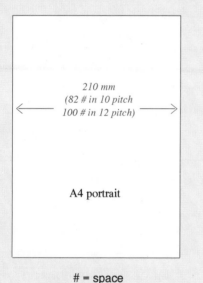

210 mm
(82 # in 10 pitch
100 # in 12 pitch)

A4 portrait

= space

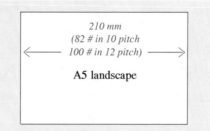

210 mm
(82 # in 10 pitch
100 # in 12 pitch)

A5 landscape

A5 portrait paper is 148 mm wide. This represents 59 spaces in 10-pitch type and 70 spaces in 12-pitch type.

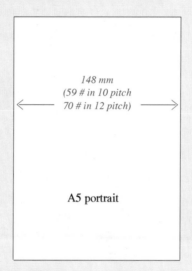

148 mm
(59 # in 10 pitch
70 # in 12 pitch)

A5 portrait

Setting the left margin

Typewriters

As the procedure for setting margins varies from machine to machine, you should refer to the instructions in your operator's manual. The following is a general guide.

- Using the return key, move the carrier to the extreme left of the machine. (You may need to use the margin release key to move to the left of any pre-set margin stop.)
- Use the space bar to move the carrier to the desired margin.
- Press the left margin set key (for separate left and right margin set keys). This sets a new margin and automatically cancels any pre-set margin.

Computers

Ask your teacher or consult your operator's manual.

In the following units a left margin is specified to give equal left and right margins. Set the left margin to the number given in the instructions using the above procedure.

Job A1

Make a rough draft of the above 3 paper size diagrams.

Keystrokes

36 Safety
(SI: 1.52)

It is no doubt true to say that attention to the health of the   62
workers in an automated office tends to centre on the correct   123
environment for screen operators, good lighting and the right   184
type of furniture, with adequate rest periods during the day.   245
But perhaps not enough thought is given to the overall safety of   309
all office workers. One of the rights of an office employee is   372
to be able to work in a safe environment. For their part,   430
workers themselves have a legal responsibility to respect safety   494
rules, use equipment correctly and for the purposes intended and   558
to take all reasonable care to avoid accidents.   Standard words: 121   605

Most people would not take it seriously when told that an office   669 64
has some very real occupational hazards. But potential accidents   734 129
are always there, ready to be triggered by a moment of   788 183
carelessness - a drawer left open, a pair of scissors perched   849 244
dangerously on a shelf, an extension cord trailing across the   910 305
floor or a cigarette left burning on a desk. A well-run office   973 368
should have a policy of making its employees safety conscious. It   1038 433
is essential to train supervisors as safety officers, giving them 1103 498
responsibility for developing safety programs and for seeing that 1168 563
staff adhere to them. This requires regular and frequent surveys 1233 628
of the workplace to spot office hazards and put them right.   1292 687
                                              Standard words: 137

When you are working in an office do not leave obstructions such   1356 64
as your bag or case, or the waste paper basket, in the aisle near 1421 129
your desk. Keep shelves tidy so there is no chance of something   1485 193
falling off the top. Do not stack things so high on shelves or   1548 256
furniture that they start wobbling. Don't use chairs as ladders, 1613 321
especially chairs with castors, as they could start rolling; and   1677 385
beware of swivel chairs that tip unexpectedly - don't lean back   1740 448
in them! Take care with electrical appliances. If there is a   1802 510
fault, do not attempt to fix it yourself but wait for a qualified 1867 575
person. One last reminder - do not rush around in corridors or   1930 638
aisles, particularly at the corners, in case you collide with   1991 699

Total standard words: 406 someone coming from the other direction.   Standard words: 148 2031 739

1 2 3 4 5 6 7 8 9 10 11 12 13

TI58

Margins

Set the left margin (LM) at 19 (10 pitch) or 28 (12 pitch). Leave the right margin (RM) on default/pre-set or set it at the extreme right. Retain these margins for the rest of Module 1.

New key procedure

Follow the procedure described under *Reaching from the home row* in Unit 1.3.

Technique, accuracy and speed

Accuracy and speed of keying depend on correct technique. If you concentrate on good technique, your accuracy and speed will gradually improve.

- Adopt the comfortable keyboarding posture illustrated on page 1.
- Your hands, arms and wrists should be almost motionless as you key.
- Curve your fingers.
- Tap the keys sharply but lightly with your fingertips.
- Return each finger to the home key after striking another key.

Errors

Remember, it is normal to make errors at first. If you make a mistake, continue keying.

New key drill pattern

The new key drills in this and other units are designed as follows.

1st line:	to teach and reinforce the reach from the home key to the new key
2nd line:	to introduce a range of common letter pairs that include the new letter
3rd line:	to give practice on short words that include the new letter
4th line:	to build skill on longer words that include the new letter.

Follow the end of session procedure.

LL: 45 • SS

Refresher: warm up on lines 1–4

1 a; sl dk fj jf kd ls ;a dk ded des jnj jnk ln
2 eel alf end ann dan; ask jan jed fen ken len;
3 jake kneels; and deane seeks; an easel falls;
4 3 keels; 33 leaks; 333 fees; 3 leases; and 33

Reach to T with F finger

5 ftt ftf ttt ftf fft ftf ttf; ftt ttt fft ttf;
6 te ta ts et at st lt nt te ta ts et at st lt;
7 eat ate sat set fat jet; ten let net ted tan;
8 seat fats tell last late tale task lent felt;

Reach to I with K finger

9 kii kik iii kik kki kik iik; kii iii kki iik;
10 ie it ia is id if il in ei ti ai si di fi li;
11 its ilk lid kid tin; lit fit inn nil sin lie;
12 isle till kits kiss tiff silt slit jill lien;

Reach to 5 with F finger

13 f5f f5 f55 f55f; f5f f5 f55 f55f; f5f f5 f55f
14 5 lids; 55 kids; 555 tins; 5 kilns; 5 kisses;
15 5 dills; 55 tints; 555 kilts; 5 fins; 5 inns;
16 tan 5; net 55; seat 555; stake 555; land 555;

Reach to 8 with K finger

17 k8k k8 k88 k88k; k8k k8 k88 k88k; k8k k8 k88k
18 8 sills; 88 tiffs; 888 isles; 8 jills; 8 nits
19 8 kills; 8 jets; 8 stiles; 8 skeins; 8 skills
20 less 8; feed 88; stain 888; need 888; slit 88

New words

21 neat tina stan salt sent sink dent silk flit;
22 anita tales; stead steak; least staff; sated;
23 slated seated; steals staked; jested fattens;

Figures

24 jan finds 3835; stan sets 5835; dan eats 8538
25 fit 585 tiles; ted tests 88 kites; 55 skates;

Build skill on phrases

26 jill is a fine kid; at least neil is in jail;
27 ann takes a late tea; let ted and ken tell it
28 see if linda and tessa still like it at tania

---

1 2 3 4 5 6 7 8 9 10 11 12 13

Keystrokes

35 The electronic office

(SI: 1.53)

The main advantage of the electronic office is that staff can   61
send information from one point in the organisation to another.   124
If in any business there is no ability to communicate between   185
terminals, then you do not have a proper office system; you just   249
have a system that types, copies and adds up.   Standard words: 59   294

If you can just tap into a database and access all you require   356 62
and not have to walk up and down stairs, travel in lifts, or go   419 125
from office to office to deliver reports and documents, or to   480 186
telephone to check that urgently required information has   537 243
arrived, that is a real saving of time. We loosely term this   598 304
ability to access information and link us with one another, both   662 368
nationally and internationally, 'electronic mail'. The telephone   727 433
was the starting point for this revolution in communication. It   791 497
has gone a long way since Bell invented his first phone.   847 553
Standard words: 111

Just as we use the telephone to dial virtually anywhere in the   909 62
world and pass on a voice message, we can now connect our office   973 126
system by means of the telephone lines to anywhere in the world   1036 189
to transmit and receive information. We may want to send a short   1101 254
telex-style message, or a long complicated report with   1155 308
statistical material presented as tables, graphs or drawings. No   1220 373
matter what the information is, it is technically possible to   1281 434
have it printed out at its destination looking just as it did   1342 495
when it left your own office. You can have confirmation that it   1406 559
has been received in seconds. A reply can be sent straight back   1470 623
to you in your office and appear on your terminal screen in no   1532 685
time at all.   Standard words: 139   1544 697

This ability to send and receive data and text is a great advance   1609 65
in office technology. The information sent electronically may   1671 127
never need to be printed out, but just be worked on at its   1729 185
destination, then forwarded on to someone else for further   1787 243
adjustment or review. If we are careful we should be able to   1848 304
save large numbers of trees by not printing out paper copies, but   1913 369

Total standard words: 387   keeping files on disk.   Standard words: 78   1935 391

1 2 3 4 5 6 7 8 9 10 11 12 13

RH4

Keying by 'touch'

Properly trained keyboard operators key by 'touch'. They keep their eyes on the copy rather than on their hands or the keyboard.

- Adopt the comfortable keyboarding posture illustrated on page 1.
- Your hands, arms and wrists should be almost motionless as you key.
- Curve your fingers.
- Tap the keys sharply but lightly with your fingertips.
- Return each finger to the home key after striking another key.

In the early stages of keyboard learning it is helpful to say the characters to yourself as you reach to the keys.

R and H

The last of the ten most commonly occurring consonants, R and H, are introduced in this unit.

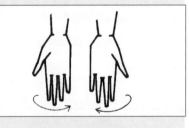

Follow the end of session procedure.

Refresher: warm up on lines 1–3
Home keys
1 sal falls; all lads ask; jak adds; a sad lass
All alpha keys
2 it is fine if jeff and len eat steak at nine;
Figures
3 d3 den 33 dad; f5 fan 55 fad; k8 kit 88 kite;

Reach to R with F finger

4 frr frf rrr frf ffr frf rrf; frr rrr ffr rrf;
5 re rt ra rs rd ri rk rl rn er tr ar dr ir kr
6 are ran jar far ark air; sir irk rat err ref;
7 rent real rink fret dirk rear tire ajar liar;

Reach to H with J finger

8 jhh jhj hhh jhj jjh jhj hhj; jhh hhh jjh hhj;
9 he ha hi th ah sh the her his has had she hit
10 hat ash half; that hear then; this than shed;
11 their there; thank these; shall think; fifth;

Reach to 4 with F finger

12 f4f f4 f44 f44f; f4f f4 f44 f44f; f4f f4 f44f
13 4 hits; 44 hats; 444 firs; 44 eras; 444 rats;
14 4 seas; 44 jars; 444 ends; 44 sins; 444 inks;
15 did 4; nail 44; field 444; date 444; her 444;

New words

16 hare hale sash kith herd jerk rain near dear;
17 after tread; later train; heard share; shift;
18 thrill sharer; shirts threes; friend strikes;

Figures

19 he has half 3458; ian hid 8543; jed risks 458
20 rae takes 44 rifles; there are 485 hares here

Build skill on phrases

21 that it did; he has his later; had less than;
22 there are these; this is hers; hear this sir;
23 after the trial he and she learnt their fate;
24 jill has lent lin and freda the three dresses
25 a friend has finished her fresh salad dessert

1 2 3 4 5 6 7 8 9 10 11 12 13

34 Noise
(SI: 1.46)

Keystrokes

Open plan offices have become more popular over the past fifteen | 64
years, but if such an office is not planned with noise levels in | 128
mind there will be a reduction in work performance rather than an | 193
improvement. When planning layout and seating in the modern | 253
office, it is essential to consider work and communication | 311
patterns. Standard words: 64 | 320

Wherever sound travels in an office, it strikes panels and walls. | 385 65
Some sound will penetrate these surfaces, and some will be | 443 123
reflected from them. Sound will also go over the top and bend | 505 185
around the sides of the panels, which means that quite often a | 567 247
great amount of sound energy travels much further than was | 625 305
thought of or desired. Standard words: 65 | 647 327

A popular way to control excess noise in an office is to use | 707 60
sound-absorbent material on the sides of panels or wall dividers. | 772 125
Another good method is to block its passage by inserting metal | 834 187
inside these panels. Standard words: 41 | 854 207

In the real world of office design, planners should try to deal | 917 63
with what can be measured and controlled. The most common source | 982 128
of noise in an office is speech. Most people will adjust their | 1045 191
speech levels to avoid excessive intrusion into other areas. | 1105 251
Office machines - copiers and printers, for example - should be | 1168 314
put in spots that do not need a high degree of privacy and are | 1230 376
away from as many people as possible. A small room, corridor or | 1294 440
alcove is an ideal place. Telephones and the tapping of | 1350 496
keyboards are a constant source of noise and are a problem to | 1411 557
those people who are sensitive to high sound levels. Standard words: 122 | 1463 609

A building, too, has sounds of its own. Its air-conditioning and | 1528 65
fluorescent lighting both produce a constant hum that should be | 1591 128
kept low enough to avoid its becoming a nuisance. Ceilings can | 1654 191
be fitted with acoustic panels which will help to moderate sound | 1718 255
levels for the office worker. It is amazing how much noise our | 1781 318
ears hear during the day. They need all the protection we can | 1843 380

Total standard words: 378

give them so that they will last for a lifetime. Standard words: 86 | 1891 428

1 2 3 4 5 6 7 8 9 10 11 12 13

Shift keys
Full stop

LL: 45 • SS

Capital (upper case) letters

This unit introduces the *shift keys*. They enable you to key capital letters. Capitals are also known as 'upper case' characters and small letters as 'lower case' characters. These were the terms used in earlier times by compositors (printers' typesetters), who stored their metal type characters in boxes above a bench. The type for the small letters was kept in a lower case above the bench and the type for the capital letters in an upper case.

There are two shift keys on your keyboard.

- The *left shift* is used to produce capitals of letters keyed with the right hand.
- The *right shift* is used for capitals of letters keyed with the left hand.

In a later unit you will see that the shifts are also used to key symbols and some punctuation marks.

You hold down the shift key as you strike the key you wish to capitalise. Release the shift key immediately after you strike the alphabetic key.

The full stop

In these exercises, space twice after keying a full stop at the end of a sentence, except at the end of a line where you should return without spacing.

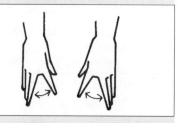

Follow the end of session procedure.

Refresher: warm up on lines 1–4

Common phrases
1 and a; as its; is it; are the; she has; if he
2 shall there; than theirs; that his; did this;
All alpha keys
3 jan and keith had their sale at nine fifteen;
Figures
4 d3 33 deaf f4 44 fear f5 55 fads k8 88 kilns;

Reach to LEFT SHIFT with A finger

5 Ja Ja Ka Ka La La Jane Jane Kate Kate Lae Lae
6 Ha Ha Ia Ia Na Na Hal Hal Ian Ian Nanna Nanna
7 Linda Leanne Freda Nathan Haden Stella Nettis
8 Jess and Kirk see Les and Nat at the Hill Inn

Reach to . with L finger

9 l.l lead l.l lids l.l lien l.l leaf l.l least
10 l.. it is ... if the ... and he ... there is. *Return without spacing* ↓
11 I tell her. ↓ *Space twice* He is late. She did. Jed said.

Reach to RIGHT SHIFT with ; finger

12 F; F; D; D; S; S; A; A; Faith Dean Seth Allan
13 T; T; R; R; E; E; Tess Rae Ena Thea Rita Elie
14 Fraser Deakin Sale Ajana Tahara Readfelt Eden
15 Freda and Sal read The Three Sisters at Hale.

Left and right shifts

16 Alf Lee and Sid Deane learn Italian at Taree.
17 Send Reid and Nairne in Alfred Lane a letter.
18 Let Faith and Esther dine at the Ti Tree Inn.
19 Janine and Delia thanked Hal Reede at Easter.

Figures

20 There are 3458. ↓ *Space twice* I had 8543. Frank has 5483.
21 Jilted all 44. Tether 583 here. Net 4 sets.

Build skill on sentences

22 Take his fare. ↓ *Space twice* The train is late at Redhill.
23 Let her share. This is its first real trial.
24 She starts first. Dial a friend in Adelaide.
25 He left Katie at the State Theatre in Kendal.
26 Dean and Shane Kale did take shelter in Fiji.

| | 1 | 2 | 3 | 4 | 5 | 6 | 7 | 8 | 9 | 10 | 11 | 12 | 13 |

Keystrokes

33 Office climate
(SI: 1.45)

The climate that we work in in the office should make us feel comfortable and relaxed. The most important conditions include temperature, air quality, light and levels of noise.

Standard words: 35

61
124
176

Office workers today are becoming more particular about the environment in which they work and how it may affect their health. Most offices have now been declared 'smoke-free' areas; those wishing to smoke have to go to specific spots in a building or may even have to go outside each time they feel the desire for a cigarette.

Standard words: 65

235 59
293 117
357 181
422 246
487 311
499 323

Air-conditioning is another cause of concern for some, with the same air constantly being recirculated among all the people in a building. Care of air-conditioning plants, to ensure that no bacteria build up in the tanks, has become important. Bacteria could be transmitted through ducts to the people inside. Perhaps the old-style buildings with windows that opened to let in outside air had some advantages, even if temperatures were not kept constant throughout the year. They may have been cheaper to run, too. Such is the price of progress.

Standard words: 108

562 63
626 127
687 188
750 251
815 316
873 374
935 436
1000 501
1041 542

Daylight was originally the prime source of light. Later oil and gas lamps were used. Today we have very sophisticated lighting levels in our workplaces. Good lighting depends on its quantity and quality. Is there enough, or do we need another lamp? Is there glare or reflection of light from outside or from some other source in the office? Windows can create glare and reflection, especially for those reading or using screens. Harsh contrasts between light and shadows can be a problem at work or at home.

Standard words: 101

1106 65
1169 128
1233 192
1295 254
1355 314
1412 371
1477 436
1540 499
1548 507

Noise levels in an office can be surprisingly high, even though you may be unaware of them after working in the building for any length of time. There is the hum of the air-conditioning, the sound of the computer and the clatter of printers, not to mention the noise of conversation.

Standard words: 56

1611 63
1675 127
1737 189
1802 254
1828 280

Total standard words: 366

| | 1 | 2 | 3 | 4 | 5 | 6 | 7 | 8 | 9 | 10 | 11 | 12 | 13 |

Checkpoint B

Vertical centring

Good formatting calls for careful *vertical* placement, with equal space above and below the work.

Some systems are capable of automatic vertical centring. Check your system for this function.

The number of single lines that can be printed on a page does not vary with pitch. For example, whether you are using 10 or 12 pitch, an A4 sheet (portrait) will take 70 lines, an A5 sheet (landscape) 35 lines and an A5 sheet (portrait) 50 lines.

The international standard for line spacing is based on the imperial inch: there are six lines to the vertical inch (approximately 25 mm).

Word processing and some electronic systems have a default page length. This is the length of the printed output that can be entered on each page, or the number of lines that can be printed on each page. The type of printer and the size of top and bottom margins will have a bearing on the number of lines of text that can be printed on a page. If your system has the default page length function, find out what your default page length is and how to reset it.

Roll-back-from-centre method

This method of vertical centring can be used on a typewriter. Follow these instructions.
- Select single line spacing.
- Starting at the top edge of the paper, space down to the vertical centre (35 lines on A4 portrait, 17 lines on A5 landscape or 25 lines on A5 portrait.
- Roll back the platen once for every two lines or line spaces in the document (or use the index up key). Ignore any odd or left-over line.
- Start keying.

Example

Do not key this example as you have not learnt all the keys.

To centre vertically:

Number of lines on an A5 landscape sheet	35
Subtract number of lines and spaces between lines in the piece to be keyed	9
	26
Divide this figure by 2 (26 ÷ 2)	13

Leave 13 blank lines at the head of the paper. (Start keying/printing on the fourteenth line.) If your computer has a default top margin, you will need to make an adjustment.

Space down 14 lines from top edge

```
Vertical centring means placing your work      1
                                               2
in a central position between the top and      3
                                               4
bottom of the paper.  Correct vertical         5
                                               6
centring is one of the first principles of     7
                                               8
good formatting.                               9
```

Double space ↓

A5 landscape • LL: 45 • DS

Job B1

Key this paragraph, centring it vertically.

```
Helen and Janine seek a third tenant in their
fine flat in Redhill.  The flat is sited in a
dear little lane near the Jindala Theatre and
a train line.  The flat is free if I like it.
At this rate I think it is safe that I shall.
```

Follow the end of session procedure.

Keystrokes

32 Office decor
(SI: 1.56)

Colour and texture play an important part in lowering stress 60
levels, lifting spirits and reducing fatigue in the work 116
environment. Modular components and screen dividers in open plan 181
offices are fine, but people still need to be able to project 242
their own personalities in their workplace. This is easier to do 307
if they have their own offices, so that they can hang pictures or 372
pin up photos, charts and posters that are important to them and 436
remind them of special places, times or events.   Standard words: 97 483

Furniture dealers offer huge ranges of colours, fabrics and 542 59
furnishings that can be combined in a wide variety of ways to 603 120
decorate an office. A basic colour can be used and then enhanced 668 185
with similar tones or contrasting colours, depending on the image 733 250
the organisation wishes to project. The effect of the colours 795 312
used will sometimes be to make the workplace seem light, airy and 860 377
casual, while others will create a dark, rich and formal 916 433
atmosphere.   Standard words: 89 927 444

Furniture, too, is used to enhance the corporate image. Modern 990 63
pieces with stark, simple lines, in glass, light-coloured wood or 1055 128
chrome will have quite a different effect from heavy or antique 1118 191
furniture with highly polished surfaces and carved legs. Not 1179 252
only is furniture bought to create an illusion; it also needs to 1243 316
be practical, serviceable and, most of all, comfortable to use 1305 378
and work with.   Standard words: 78 1319 392

With the intelligent use of colour, fabric and finish, the modern 1384 65
office can have a totally different aesthetic appearance to suit 1448 129
the type of business, whether it be a law office, an advertising 1512 193
agency or consulting rooms. A tastefully coloured and decorated 1576 257
environment can be very satisfying and do a lot for both employee 1641 322
morale and client perception of the firm. Look at the next 1700 381
office you enter and see what impact the decor makes on you when 1764 445

Total standard words: 359   you first step through the door.   Standard words: 95 1796 477

O C 9

Posture and technique

- Adopt the comfortable keyboarding posture illustrated on page 1.
- Your hands, arms and wrists should be almost motionless as you key.
- Curve your fingers.
- Tap the keys sharply but lightly with your fingertips.
- Return each finger to the home key after striking another key.

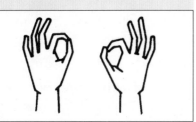

Refresher: warm up on lines 1–3

e/r/t/i
1 de fr ft ki era earn rat rid tea tin ilk isle
All alpha keys
2 Ita Keen is in Deakin. She flies a Lear Jet.
Figures
3 all 35 seats; less than 543; sell the 84 tins

Reach to O with L finger

4 loo lol ooo lol llo lol ool; loo ooo llo ool;
5 on or ot oa os od of io ho no ro to so do fo;
6 one off too son for not ion lot nor soon does
7 done took look order tote those effort notion

Reach to C with D finger

8 dcc dcd ccc dcd ddc dcd ccd; dcc ccc ddc ccd;
9 ca ce cr ct ci co ch ck cl ac sc ec ic oc nc;
10 can act ace car case care cold coin tick sick
11 fact race once each cheer ocean choice attach

Reach to 9 with L finger

12 l9l 19 199 1991; l9l 19 199 1991; l9l 19 1991
13 9 sons; 99 lots; 999 cans; 99 loans; 999 cots
14 9 oars; 99 tots; 999 coats; 99 orders; 9 ices
15 check 9; sack 99; trace 999; join 9; toast 99

New words

16 coal rack face cake lack fore joke knot tonne
17 alone child stool short closes sliced jointed
18 chill rotors certain contact another occasion

Figure review

19 3 or 4 or 5 or 8 or 9; 35 or 84 or 95 or 4539
20 Nola sold 99 noodles. Ollie loans 39 stools.

Build skill on a paragraph. Retain this exercise – you will need it for Checkpoint C.

21 Claire Olsson joined this office last Easter.
   Her role is to assist Oscar Ace in the Orders
   Section. This section looks after all direct
   school orders. Her close contact is Jo Cook.
   All orders are sent to Jo for action. Jo has
   to check each one for error. She takes care.

Follow the end of session procedure.

Keystrokes

**31 Office
automation**
(SI: 1.56)

Automation of any office will cause a great upheaval and, though   64
technology may play a large role in the raising of productivity   127
levels, it cannot bypass people and the way they react to their   190
work. Introducing screen-based technology to a work group in any   255
office will cause some changes to the staff, their roles,   312
functions, responsibilities and relations with each other, as   373
well as their whole work environment.   Standard words: 82   410

There is always some resistance to change, so the key things to   473 63
be aware of when planning for it are not technological but   531 121
behavioural. Change at work can be accomplished smoothly and   592 182
efficiently with the cooperation of staff who know what is going   656 246
to happen, and when and how they will be affected by it. Many   718 308
new changes may override set behaviour patterns which have become   783 373
entrenched in the habits and social relationships of the staff   845 435
within the specific office or firm. Communication is vital to   907 497
the smooth introduction of new office technology. Meetings   966 556
should be held often to keep employees informed of all changes to   1031 621
their working environment and their proposed involvement in these   1096 686
changes.   Standard words: 139   1104 694

Many firms do not understand that a large amount of time and   1164 60
money must be set aside to prepare people for change in their   1225 121
workplace. Staff are the most vital, most costly and least   1284 180
predictable element when changes are being planned for any firm   1347 243
or work group. It is therefore essential that adequate,   1403 299
systematic consideration be given to people's needs when new   1463 359
technology is being introduced, and those who are to be involved   1527 423
with the change are part of the process right from the start. A   1591 487
carefully planned awareness program that keeps staff informed and   1656 552
involved will allay much of the fear of the unknown that is   1715 611
brought about by any proposed change to their working   1768 664

Total standard words: 356 environment.   Standard words: 135   1780 676

1| 2| 3| 4| 5| 6| 7| 8| 9| 10| 11| 12| 13|

Checkpoint C

Proofreading

The purpose of proofreading is to identify and mark keying errors. Carefully proofread all your finished work from now on. Proofread on the screen using the scroll facility or, if you are using a typewriter, before you remove the paper from the machine.

Job C1

1 Proofread the work that you keyed in Unit 1.7 (paragraph 21) and circle any errors.
2 If you made three or more errors, re-key the paragraph, aiming for a perfect copy.
3 *Alternatively*, if you made no more than two errors, key a corrected version of the example above. If you key it without error, your copy will have an even right margin.

LL: 45 • DS • centre vertically

(Clare) (Olssen) joined this (offfice) last Easter. Her role is to (to) assist Oscar Ace (inthe) Orders Section. This section looks after direct school (O)rders. Her close contact is Jo Cook. (all) orders are sent to Jo for action. Jo has to check each one for error. She takes care.

The paragraph above shows the kinds of errors trainee keyboard operators make.

1 letter omitted	4 word repeated	7 upper case instead of lower case
2 wrong letter	5 space omitted	
3 letter repeated	6 word omitted	8 lower case instead of upper case

Job C2

Do not key this paragraph (it contains letters you have not learned), but compare the finished work with the handwritten copy and note the 11 errors.

Proofread the paragraph only

Thank you for your letter of 4 May, addressed to Philip Coe, who passed it to me this morning. Unfortunately, your Order No G3286 was not received until 30 May so it has not been processed. I will, however, ensure that it leaves today.

Thank you for you're letter of 4 May, adressed to Phillip Coe, who past is to me this morning. Unfortunatly, your Order No G3826 was not recieved untill 30 May so it had not been processed. I will, however, insure that it leaves today.

Measure your speed

You can now find your keying rate on selected exercises. Measure your rate by the number of standard *words* keyed in a *minute* (wpm). A standard word comprises five keystrokes.

The speed test paragraph in Job C3 has four lines of nine words each, 36 words in all. If you just completed the paragraph in two minutes your keying rate would be 18 wpm. Find the number of words keyed in the time allowed by reading the scales at the right and the foot of the paragraph. An uncompleted word counts as a complete word if you have keyed at least three strokes. Divide the number of words keyed by the number of minutes in the timing.

Job C3 (SI 1.24)

1 First key this paragraph, concentrating on accuracy.
2 Then take a 1-minute *speed test*, aiming for *controlled* speed.

Follow the end of session procedure.

LL: 45 • DS

	Words
The last train for Riddle Creek is late. All	9
ticket holders are asked to take the train to	18
Jones Hill instead. At Jones Hill there is a	27
fast rail connection to Riddle Creek station.	36

1 2 3 4 5 6 7 8 9

1 | 2 | 3 | 4 | 5 | 6 | 7 | 8 | 9 | 10 | 11 | 12 | 13

Keystrokes

30 Care of floppy disks
(SI: 1.43)

Most small businesses with personal computers use magnetic disks 64
for storing their data. Damage to a disk can mean loss of vital 128
information. There is now a huge amount of data stored on floppy 193
disks throughout the world and, sadly, too many people fail to 255
treat their disks carefully. This can lead to loss of valuable 318
data. 323

Standard words: 65

Disks are formatted or initialised before they can hold data. 384 61
Formatting divides the disk into tracks, which are concentric 445 122
circles drawn around the disk. Each of these tracks is then 505 182
divided into sectors on which bytes of data can be stored. 563 240

Standard words: 48

Floppy disks are covered by a vinyl jacket, which is never 621 58
removed. The read/write head on the computer comes into contact 685 122
with the recording surface through the long hole in this jacket. 749 186
Information is written to or read from the magnetic surface of 811 248
the disk in a way similar to the way a tape recorder works. 870 307

Standard words: 61

Even though these disks are quite durable they do need to be 930 60
handled carefully. For long life and security of recorded data 993 123
they should be stored in dust-proof containers in a vertical 1053 183
position. Never force a disk into a disk drive, and always make 1117 247
sure it is fully inserted into the drive before closing the 1176 306
latch. Do not touch the exposed areas, as this can damage the 1238 368
magnetic coating and lead to loss of valuable data. When 1295 425
labelling a disk use a felt-tipped pen and then attach the stick- 1360 490
on label to the disk. Do not expose the disk to too much heat or 1425 555
sunlight or place magnetic objects near it. Never use rubber 1486 616
bands or paper clips on disks, and do not bend them or place 1546 676
heavy objects on them. Another hazard to floppy disks is 1603 733
liquids: never use alcohol or thinners to clean the disk, and be 1668 798

Total standard words: 342 very careful of your cup of tea or coffee! Standard words: 168 1710 840

1 | 2 | 3 | 4 | 5 | 6 | 7 | 8 | 9 | 10 | 11 | 12 | 13

U G 7

LL: 45 • SS

Review your technique

- Try not to look up at the end of each line. Be strict about keeping your eyes on the copy.
- Remember that the home keys are your 'base'. Keep your fingers in their home key positions when you are not striking other keys.
- Your hands, wrists and arms should be almost motionless as you key.
- Keep your fingers curved.

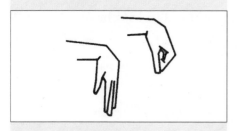

Refresher: warm up on lines 1–3

Common words
1 do so to no of on one too for not can at once
Capitals
2 This is Dr Colin Rice. Face Sir Jock Clarke.
Figures
3 Call 43 5984. Add 89 to 453. 5985 less 348.

Reach to U with J finger

4 juu juj jjj juj jju juj uuj; juu uuu jju uuj;
5 ur ut us ud uf ul un ru su du fu cu lu ou hu;
6 us use our out cut fun run sun just such full
7 sure fuel rule ruin used dual cult unit studs

Reach to G with F finger

8 fgg fgf fff fgf ffg fgf ggf; fgg ggg ffg ggf;
9 ge gr ga gs gu gh go gn gl eg ng ag ug ig og;
10 got get age ago jog goes sign good gone gain;
11 sign sang grant rough light large thing again

Reach to 7 with J finger

12 j7j j7 j77 j77j; j7j j7 j77 j77j; j7j j7 j77j
13 7 jugs; 77 jags; 777 glues; 77 gulls; 7 gusts
14 7 chairs; 77 stars; 777 designs; 77 articles;
15 settle 7; heat 77; cook 777; fold 77; case 77

New words

16 sag gas lug gin fog rug rut gel hut dug egos;
17 juke duke dour goal gaol cage gold golf gale;
18 usual under house should going thing against;

Figure review

19 I think he caught 759 fish at 8.37 on 4 June.
20 He did 35 48 hours ago. I found 873 at 9.47.

Build skill on a paragraph

21 Golf is great fun; or so Gretel thought until she sliced into the rough grass at the fourth hole on the South Leagues Course at Greenock. I had to laugh. She groaned. Then her anger changed to a grin as I struck into that rough ground also. Golf and laughter go together.

Speed test: page 40.
Follow the end of session procedure.

Level 3

| | | | | | | | | | | | | |
|1|2|3|4|5|6|7|8|9|10|11|12|13|

Keystrokes

29 Computers and keyboarding
(SI: 1.52)

Europeans and the rest of the world are at present right in the   63
midst of a technological revolution. More and more of our jobs   126
are becoming automated and there is a much greater reliance on   188
the computer. It is expected that in the next few years about   250
three-quarters of all workers will need to use a keyboard in   310
their jobs.   Standard words: 64   321

In fact, it will be hard for people to avoid using a computer in   385 64
the future. A lack of skill in keyboarding will limit their   445 124
chances of finding a job or of performing a task with maximum   506 185
efficiency.   Standard words: 39   517 196

A large number of homes have microcomputers. Many are put to   578 61
personal use in games or hobbies; others are an extension of   638 121
their users' work environment or even the means of earning a   698 181
living from home. Home computers also play an important part in   762 245
study and have a vital role in distance education.   Standard words: 59 812 295

Keyboarding has become a basic communication tool for all. More   876 64
and more careers, from entry-level jobs to top-level management,   940 128
require the ability to keyboard. The demand for people who can   1003 191
enter data accurately and at high speed will continue to   1059 247
increase. Efficient keyboarding calls for a high level of   1117 305
automatic recall of the keys so as to free the user's mind to   1178 366
concentrate on the task in hand. Sadly, not enough people learn   1242 430

Total standard words: 252   to do this properly.   Standard words: 90 1262 450

| | | | | | | | | | | | | |
|1|2|3|4|5|6|7|8|9|10|11|12|13|

WM2

Proofreading

As a proofreading exercise, count the number of w's and the number of m's in paragraph 20.

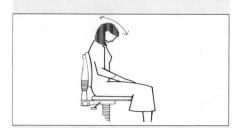

LL: 45 • SS

Refresher: warm up on lines 1–4

c/n
1 can con nice once coin chin clan since centre
All alpha keys
2 Alf can join us at our lodge in Duke Heights.
Figures
3 Flight nos 738 and 549 are on schedule no 37.

Reach to W with S finger

4 sww sws www sws ssw sws wws; sww www ssw wws;
5 we wa wf wu wi wo wh wn ew tw aw ow we wa wh;
6 was win few two how who owe awe low law news;
7 We saw where Lew wed. Wes knows what we own.

Reach to M with J finger

8 jmm jmj mmm jmj jjm jmj mmj; jmm mmm jjm mmj;
9 me ma ms mu mi mo em rm am sm um im om lm me;
10 him met man aim jam come same home time milk;
11 Most men made music. More women manage them.

Reach to 2 with S finger

12 s2s s2 s22 s22s; s2s s2 s22 s22s; s2s s2 s22s
13 2 laws; 22 firms; 222 wags; 22 arms; 22 wins;
14 22 locks; 2 canes; 22 deeds; 2 nights; 2 jigs
15 catch 22; make 222; sort 22; watch 22; aid 22

New words

16 mar alm mat ham mad ohm dew owl sew won wells
17 mare came form from firm when with will known
18 model claim metre meant which while would wit

Figure review

19 Check item 28 on docket 4579. It should read
   35 tonnes not 38. Delete no 32 on note 2798.

Build skill on a paragraph

20 New formula Grime adds scum to washing. With
   Grime in their water home makers wonder where
   the white went. Some men and women now claim
   new Grime smears their washing much more than
   most other known makes on the market. Demand
   in the month of March as a whole was awesome.

Speed test: page 40.
Follow the end of session procedure.

	1	2	3	4	5	6	7	8	9	10	11	12	13	

Keystrokes

27 Relief of tension
(3I. 1.57)

Studies have shown that the right exercises improve the ability 63
of a person to relax, and that a relaxed person works and thinks 127
more efficiently. Increased physical activity stimulates 184
circulation throughout the body and helps all the brain cells 245
receive the nutrients they need, as well as relaxing tension- 306
filled limbs. During a busy day, muscles store up tension which 370
can lead to back, arm and hand pains, a stiff neck or headaches. 434
Exercises can relieve these areas of tension. You can select 495
those that fit your needs.   Standard words: 104 521

Some can be performed at your work station, either sitting or 582 61
standing. You can do others while driving home, travelling on 644 123
public transport or even as you watch TV. Get into the habit of 708 187
doing them regularly throughout the day and you will be amazed at 773 252
the difference to your mental attitude, physical well-being, 833 312

Total standard words: 174 concentration and performance levels.   Standard words: 70 870 349

	1	2	3	4	5	6	7	8	9	10	11	12	13	

28 Wind energy
(SI: 1.53)

Only 1-2 per cent of all solar energy results in wind energy; but 65
if all this wind energy were harnessed efficiently and used to 127
make electricity, it could produce 10 times more power than all 190
the people on Earth use in one year.   Standard words: 45 226

The wind been used for centuries as an energy source. It was 287 61
used as early as 5000 years ago, when it gave the power for such 351 125
tasks as pumping water for irrigation, grinding grain and sailing 416 190
ships. In more recent times, wind has become an important energy 481 255
source for generating electricity, especially in far-flung areas, 546 320
and as part of national electricity supply grids. The use of 607 381
wind energy is growing as fossil fuels become dear and in short 670 444
supply. Pollution caused by these fuels is also of concern. 730 504
                                                 Standard words: 101

Like solar energy, the wind can be thought of as free, but 788 58
because special equipment is needed to extract the energy from 850 120

Total standard words: 179 the wind there is a cost in using wind energy.   Standard words: 33 896 166

	1	2	3	4	5	6	7	8	9	10	11	12	13	

Appendix 1 cont *Speed tests Level 2*   **180**

Checkpoint D

Proofreading marks 1

The trained keyboard operator should not only be a competent proofreader, but also

- know how to mark work for correction
- be able to interpret the marks made by others.

Study the proofreading marks opposite and make sure you understand them before attempting Jobs D1 and D2.

Word processing functions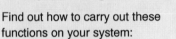

Find out how to carry out these functions on your system:

- *deleting* a character
- *deleting* a word
- *adding* a character
- *adding* a word
- *substituting* a character or word for another (also called *overwriting* or *overtyping*).

Proofreading marks

Mark in text	Mark in margin	Corrected passage
Inset a character.	r /	Insert a character.
Insert aspace.	#	Insert a space.
Deleted a character.	♌ or del	Delete a character.
Delete and close up.	♌ or del	Delete and close up.
Insert a /.	word /	Insert a word.
Delete a ~~word~~ word.	♌ or del	Delete a word.
Cancel a change. '	' ⅄	Cancel a change.
Insert a full stop		Insert a full stop.
Insert a word/	or words	Insert a word or words.

Note that sometimes proofreading marks are used in the text with no marginal instructions.

Job D1

1 If your system allows, name this document.
2 Key a corrected copy, *keeping to the same line endings.*
3 Proofread. If you key a perfect copy, you will have an even right margin.
4 If your system allows, save the document.

A5 landscape • LL: 45 • DS • centre vertically

In this an later units the common correction
marks are introduced demonstrated. These are
signs are the standard ones words in use. Some are
taught in each lesson to make them easier for
the student to learn From this stage on use
these signs to mark all errors in a document.

Job D2

1 If you saved the document in Job D1, retrieve it and edit as follows, *keeping to the same line endings.*
2 If you did not save it, key a corrected copy of the complete paragraph.
3 Proofread. If you key a perfect copy, you will have an even right margin.

A5 landscape • LL: 45 • DS • centre vertically

Here
~~In this~~ and later units the common correction
marks are introduced and demonstrated. These
signs are the standard ones in use. Some are
taught in each lesson to make them ~~easier~~ for stet
the student to learn. From this stage on use
stet these signs to ~~mark all~~ correct errors in a document.

Follow the end of session procedure.

	1	2	3	4	5	6	7	8	9	10	11	12	13	

Keystrokes

25 Training adults
(SI: 1.56)

The training of adults is a specialised field of study - the   60
trainer is not catering for a group of large children waiting to   124
be taught. Rather, they are usually highly self-motivated and   186
self-directed learners who may be forced to join a course in   246
which they see no great benefit.   Standard words: 56   278

The emphasis for the trainer should be on providing a learning   340 62
atmosphere for the group of adults which assists the learning   401 123
process, is non-threatening, and which enables the people in the   465 187
group to achieve their maximum potential.   Standard words: 46   506 228

Each person in the group will perform differently. Some may be   569 63
slower than others; some show more anxiety; some are less willing   634 128
to seek help; some may even appear indifferent to the task. The   698 192
positive, effective and sympathetic trainer will be able to cater   763 257
to these differences and still achieve good results in the   821 315

Total standard words: 168   training program.   Standard words: 66   838 332

	1	2	3	4	5	6	7	8	9	10	11	12	13	

26 Spreadsheets
(SI: 1.5)

Spreadsheets are not new to business. A spreadsheet is a form   62
set out in columns and rows which accountants have used for years   127
to compare costs and revenues and to predict future performance.   191
It is not hard to see, though, that without the aid of a computer   256
using a spreadsheet would be a slow and tedious process. Their   319
application to the computer has encouraged much more widespread   382
use in recent times.   Standard words: 80   402

Electronic spreadsheets have become popular because they have so   466 64
many applications in business and are so easy to use. All   524 122
calculations are performed in an instant once the figures are   585 183
keyed into the columns. If a figure is changed the computer   645 243
recalculates the rest of the figures. Spreadsheets save time and   710 308
allow the user to apply, for example, different sales volumes,   772 370
prices and discounts to a sales budget to give a more precise   833 431

Total standard words: 170   forecast of profit.   Standard words: 90   852 450

	1	2	3	4	5	6	7	8	9	10	11	12	13	

BY 6

Do not attempt to key the vertical strokes in lines 1 and 18. Leave a space where a stroke is shown.

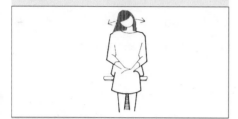

LL: 45 • SS

Refresher: warm up on lines 1–3
Simple phrases
1 I am |of the |for her |he was |she will |if it can
All alpha keys
2 Jamie seeks the aid of Cleo in working hours.
Figures
3 Figures 8.23 and 9.45 are now 7.32 and 24.59.

Reach to B with F finger
4 fbb fbf bbb fbf ffb fbf bbf; fbb bbb ffb bbf;
5 be br ba bs bu bi bo bl eb rb ab ub ib ob lb;
6 but big bar job bag bet bob bin tub able curb
7 Bob and Bess grabbed both the bank bags back.

Reach to Y with J finger
8 jyy jyj yyy jyj jjy jyj yyj; jyy yyy jjy yyj;
9 ye ys ey ry ty ay sy dy fy gy cy by ly ny my;
10 why lay way say day may hay fly any try they;
11 Kay and Ray always carry ninety trays to Rye.

Reach to 6 with J finger
12 j6j j6 j66 j66j; j6j j6 j66 j66j; j6j j6 j66j
13 6 days; 66 boats; 666 birds; 6 kerbs; 6 bulls
14 take 6; sign 66; back 666; fill 66; test 666.

New words
15 bay sty dry sky gay beg bog bad bed bow bees;
16 yell york yank body yolk been bunk book noble
17 yacht hurry yeast jelly being doubt about bud

Review all figures
18 32 years ago |in Section 54 |in Unit 67 |line 98
19 I am 34. He is 65. She was 27. They own 9.

Build skill on a paragraph
20 Yesterday Yolanda Yea bought the yellow brick
   bungalow you built in the back yard in Yarrah
   Mews. Because her bank balance is buoyant it
   is my belief that Yolanda will easily be able
   to buy the bungalow without any necessity for
   borrowing from my bank or a building society.

Speed test: page 40.
Follow the end of session procedure.

| | 1 | 2 | 3 | 4 | 5 | 6 | 7 | 8 | 9 | 10 | 11 | 12 | 13 |

Keystrokes

23 Ergonomics
(SI: 1.47)

Office workers need more than the right type of ergonomic chair; 64
they should also have work stations or desks that are tailored to 129
their particular needs. Workers vary in size, shape and weight 192
and to accommodate this wide variety of people there must be a 254
good deal of adjustability in furniture.   Standard words: 59   294

The posture of any office worker is affected by the placement of   358 64
documents, keyboard, screen (both height and distance), work   418 124
surface and chair. The feet should rest directly on the floor or 483 189
footrest, with the forearms parallel to the floor; eyes should be 548 254
level with the screen. Rest breaks should be taken as often as   611 317
needed. Get up and file something. Talk to an associate.   669 375
Answer the telephone. These activities all give the back, arms   732 438

Total standard words: 157   and neck that necessary pause from tension and use.   Standard words: 98   783 489

| | 1 | 2 | 3 | 4 | 5 | 6 | 7 | 8 | 9 | 10 | 11 | 12 | 13 |

24 Rest pauses
(SI: 1.55)

Rest pauses are a necessary part of an effective work routine.   62
Answering the phone, talking to a visitor, a trip to the   118
photocopier or a break for tea or coffee relieve mental stress   180
and should be viewed as a natural part of the working day.   238
                                                Standard words: 48

Rest pauses and changes of task are essential for those who are   301 63
continually working at screen-based equipment. The nature,   360 122
length and frequency of rest pauses will depend on the person,   422 184
the task, the environment, the equipment and a range of other   483 245
factors.   Standard words: 51   491 253

It is important to create an atmosphere in which computer   548 57
operators feel they can take a break whenever they need to.   607 116
Evidence shows that suitable rest pauses and changes of task   667 176
increase total productivity and reduce tension and stress.   725 234
Wherever possible screen-based work should be part of the user's 789 298

Total standard words: 165   daily routine, rather than all of it.   Standard words: 67   826 335

| | 1 | 2 | 3 | 4 | 5 | 6 | 7 | 8 | 9 | 10 | 11 | 12 | 13 |

PVO

Do not attempt to key the vertical strokes in line 3. Leave a space where a stroke is shown.

LL: 45 • SS

Refresher: warm up on lines 1–3

ing
1 ring thing being doing baking having knowing
All alpha keys
2 Mohair jerseys make Hans Ludwig comfortable.
Figures
3 7.8 metres|3.6 tonnes|4.2 grams |9.5 hectares

Reach to P with ; finger

4 ;pp ;p; ppp ;p; ;;p ;p; pp; ;pp ppp ;;p pp; p
5 pe pr pa py pu pi po pl ep rp ap sp mp ip op;
6 up pa put pen pot pan ape opt sap nip rip map
7 Phillip will help to pass the open span plan.

Reach to V with F finger

8 fvv fvf vvv fvf ffv fvf vvf; fvv vvv ffv vvf;
9 ve va vy vu vi vo lv ev rv av uv iv ov lv eve
10 via vet vat vim view live over ever even have
11 Give Vick veal vol au vents; serve Viv liver.

Reach to 0 with ; finger

12 ;0; ;0 ;00 ;00; ;0; ;0 ;00 ;00; ;0; ;0 ;00; 0
13 20 trips 80 ports 30 packs 40 love 90 carpets
14 200 places 800 hovels 300 ploughs 400 shovels
15 divide 202 into 404; 303 plus 707; 606 is all

New words

16 trap pair pats pace opal vain oven very every
17 group spent apple proof govern events sheaves
18 appeal person public seventy heavenly vinegar

Figure review

19 206 Mill Lane; 738 High Street; 45 Elm Avenue
20 on pages 390 and 468 of her report of 27 June

Build skill on a paragraph

21 Valda and Vince have packed apple and apricot pies for our picnic at Belvue Park. I prefer peach and pawpaw but will have to put up with whatever filling Vincent plumps for. My view on picnic pies and pasties has never received the points it deserves. It gives me the pip.

Speed test: page 40.
Follow the end of session procedure.

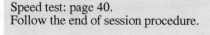

Level 2

| | 1 | 2 | 3 | 4 | 5 | 6 | 7 | 8 | 9 | 10 | 11 | 12 | 13 |

Keystrokes

21 Business letters
(SI: 1.57)

The written word is at least as important as the spoken word, but 65

we often do not pay enough attention to the art of writing 123

effective business letters. Standard words: 30 150

The style in which you write your letters is vital to the 207 57

reader's understanding of your message. Never talk down to the 270 120

reader: you can make suggestions without being condescending. 332 182

Whatever your style, your letters should provide information that 397 247

is correct and useful to the receiver. When you write a reply, 460 310

respond to all questions in clear, concise language that cannot 523 373

be misunderstood. Standard words: 78 540 390

Use grammatical language. Avoid jargon or slang. Choose your 602 62

words with care to convey the message so far as possible in 661 121

Total standard words: 136 everyday language. Standard words: 28 679 139

| | 1 | 2 | 3 | 4 | 5 | 6 | 7 | 8 | 9 | 10 | 11 | 12 | 13 |

22 Information
(SI: 1.49)

The amount of information available to humankind has more than 62

doubled in the past ten years and it is likely at least to double 127

again by the end of the century. Much of this flood of 182

information has been created by advances in office automation in 246

the past four decades and especially since the early 1970s. 305

Office machines today do things much faster and they do them with 370

less effort. It used to take days - sometimes weeks - to get 431

accurate answers to the simplest questions; for example, who the 495

firm's 200 best customers were; how much was owed by country 555

customers; and so on. Because people knew it would take so long 619

to get the answers, the questions were not asked unless they were 684

essential. Most firms worked under handicaps that would not be 747

Total standard words: 153 tolerated today. 763

| | 1 | 2 | 3 | 4 | 5 | 6 | 7 | 8 | 9 | 10 | 11 | 12 | 13 |

Checkpoint E

Proofreading marks 2

Study the proofreading marks opposite and make sure you understand them before attempting Jobs E1 to E4.

Proofreading marks		
Mark in text	**Mark in margin**	**Corrected passage**
Transpose adjacent characters.	trs	Transpose adjacent characters.
Transpose words adjacent.	trs	Transpose adjacent words.
blue red green yellow	trs	yellow red green blue
Move to left. Move to right.		Move to left. Move to right.
to the previous line. This means 'no new paragraph'.	run on	to the previous line. This means 'no new paragraph'.
mark means 'run on'. This is the mark for a new paragraph.	NP or ||	mark means 'run on'. This is the mark for·a new paragraph.
Parallel vertical lines mean 'straighten the margin'.		Parallel vertical lines mean 'straighten the margin'.
These letters, written in the margin, mean 'key in single spacing'.	S|S	These letters, written in the margin, mean 'key in single spacing'.
These indicate that the passage is to be keyed in double spacing.	D|S	These indicate that the passage is to be keyed in double spacing.
When you want a passage keyed in triple spacing, use these letters.	T|S	When you want a passage keyed in triple spacing, use these letters.

Job E1

1 If your system allows, name this document.
2 Key a corrected copy, *keeping to the same line endings.*
3 Proofread. If you key a perfect copy, you will have an even right margin.
4 If your system allows, save the document.

A5 landscape • LL: 45 • DS

trs Should you ahve to proofread hard copy from a
trs word processor include always the appropriate
\|\| marginal mark as well as the mark in the body
\|\| of the passage. This enables the operator
to take in at a glance what changes must be made
and where.
run on It is then an easy matter to call the document up
and key in all these corrections.

Keystrokes

17
(SI: 1.52)

A scanner is a device that reads text or other images from a page   65
straight into a computer. Typewritten or printed documents or   127
those with graphics in them do not have to be keyed into the   187
computer or redrawn if a scanner is part of the system. By means   252
of a scanner you can convert typewritten or printed matter, line   316
drawings or photographs directly onto the screen. Apart from   377
being a time saver, a scanner can give a report or other   433

Total standard words: 93   publication a professional look.   465

18
(SI: 1.6)

Desktop publishing has emerged as one of the most important   59
developments in computing. It borrows from computing, television   124
and communications to provide a complete system for creating   184
printed matter. 'Desktop' is part of the description because the   249
whole system can be assembled on a desktop. Photographs,   306
drawings and text can be combined on the screen in a few minutes   370
instead of the hours or days it used to take. A single user is   433

Total standard words: 95   in complete control of the entire process.   475

19
(SI: 1.59)

Data and images can be transmitted from one place to another by   63
using electronic mail. It removes the need to send hard copies   126
of letters and other messages through the usual mail system. A   189
major advantage of electronic mail is that data can be sent and   252
received almost instantaneously. Computer-based messaging is an   316
aspect of electronic mail which provides electronic mail boxes.   379
A blinking light on the screen signals to the receiver that a   440

Total standard words: 100   message is in the mail box and can be viewed on the screen.   499

20
(SI: 1.47)

Database management is the pooling of the files of a business in   64
a computerised file centre in a central place. All the files in   128
the business are part of the system. There is no need for   186
separate departmental systems to be set up in each department.   248
Files are created, maintained, stored and deleted at this source.   313
All authorised staff have access to the data. Database   368
management puts a filing system in the hands of specialists and   431
cuts out the waste of time and effort that results from the   490

Total standard words: 104   duplication of data and files.   520

Job E2

1 If you saved the document in Job E1, retrieve it and edit as follows, *keeping to the same line endings.*
2 If you did not save it, key a corrected copy of the complete paragraph.
3 Proofread. If you key a perfect copy, you will have an even right margin.

A5 landscape • LL: 45 • DS • centre vertically

Should you have to proofread hard copy from a word processor always include the appropriate marginal mark as well as the ~~sign~~ mark in the body of the ~~passage~~. This enables the operator to take in at a glance what changes must be made and where. It is then an easy matter to call the document up and key in these corrections.

Different rules do apply to handwritten copy.

Keying from handwritten copy

Job E3

1 Proofread the typed paragraph against the handwritten copy.
2 Find and mark eight errors.
3 Now key a correct version.

A5 landscape • LL: 30 • DS • centre vertically

Ms G Wild of Desert Flora came to see you this afternoon. As you were in conference I asked her to leave her card. She is very enthusiastic about cactus arrangements and says they can withstand even the harshest of heating systems.

Mr C Wild of Dessert Flora came to see you this afternoon. As you were inconference I asked her to leave her card. She is really enthusiastic about cacti arrangements and said they can withstand even the harshest heating systems.

Job E4

1 Key an accurate copy of the following paragraph.
2 Proofread, and mark any errors with standard proofreading signs.
If you key a perfect copy you will finish with an even right margin.

A5 landscape • LL: 45 • DS • centre vertically

When making alterations to manuscript copy there is no need to make marks in the margin unless there is not room in the copy itself. This is because whoever has the task of typing it must read each line in detail anyhow. You do not need to alert the operator to the corrections by writing a note in the margin.

Follow the end of session procedure.

1 | 2 | 3 | 4 | 5 | 6 | 7 | 8 | 9 | 10 | 11 | 12 | 13

Keystrokes

13
(SI: 1.53)

Job performance appraisals are quite commonly used in business to   65
assess the strengths and weaknesses of the firm's employees. At   129
least once a year the supervisor prepares a written appraisal for   194
each member of the staff who reports to him or her. Some   251
suggestions for improving performance may be added. The   307
appraisal is normally discussed with the employee, who should be   371

Total standard words: 83   given the chance to express his or her views.   416

1 | 2 | 3 | 4 | 5 | 6 | 7 | 8 | 9 | 10 | 11 | 12 | 13

14
(SI: 1.6)

The initial introduction of a new employee to his or her   56
workplace is called induction or orientation. There is often a   119
formal induction program that deals with the introduction of more   184
than one new staff member at a time. In it the policies of the   247
firm are spelt out and so are the organisational structure and   309
such things as staff benefits and amenities. Procedures that   370

Total standard words: 84   relate to specific positions are covered as well.   419

1 | 2 | 3 | 4 | 5 | 6 | 7 | 8 | 9 | 10 | 11 | 12 | 13

15
(SI: 1.5)

Do you realise what an admission of weakness it is to say that   62
someone has made you angry? You are really demonstrating that   124
someone else has taken control of your feelings. It is true that   189
other people can influence your emotions, but they should not be   253
permitted to exert control over them. Displaying anger is not in   318
itself a sign of weakness; you are only being weak if you allow   381

Total standard words: 84   someone else to dictate your behaviour.   420

1 | 2 | 3 | 4 | 5 | 6 | 7 | 8 | 9 | 10 | 11 | 12 | 13

16
(SI: 1.45)

An icon is a picture on a computer screen which allows the user   63
to direct the computer to perform a task. The icon for a file   125
might be a file folder. Other icons commonly used are calculator   190
pads, clip boards and even waste paper baskets. The user moves a   255
pointer to the symbol that represents the task to be carried out   319
and presses the button on a hand-held mouse. Users with good   380

Total standard words: 85   keyboard skills may find this exercise tedious.   427

1 | 2 | 3 | 4 | 5 | 6 | 7 | 8 | 9 | 10 | 11 | 12 | 13

Appendix *1* cont *Speed tests Level 1*

Q Comma 1

LL: 45 • SS

Refresher: warm up on lines 1–3
Double letters
1 ebb err access eddy eel Emma egg huff all Ann
All alpha keys
2 Jeff will make a very good branch post issue.
Figures
3 Flights 48 and 967 are due at 2305 hrs today.

Reach to Q with A finger
4 aqq aqa qqq aqa aaq aqa qqa; aqq qqq aaq qqa;
5 qu'aq sq iq cq eq quad aqua quit quip quay qu
6 queue quite quote quirk quaff mosque quarrel;
7 Quentin acquires a unique squeak in a squall.

Reach to , with K finger
8 k,, k,k ,,, k,k kk, k,k ,,k k,, ,,, kk, ,,k ,
9 kith, kin, kind, akin, kindred, kinship, key,
10 Have knife, fork and spoon, and form a queue.
11 I am, as a rule, kind, gentle and quite calm.

Reach to 1 with A finger
12 a1a a1 a11 a11a a1a a1 a11 1aa1 a1a a1 a11a 1
13 1 ace, 11 asps, 111 ants, 11 ages, 111 altos,
14 Request 11 more, 1 for each of the 11 squads.
15 On 11 May 1911; figure 1.11; 11 am; 1111 hrs.

New words
16 quin quid quill quest squat quell quick pique
17 quack quiff queen equal quire squeal required
18 sequel requisite squeamish quivered querulous

Review all figures
19 Unit 14, 208 Ash Street; Flat 25, 96 Rye Road
20 75 kg, 98 mm, 46 g, 27 t, 10 cm, 38 L, 23 mL;

Build skill on a paragraph
21 We request your quotation for a quire of high
quality paper, as well as a quantity of pens,
pencils, pads and markers, all Quentin brand,
required in this quarter. This request will,
I hope, qualify for quite quick action as our
requirements are, genuinely, uniquely urgent.

Speed test: page 40.
Follow the end of session procedure.

| | 1 | 2 | 3 | 4 | 5 | 6 | 7 | 8 | 9 | 10 | 11 | 12 | 13 |

Keystrokes

9
(SI: 1.56)

Stress is an unavoidable fact of life. But research has shown 62
that a limited amount of stress does us no harm; in fact it may 125
be quite good for us. However, different people have different 188
stress thresholds. One person's enjoyment level may be someone 251
else's anxiety point. We should all learn to recognise our 310
particular threshold and how to exercise control over situations 374

Total standard words: 81 | that may cause us to exceed it. 405

| | 1 | 2 | 3 | 4 | 5 | 6 | 7 | 8 | 9 | 10 | 11 | 12 | 13 |

10
(SI: 1.57)

Excessive stress can show itself in quite a few ways: fatigue, 63
feelings of anxiety, moments of panic, an inability to 117
concentrate, sudden mood swings, bouts of depression, sleepless 180
nights and even an obsessive drive for perfection. People 238
suffering from stress are putting their health at risk. 293
Excessive stress is thought to be a factor contributing to heart 357

Total standard words: 81 | disease as well as to all sorts of minor ailments. 407

| | 1 | 2 | 3 | 4 | 5 | 6 | 7 | 8 | 9 | 10 | 11 | 12 | 13 |

11
(SI: 1.5)

An office can be a stressful place in which to work. This is 61
because it is an environment where people with different 117
personalities work together as part of a team. Being assertive 180
is one way to counter stress. It will help you to relax, and you 245
will not waste any energy putting a clamp on your personality. 307
Regular exercise, fresh air and a sensible diet will also help 369

Total standard words: 82 | you cope with any stress that may arise. 409

| | 1 | 2 | 3 | 4 | 5 | 6 | 7 | 8 | 9 | 10 | 11 | 12 | 13 |

12
(SI: 1.53)

Psychologists say that folded arms are often a signal that, 59
subconsciously at least, a person is trying to put up a barrier 122
between herself and the other party to a conversation. Such a 184
posture may suggest resentment and unwillingness to listen to the 249
other person's views. Drumming the desk with your fingers or 310
tapping it with the end of a pencil is a sign of impatience; it 373

Total standard words: 82 | is a good idea to control these habits. 412

| | 1 | 2 | 3 | 4 | 5 | 6 | 7 | 8 | 9 | 10 | 11 | 12 | 13 |

X Colon Shift lock

The colon

Leave one space after a colon. In these exercises, if a colon occurs at the end of a line return without spacing.

The shift lock

The shift lock allows you to key in a succession of capital letters without having to hold down the shift key.

- On a *computer* release the shift lock by striking the shift lock key again.
- On an *electronic typewriter* release the shift lock by striking the shift key.

LL: 45 • SS

Refresher: warm up on lines 1–3
Comma/ion
1 ion, action, motion, nation, vision, fashions
All alpha keys
2 Megan Quick and Jeff Provis will both comply.
Figures
3 Please call Justin on 438 9762 after 5.30 pm.

Reach to X with S finger
4 sxx sxs xxx sxs ssx sxs xxs; sxx xxx ssx xxs;
5 xe xt xc xi xp xh ex ax ix ox xe xt xc xi xp;
6 fix six fox lax mix hex sex axe box sax waxen
7 Alex Marx, tax expert, expects sixty at Expo.

Key : with LEFT SHIFT and ; finger
8 ; ;   : : To: From: Date: Subject: Reference:
9 Note these names: Tess Rix; Rex Fox; Sid Day.
10 Her address is: Falls Lodge, Perth, Tayside.

Reach to SHIFT LOCK with A finger
12 This is the MAXIMUM speed now; do NOT exceed.
13 Their names are: CLAIRE, EDWINA and RUTH LEA.
14 The commands are: CREATES, CLEAR and DISPLAY.

New words
15 text prix flax flex minx axle jinx hoax exact
16 index extra excel excess explain complex exit
17 export excite sphinx exhumes explore exclaims

Review all figures
18 The ingredients are: 125 g SLICED AUBERGINES,
    90 g MINCED BEEF, 647 g LASAGNE, 83 g CHEESE.

Build skill on a paragraph
19 In an exclusive briefing next week, MAX RIXON
    will explain his excellent new TAX INDEXATION
    SCHEME. This complex plan is expected to aid
    executives over sixty whose income, exclusive
    of exceptional expenses, did not exceed forty
    thousand pounds for this year of examination.

Speed test: page 40.
Follow the end of session procedure.

Keystrokes

5
(SI: 1.6)

Eye contact is an important element of body language. Look 59
directly at the person with whom you are speaking; but don't make 124
the mistake of fixing him or her with an unwavering stare. That 188
would be unnerving! To look everywhere but at the other person 251
would be just as disconcerting. Try to strike a happy medium by 315
making frequent eye contact - and maintaining an interested 374

Total standard words: 78   facial expression. 392

6
(SI: 1.45)

Everyone uses body language, although some of us may not be 59
conscious of it. Facial expression, tone of voice, posture, eye 123
contact, not to mention the way we use our arms and hands, are 185
all indications of our emotional state when we are carrying on a 249
conversation with someone. Since we can't really avoid using 310
body language in one way or another, the least we can do is to 372

Total standard words: 79   use it in a positive way. 397

7
(SI: 1.57)

Most places of work have a strict rule forbidding the passing of 64
personal information about members of staff to outsiders. It is 128
the duty of a receptionist or a secretary to be as helpful as 189
possible to callers, but such assistance should not extend to 250
giving out such details as private addresses or telephone numbers 315
of staff, no matter how much the caller insists, or how genuine 378

Total standard words: 80   the request seems to be. 402

8
(SI: 1.48)

When speaking to someone the words we use are not the only form 63
of language we employ. Although we may not be conscious of it, 126
we reinforce our words with what psychologists call 'body 183
language'. We use facial expressions and gestures to communicate 248
meaning. When you sit on the edge of your chair at a job 305
interview, for example, you are signalling to your prospective 367

Total standard words: 81   employer that you are feeling nervous. 405

Z Question mark

LL: 45 • SS

The question mark

Space twice after a question mark at the end of a sentence. In these exercises, if a question mark occurs at the end of a line return without spacing.

Refresher: warm up on lines 1–3
Phrases
1 such as: for example: but to sum up: it was this:
xc/cv/vb
2 excel coax cave cove vice verbs behave beaver
Figures/colon
3 2:3 equals 4:6; 5:1 is 10:2; 79 minus 8 is 71

Reach to Z with A finger
4 azz aza zzz aza aaz aza zza azz zzz aaz zza z
5 ze zy zu zi zo ez rz tz az uz iz oz zl az zip
6 zap zoo zag zed gaze zone size zinc quiz zero
7 Seized with a dozen sneezes, Zoe became hazy.

Key ? with LEFT SHIFT and ; finger
8 ;; ?? how? why? where? which? when? who?
↓*Space twice*
9 Are you? Can it? Could they? Will he? No?
10 Shall I call? Did you order? May we supply?
11 Did Liz win a prize? Fancy a pizza, Zenobia?
12 Why laze and doze when we can hear zany jazz?
13 Did dazzling Kez give Zulus a buzz in Zambia?

Upward and downward reaches
Home row
14 Ask sad Hal; Glad has a Jag; Dad had a flask.
Top row
15 We were quite true to our two pretty poppies.
Bottom row
16 Can Max sneeze? No, but Vince and Brian can.

Figure review
17 Wendy Dixon ran the 42.2 km course in 2 hours
   38 minutes and 15 seconds, just 4 minutes and
   26 seconds faster than her best time in 1989.

Build skill on a paragraph
18 Fancy a lazy holiday in New Zealand? Keen to
   get behind the wheel of the amazing new Mazda
   or squeeze into a snazzy Suzuki? Itching for
   a jumbo size freezer in your home? These are
   only some of the dazzling prizes to be seized
   at the Pizza Parlour Crazy Quiz next Saturday
   on the mezzanine of the Plaza Hotel, Fitzroy.

Speed test: page 41.
Follow the end of session procedure.

Level 1

Keystrokes

1
(SI: 1.52)

Assertive people respect the rights of others but in return | 59
expect other people to show respect for them. They are not too | 122
self-conscious to let their views be known and do not allow | 181
others to impose on them. They refuse unreasonable requests and | 245
are not afraid of going against the other person's wishes in | 305

Total standard words: 74

doing so. Assertion is really the expression of self-confidence. | 370

2
(SI: 1.44)

Self-assertive people neither surrender their rights to others | 62
nor behave with aggression. Self-assertiveness is a positive | 123
rather than a negative trait which we should all try to nurture. | 187
Some people find it quite painful to 'stick up for themselves'. | 250
They take the easy way out and 'give in' to others. But it is | 312

Total standard words: 74

worth making the effort in order to improve your self-image. | 372

3
(SI: 1.45)

Aggressive behaviour is to be deplored. Yet so is the behaviour | 64
of people at the other end of the scale: those who adopt a | 123
submissive approach in their dealings with others. They very | 184
rarely express their opinions on an issue, often allowing their | 247
colleagues or friends to speak for them; they allow others to | 308
'use' them. This is their way of avoiding conflict in their | 368

Total standard words: 75

lives. | 374

4
(SI: 1.52)

Some people adopt an aggressive manner and mistake this for | 59
assertiveness. They demand their own way on every issue with no | 123
thought for the views or needs of their fellow human beings. | 183
They may use sarcasm, ridicule, threats or even violence to force | 248
their point of view on others. Although they may not always show | 313

Total standard words: 75

it, they are usually unhappy people – and often lack confidence. | 377

Checkpoint F

Proofreading marks 3

Study the proofreading marks opposite and make sure you understand them before attempting Jobs F1 and F2.

Proofreading marks		
Mark in text	**Mark in margin**	**Corrected passage**
this is the sign for 'change to a capital letter' . . .	cap or UC	This is the sign for 'change to a capital letter' . . .
. . . And this is the sign for 'change to a small letter'.	lc	. . . and this is the sign for 'change to a small letter'.
To insert a comma, write this.	(,)	To insert a comma, write this.
This is the sign for a semicolon and a colon is marked thus	(;) (:)	This is the sign for a semicolon; and a colon is marked thus:
This sign means 'close up space between characters'.	⌒	This sign means 'close up space between characters'.

Job F1

1 If your system allows, name this document.
2 Key a corrected copy, *keeping to the same line endings.*
3 Proofread. If you key a perfect copy, you will have an even right margin.
4 If your system allows, save the document.

A5 landscape • LL: 45 • DS • centre vertically

uc it is good practice to proofread long reports
double handed. It is done like this. one of uc
the checkers reads out loud from the Original
(;) Copy meanwhile the other reads the Printout.
This way it is easy to be certain nothing has #
been omitted and to find any errors. Lots of ⌒
people find it difficult to do the job alone.

Job F2

1 If you saved the document in Job E1, retrieve it and edit as follows, *keeping to the same line endings.*
2 If you did not save it, key a corrected copy of the complete paragraph.
3 Proofread. If you key a perfect copy, you will have an even right margin.

Follow the end of session procedure.

A5 landscape • LL: 45 • DS • centre vertically

It is good practice to proofread long reports
caps double handed. It is done like this. one of
the checkers reads out loud from the Original lc
lc Copy; meanwhile the other reads the Printout. lc
(,) This way it is easy to be certain nothing has
been omitted and to find any errors. Lots of
stet people find it difficult to do the job alone.

Appendix 1 Speed tests

Contents

Introduction
Level 1 Passages 1–20 (number of standard words: approximately 75–100)
Level 2 Passages 21–28 (number of standard words: approximately 135–220)
Level 3 Passages 29–36 (number of standard words: approximately 250–400)

Introduction

The speed test passages in Appendix 1 are intended to build accuracy and speed in keystroking.

Passages in this appendix are graded as follows:

- Level 1 (approximately 75–100 standard words)
- Level 2 (approximately 135–220 standard words)
- Level 3 (approximately 250–400 standard words).

It is left to the teacher to select passages of suitable length and difficulty at appropriate intervals.

Format

- A 10-pitch typewriter font, not proportionally spaced, is to be used.
- The maximum line length is 65 keystrokes.
- Progressive stroke counts are provided in the right margin and at the foot of the passage.

Content

- The content is of a business or social nature.
- Where headings are included they are not part of the speed test.
- The average syllabic intensity of the passages falls between 1.4 and 1.6 syllables per actual (ie not standard) word.
- The passages do not contain an unusually high number of technical or unusual words or an unusually high proportion of common words.
- Numbers and signs do not constitute more than 1 per cent of the total words in a passage.

Test conditions

- Under test conditions students should be allowed a warm-up of at least 5 minutes.

- They should be allowed a 1-minute pre-reading of the passage.
- The duration of the test is 5 minutes.
- It is not necessary to key the passages line for line, although the student will find it convenient to set a 65-space line.

Speed calculation

1 Calculate the number of standard words completed in 5 minutes by dividing the number of keystrokes by 5.
2 Divide the number of standard words by 5 to calculate the number of standard words keyed per minute.

Accuracy calculation

In order for students to achieve at least 98 per cent accuracy, no more than two errors are allowed in every 100 standard words.

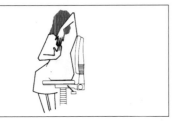
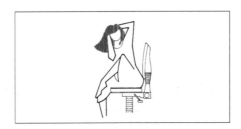
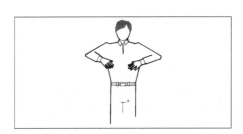

Hyphen/dash Backspace and underscore Exclamation mark

LL: 45 • SS

Variation of keyboards

The position of certain characters and symbols may vary with different machines. When practising these keys:

- locate the key on your machine
- practise the reach from the appropriate home key
- ensure you know whether or not you have to use the shift key.

The hyphen/dash

- The *hyphen* on a computer or electronic typewriter keyboard also serves as a *dash*.
- When the dash is used to indicate a span of figures, no space is left on either side (see line 8). When it is used for emphasis, one space is left before and after the dash.

The underscore

Word processing systems and most electronic typewriters have an *automatic underscore*. If necessary, consult your operator's manual to find out how to use this facility on your system.

If there is no automatic underscore on your system, locate the underscore key on your machine. Backspace to the character at which the underscoring is to begin. After underscoring tap space bar.

Note: some electronic equipment does not underscore word spaces.

The exclamation mark

Leave two spaces after an exclamation mark at the end of a sentence.

Speed test: page 41.
Follow the end of session procedure.

Refresher: warm up on lines 1–6

Colon/shift lock
1 Enter DISKCOPY A:B: and this message appears:
x
2 Was Maxwell vexed to miss the next six taxis?
y
3 On Monday or Tuesday Joy may try to fly away.
z
4 In Zambia I gazed at dozens of grazing zebra.
Figures
5 At 10.35 pm on 28 June I called her on 67490.
Aim for speed
6 Thank you so much for your very kind letters.

Reach to - with ; finger

Hyphen
7 ;-; ;- ;-; ;-;- well-to-do; son-in-law; X-ray
Dash used in a span of figures
8 During the week 18-25 May she ran 200-210 km.
Dash used for emphasis
9 Charlotte paused - turned - then ran further.

Key _ with LEFT SHIFT and ; finger

10 The Right Word and Write This Up were chosen.
11 Key employee or employer to recall the files.

Key ! with RIGHT SHIFT and A finger

12 a!a a! a!! a!!a No! Go! Oh! Ah! Hi! Run!
↓Space twice
13 Happy New Year! What a pity! Whatever next!
14 No, it is not! What a surprise! How lovely!

Build skill on a paragraph

15 Congratulations on achieving the well-merited first-class pass in Communications 1! What a surprise - to us at least! Jane and I almost choked on our pre-dinner soda water when your sister-in-law gave us the news! I understand you did well in the one-hour essay. You told me - or I think you did - that writing essays was your weak spot. Your ability was a well-kept secret - even from your own family! Can we ever really believe what you tell us - you dark horse! Quite seriously though, Jane and I are very proud of you!

Job 10.4.2 cont

Thu 7 Jan	0730 hrs	Working breakfast with Ed Schwarz
	0900 hrs	Head office of Cisceau Corporation, 116 East Fortitude St, San Diego (Ph 863 9211)
	0915 hrs	With Alison Jones (Vice-President, Marketing)
	1230 hrs	Lunch with Paul S Cato (Vice-President, Production)
	1430 hrs	With Lee Jacques (Assistant Vice-President, Personnel)
	1930 hrs	Host dinner at hotel for Ed Schwarz
Fri 8 Jan	0830 hrs 1730 hrs	Attend Cisceau Corp Sales Conference at Winston Hotel, 18 Kennedy St, San Diego

Sun 10 Jan	0900 hrs 1700 hrs	Attend American Textiles Association Trade Fair, Passmore Hotel, 1127 Connors St, Phoenix
Mon 11 Jan	0900 hrs 1700 hrs	American Textiles Association Trade Fair
	1230 hrs	Lunch at fair with Gerald H DiMarco (President, ATA)
Tues 12 Jan	0900 hrs 1700 hrs	American Textiles Association Trade Fair
	1300 hrs	Lunch at fair with Frances Anjou (President R C Wasson Inc)
	1930 hrs	Host dinner at hotel for Mr & Mrs J R Brown

ACCOMMODATION

La Jolla Marriott
SAN DIEGO (Ph 863 1100)
IN 6 Jan   OUT 9 Jan

Sat 9 Jan	0920 hrs	Depart SAN DIEGO	America West Airlines
	1125 hrs	Arrive PHOENIX (Sky Harbor)	Flight HP 203 First Class (Confirmed)

ACCOMMODATION

Windham Paradise Valley Resort
SCOTTSDALE
IN 9 Jan   OUT 13 Jan

Wed 13 Jan	0840 hrs	Depart PHOENIX (Sky Harbor)	United Airlines Flight UA 884
	1245 hrs	Arrive CHICAGO (O'Hare)	First Class (Confirmed)
Wed 13 Jan	1350 hrs 1635 hrs	Depart CHICAGO (O'Hare) Arrive ALBANY	United Airlines Flight UA 644 First Class (Confirmed)
Wed 13 Jan	1800 hrs 2100 hrs	Depart ALBANY Arrive NEW YORK	Train

ACCOMMODATION

Kozminski's Hotel
Fifth Avenue
NEW YORK (Ph 907 3862)
IN 13 Jan   OUT 17 Jan

Sun 17 Jan	1130 hrs	Depart NEW YORK (La Guardia)	Continental Airlines Flight CO 125
	1735 hrs	Arrive LOS ANGELES	First Class (Confirmed)
Sun 17 Jan	1910 hrs	Depart LOS ANGELES	Continental Airlines
Tue 19 Jan	0935 hrs	Arrive MELBOURNE	Flight CO 015 First Class (Confirmed)

Your travel consultant is Leon Abdullah. Please inform Leon immediately on 380 1611 if this itinerary does not meet your precise needs.

(TS.46)

Thu 12 Jan	0900 hrs 1600 hrs	Visit dyeworks of The Conrad Corporation, 718 East Street, Albany (host: Ms Kerstin Burroughs, Vice-President)
Fri 13 Jan	0900 hrs 1700 hrs	Visit Oban Knitting Mills Inc, 2738 Washington Street West, Albany (host: Lee Huang, Sales Manager)
Sat 14 Jan		At leisure

Quotation marks Apostrophe

Quotation marks

Either *single* or *double quotation marks* may be used in keyboarding but it is important to keep to the same style (either single or double) in a piece of work.

It may be necessary to use double quotation marks within single quotation marks, or single within double.

The apostrophe

Take care in keying the apostrophe as it is often misplaced. See page 59 for guidelines on the use of the apostrophe.

LL: 45 • SS

Refresher: warm up on lines 1–6

Question mark/exclamation mark
1 What breeds success? Work! Really? Really!
t
2 Tell the truth and Thea will truly trust you.
y
3 Even Vivien gave voice to her views on vices.
w
4 Who washes a well-worn sweater in warm water?
Figures
5 Read pp 124-58 - then write a 900-word essay.
Aim for speed
6 Please ask Liza if she wants to join a group.

Reach to '

7 ;'; ;' ;'' ;''; don't, can't, shan't, they're
8 isn't wasn't Sue's let's they've Dad's Jack's
9 'What's the time?' asked Jody. 'Is he late?'

Key "

10 "The Herald"|"The Age"|"The Sun"|"The Mirror"
11 "May I go to Florence?" said Kaz. "Not this time," answered Max, "next November perhaps."

Build skill on a paragraph

12 Of all the punctuation marks in our language, the apostrophe is the most commonly confused. It is used to denote 'possession' as in 'that day's paper', as well as in contractions such as 'it's' to show that a letter is 'missing'. Many people do not know where to put the mark in, for example, 'children's shoes' or 'men's team'. They forget that 'children' and 'men' are plural forms, and make the basic error of positioning the apostrophe after, rather than before, the 's'. If you have this difficulty ask yourself 'Who is the "owner"?', and place the apostrophe right after that word. People also confuse the possessive 'its', as used in the phrase 'its place', with 'it's' which, as we have already said, can only mean 'it is'.

Speed test: page 41.
Follow the end of session procedure.

Job 10.4.1 cont

ACCOMMODATION

Windham Paradise Valley Resort
SCOTTSDALE
IN 9 Jan   OUT 13 Jan

Wed 13 Jan	0840 hrs	Depart PHOENIX (Sky Harbor)		United Airlines Flight UA 884
	1245 hrs	Arrive CHICAGO (O'Hare)		First Class (Confirmed)
Wed 13 Jan	1350 hrs	Depart CHICAGO (O'Hare)		United Airlines Flight UA 644
	1635 hrs	Arrive ALBANY		First Class (Confirmed)
Wed 13 Jan	1800 hrs	Depart ALBANY		Train
	2100 hrs	Arrive NEW YORK		

ACCOMMODATION

Kozminski's Hotel
Fifth Avenue
NEW YORK (Ph 907 3862)
IN 13 Jan   OUT 17 Jan

Sun 17 Jan	1130 hrs	Depart NEW YORK (La Guardia)	Continental Airlines Flight CO 125
	1735 hrs	Arrive LOS ANGELES	First Class (Confirmed)
Sun 17 Jan	1910 hrs	Depart LOS ANGELES	Continental Airlines
Tue 19 Jan	0935 hrs	Arrive MELBOURNE	Flight CO 015 First Class (Confirmed)

If your system has no bolding function, key this paragraph in upper case.

Your travel consultant is Leon Abdullah. Please inform Leon immediately on 380 1611 if this itinerary does not meet your precise needs.

(TS:46)

Job 10.4.2

Edit the travel agent's itinerary you prepared in Job 10.4.1 to produce Cisceau Australia's more detailed document.

American companies are commonly called corporations. A president is the chief executive officer (a position equivalent to a managing director in the U.K.).

This document is continued on the next page.

Plain A4 portrait • LL: 66

AUSTOURS

DRAFT ITINERARY FOR MR EDWIN POWER
Managing Director, Cisceau Australia Pty Ltd

6-19 January 1993

Wed 6 Jan	1435 hrs	Depart MELBOURNE		Continental Airlines
	0600 hrs	Arrive HONOLULU		Flight CO 016 First Class (Confirmed)
Wed 6 Jan	0810 hrs	Depart HONOLULU		Continental Airlines
	1510 hrs	Arrive LOS ANGELES		Flight CO 002 First Class (Confirmed)
Wed 6 Jan	1700 hrs	Depart LOS ANGELES		Delta Air Lines
	1740 hrs	Arrive SAN DIEGO		Flight DL 5655 First Class (Confirmed)

Met by Ed Schwarz (President, Cisceau Corporation) and taken to hotel

Checkpoint G

Proofreading marks 4

Study the proofreading marks opposite and make sure you understand them before attempting Jobs G1 to G4.

Italic and bold type

'Roman' is the name given to type which is not bold or italic. Word processors and most electronic type-writers have the facility to print in bold. By changing the daisy wheel on an electronic typewriter you can switch to italic type.

Find out from your operator's manual how to key in bold and italic on your system.

Proofreading marks		
Mark in text	**Mark in margin**	**Corrected passage**
A wavy line shows that a word - or words - is to appear in <u>bold</u>.	bold	A wavy line shows that a word - or words - is to appear in **bold**.
This combination of marks instructs the operator to re-key bold or italic type in ordinary (roman) type.	rom	This combination of marks instructs the operator to re-key bold or italic type in ordinary roman type.
Here's how you tell the operator to insert an apostrophe . . .	;	Here's how you tell the operator to insert an apostrophe . . .
. . . and similarly for quotation marks (also called ˄inverted commas˄.	⟨ ⟩ *or* ⟨⟨ ⟩⟩	. . . and similarly for quotation marks (also called 'inverted commas'). *or* "inverted commas").
<u>This</u> is all you do to indicate underscoring (or italics).	u|score *or* ital	<u>This</u> is all you do to indicate underscoring (or italics).
This is how you mark <u>underscored capitals</u>.	caps + u|score	This is how you mark <u>UNDERSCORED CAPITALS</u>.

Job G1

1 If your system allows, name this document.
2 Key a corrected copy in double spacing, *keeping to the same line endings.*
 If your system has no bold type facility, underscore the words marked for bold.
3 Proofread. If you key a perfect copy, you will have an even right margin.
4 If your system allows, save the document.

A5 landscape • LL: 45 • DS • centre vertically

Most word processing software packages have a
spell checker. It may be an option on the
electronic typewriter, as well. But, spelling
checkers are not foolproof. Do you know why?
Its because some sets of words, such as role
and roll, born and borne, canvas and canvass,
may be confused by the writer or the keyboard
operator. You must therefore keep a watchful
eye for trap words like these because you can
bet a spell checker won't recognise them.

Itinerary

An itinerary is a travel plan. If prepared by a travel agent it will provide departure and arrival dates and times and, where appropriate, the names of airlines and flight numbers.

A more detailed itinerary, based on the travel agent's itinerary but providing information about meetings that form part of the travel plan, may be prepared by the travelling executive's own office.

Refresher

All alpha keys
1 Verdi and Mozart both wrote exceptional requiems. They are enjoyed by people who like great live performances.

Second and third fingers
2 Lew Dodds excelled; Kel Wilde's widow closed six deals.

Quotation marks/ellipsis
3 'Quote Pope's words: "To err is human . . ."', Jo said.

Aim for speed
4 Express your point of view but do listen to others too.

Job 10.4.1

If your system allows, save this document.

AUSTOURS

DRAFT ITINERARY FOR MR EDWIN POWER
Managing Director, Cisceau Australia Pty Ltd

6-19 January 1993

> The 24-hour clock is commonly used in itineraries.

> In an itinerary, abbreviated forms (eg of days and months) are acceptable.

Wed	6 Jan	1435 hrs 0600 hrs	Depart MELBOURNE Arrive HONOLULU	Continental Airlines Flight CO 016 First Class (Confirmed)
Wed	6 Jan	0810 hrs 1510 hrs	Depart HONOLULU Arrive LOS ANGELES	Continental Airlines Flight CO 002 First Class (Confirmed)
Wed	6 Jan	1700 hrs 1740 hrs	Depart LOS ANGELES Arrive SAN DIEGO	Delta Air Lines Flight DL 5655 First Class (Confirmed)

> IN: the traveller is expected to arrive at the hotel on that date.
> OUT: the traveller is expected to depart on the morning of that date.

ACCOMMODATION

La Jolla Marriott
SAN DIEGO (Ph 863 1100)
IN 6 Jan   OUT 9 Jan

> This document is continued on the next page.

Sat	9 Jan	0920 hrs 1125 hrs	Depart SAN DIEGO Arrive PHOENIX (Sky Harbor)	America West Airlines Flight HP 203 First Class (Confirmed)

Job G2

1 If you saved the document in Job G1, retrieve it and edit as follows, *keeping to the same line endings.*

2 If you did not save it, key a corrected copy of the complete paragraph.

3 Proofread. If you key a perfect copy, you will have an even right margin.

Most electronic typewriters have a half backspacing function. This moves the carrier half a space to the left and is useful for combining characters and making corrections, eg:

This ĵ̷ś the *was*
This was the

æsthetic

Most word processing software packages have a
bold spelling checker. It may be an option on the
electronic typewriter, as well. But, spelling *bold*
checkers are not foolproof. Do you know why?
It's because some sets of words, such as **role** *ital*
ital and **roll**, **born** and **borne**, **canvas** and **canvass**,
may be confused by the writer or the keyboard
operator. You must therefore keep a watchful
open| s) eye for trap words like these because you can
bold bet a spelling checker won't recognise them!

Job G3

1 If your system has a spelling checker, try it out on the following paragraph in which there are ten spelling errors. You will normally correct errors in the copy, but for this exercise key in the copy exactly as it is here. This will show you the kinds of errors a spelling checker will not pick up.

2 Name the document.

3 Keep to the same line endings.

4 Print a copy.

'Practise makes perfect' may be an overworked
old peace of advise but that's not to suggest
it doesn't make pretty gd cents. What will
practise do for you? Will it insure sucess?
No. But you surely won't succede with-out it.

Job G4

1 If you saved the document in Job G3, retrieve it.

2 Mark and correct the remaining errors.

3 What kind of error did the spelling checker fail to pick up?

4 Print a final copy in single spacing.

No copy can't find and the copy in the
australian book is empty

Follow the end of session procedure.

Job 10.3.1 cont

6 <u>Appointment of Auditor</u>

Moved that Mr W J Oakley be appointed as Hon Auditor for the season 1994-95. PROPOSED J Wendt, SECONDED P Meyer. CARRIED.

The Secretary was asked to write to Mr Oakley thanking him for his past year's service and advising him of his reappointment.

Head the continuation page in this condensed form: 'Minutes of CYA AGM – 6 August 1993 – page 2' (in one line, blocked left).

7 <u>President's Report</u>

D Tuohy presented his report on the past year's activities.

It was moved that the President's report be received. PROPOSED P Meyer, SECONDED A Bishop. CARRIED.

8 <u>Fleet Report</u>

P McShann presented her report.

It was moved that the fleet report be accepted. PROPOSED J Wendt, SECONDED A Starcevic. CARRIED.

9 <u>Election of Office Bearers</u>

President - D Noonan (PROPOSED F Radford, SECONDED P McShann. CARRIED)

Treasurer - J Wendt (PROPOSED F Radford, SECONDED N Wood. CARRIED)

Secretary - G O'Connell (PROPOSED D Ludowyk, SECONDED L Webb. CARRIED)

Committee Members - A Pryse, L Webb, N Wood, D Ludowyk, B Rosario (PROPOSED D Tuohy, SECONDED F Radford. CARRIED)

Questions from the 'floor' are questions put to the committee or board of an association or company from ordinary members present.

10 General Business

A Bishop reminded members of the casserole night on Saturday 18 August at 8 pm.

The meeting closed at 9.35 pm.

D Tuohy
President

8 August 1993

Numeric keys
3 5 8 4

If you have already covered the numeric keys, you can skip Units 1.17–1.19 or use these units as a review.

Numeric keys technique

Follow the new key procedure described in Unit 1.3.

As the numeric keys are on the top row of the keyboard, you will have to reach further to strike them. Keep your hands in their normal position, with the fingers on the home keys except when they are reaching out to strike another key.

LL: 45 • SS

Refresher: warm up on lines 1–3
Question mark/ze/za
1 Why not? Can you? daze laze pizza plaza zero
Phrases
2 are lazy, have queried, will quiz, one dozen,
All alpha keys
3 Patrick bought fresh quince jelly jam to take
  for Devonshire tea with Zoe, Xavier and Gwen.

Reach to 3 with D finger
4 d3d d3 d33 d33d; d3d d3 d33 d33d; d3d d3 d33d
5 3 dads; 33 deeds; 333 dips; 33 dolls; 3 dues;
6 So 3 ducks, 3 ibis and 3 eels were destroyed.
7 The 33 drakes dive for 33 dandelions for tea.

Reach to 5 with F finger
8 f5f f5 f55 f55f; f5f f5 f55 f55f; f5f f5 f55f
9 5 farms; 55 fell; 555 films; 55 forks; 5 furs
10 See 5 men fix 55 bald tyres on 5 fire trucks.
11 The 5 friendly flies flew past 55 fresh fish.

Reach to 8 with K finger
12 k8k k8 k88 k88k; k8k k8 k88 k88k; k8k k8 k88k
13 8 kites; 88 keys; 888 kettles; 8 kings 8 inns
14 In all, 8 women, 8 boys and 88 girls arrived.
15 Join the 8 vans and 888 trucks in the convoy.

Reach to 4 with F finger
16 f4f f4 f44 f44f; f4f f4 f44 f44f; f4f f4 f44f
17 4 frogs; 44 families; 444 fences; 44 finished
18 Add 4 chillies, 4 shallots and 44 fresh eggs.
19 The 44 yachts sailed in the 444 km challenge.

Review sentences
20 Zoe lives at Unit 3, 5 Cliff Street, Glenelg.
21 Later, 33 tests were taken by 548 volunteers.
22 The vehicle drove slowly up the 4:8 gradient.
23 The session is held in room 45, level 3 at 8.
24 The cancelled delivery docket is number 8354.
25 Invoice nos 3548 and 8453 were paid on 8 May.

Speed test: page 41.
Follow the end of session procedure.

Minutes

Minutes are the official record of the proceedings of a meeting. They are usually sent to members either immediately after the meeting or just prior to the following meeting, together with the notice and agenda. The minutes are signed by the chairperson after they have been adopted (ie approved as an accurate record) by members present at the next meeting.

Refresher

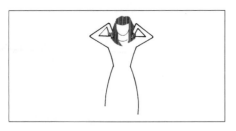

All alpha keys
1 Jacaranda trees have beautiful purple flowers that make an exciting picture in a squally storm with hazy skies.

Second and third fingers
2 Del Kidd and Les Dew do like Will Wescock's cool colas.

Symbols/figures
3 Dimensions: 1175 x 280 x 46 mm; tuning range 86-98 MHz.

Aim for speed
4 Do choose your words with great care and speak clearly.

Job 10.3.1

Prepare an exact copy of these minutes.

This document is continued on the next page.

CENTENARY YACHT ASSOCIATION

MINUTES OF THE ANNUAL GENERAL MEETING

Held at Parkville Yacht Club on Thursday 6 August 1993

1 Present

   D Tuohy (President), F Radford (Honorary Secretary),
   J Wendt (Treasurer), A Bishop, D Ludowyk, P McShann,
   P Meyer, D Noonan, G O'Connell, A Pryse, B Rosario,
   A Starcevic, S Van De Kuyt, L Webb, N Wood

2 Apologies

   A Dunstan, M Greco, W Hitchins, L Homann

3 Minutes of Annual General Meeting 15 August 1992

   It was moved that the minutes, as distributed, be taken
   as read and approved. PROPOSED A Bishop, SECONDED
   B Rosario. CARRIED.

4 Business Arising

   The President reported that enquiries had shown that the
   current spinnaker was adequate for the Club's class.
   Sailmakers were of the opinion that little could be done
   in the way of improvement.

5 Treasurer's Report

   The Treasurer, J Wendt, presented her report and thanked
   A Pryse, G O'Connell and S Van De Kuyt for their
   assistance.

   It was moved that the Treasurer's report be received.
   PROPOSED D Noonan, SECONDED P McShann. CARRIED.

A *motion*, ie a proposed course of action, must be *proposed* and *seconded* by members present at the meeting. A vote is then taken. If the motion is approved (ie *carried*) it becomes a decision of the meeting.

It is common to key the words *proposed*, *seconded* and *carried* in capitals.

Numeric keys
9726

LL: 45 • SS

Refresher: warm up on lines 1–4

Review figures
1 3 dandelions, 5 fixtures, 8 koalas, 4 fruits,
ou
2 house, joust, carousel, about, flout, pounce,
All alpha keys
3 The taxi whizzed quickly along the busy road.
Shift keys
4 Gerald, Flora and Vern jumped out of the way.

Reach to 9 with L finger

5 l9l l9 l99 l991; l9l l9 l99 l991; l9l l9 l991
6 9 laws, 99 less, 999 lids, 99 lollies, 9 lugs
7 Buy 9 quinces, 99 mangoes and 999 pineapples.
8 Thus 9 little lasses ironed 99 handkerchiefs.

Reach to 7 with J finger

9 j7j j7 j77 j77j; j7j j7 j77 j77j; j7j j7 j77j
10 7 jackets, 77 jellies, 777 jigsaws, 7 January
11 The 7 women left room 7 on 7 January at 7 am.
12 Of the 77 who paid only 7 actually came at 7.

Reach to 2 with S finger

13 s2s s2 s22 s22s; s2s s2 s22 s22s; s2s s2 s22s
14 2 shawls, 22 seas, 222 sips, 22 songs, 2 sums
15 These 22 gents need 22 pairs of size 2 shoes.
16 Those 2 companies bought 22 2-metre dividers.

Reach to 6 with J finger

17 j6j j6 j66 j66j; j6j j6 j66 j66j; j6j j6 j66j
18 6 jays, 66 jets, 666 join, 66 jumpers, 6 jugs
19 We need 6 pens, 66 pads and 666 pencils soon.
20 Why did 6 queue for 66 green quilts in lot 6?

Build numeric skills on sentences

21 With 976 sheep, 2 drovers rode into the yard.
22 The 6 cars averaged 97 mph in these 2 trials.
23 It took 6 months and 2 weeks to construct it.
24 Last month 9 sheets and 7 towels were stolen.
25 Joe collected 79 old stamps and Frederick 62.
26 Numbers at the meeting on 9 May were 542 367.

Sped test: page 42.
Follow the end of session procedure.

Job 10.2.2

This combined notice and agenda is to be signed by Frances Pannuzzo, Executive Officer. Date it 25 July this year.

If necessary, check the meanings of these words in your dictionary: *revue   review.*

Plain A4 portrait • centre vertically/horizontally

ANNERLEY INSTITUTE OF HIGHER EDUCATION
COURSE COMMITTEE M
for the
DIPLOMA OF TECHNICAL TEACHING (ADVANCED)

The next meeting will be held on Monday 3 Aug 19_ _ at 5·30 pm in the conference rm. Papers will be circulated prior to the mtg
prior

AGENDA

1 APOLOGIES
2 1 CORRESPONDANCE
   E

3 2 MINUTES OF THE MEETING HELD ON 4 MAY 19_ _
   4 BUSINESS ARISING
5 3 COURSE COORDINATOR'S REPORT

6 4 DIPLOMA OF TEACHING (TECHNOLOGY)
   Draft submission revue   review
   7 OTHER BUSINESS
8 5 NEXT MTG
   Mon 7 Sept 19_ _ at 5·30 pm

Job 10.2.3

Prepare this as a chairperson's agenda (ie leave space at right hand side of each agenda item for the chairperson to write notes).

Plain A4 portrait • centre vertically/horizontally

RAWCLIFFE ENTERPRISES

The next meeting of sales representatives for the north-east region will be held in the board room of the Blenheim Road building at 10·30 am on Wednesday, 15 October 199-.

AGENDA	NOTES
1 Apologies	1
2 Minutes	2
3 Matters arising	3
4 Receive reports from Alan Knight and Kerry Anderson	4
5 Any other business	5
6 Date of next meeting	6

Numeric keys
0 1

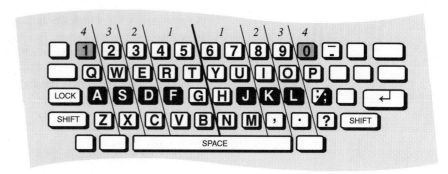

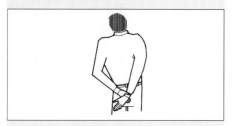

LL: 45 • SS

Refresher: warm up on lines 1–4

Figures
1 Convert 92 pounds and 76 francs into dollars.

2 I spent 35 yen and 84 pounds when on holiday.

ea/ai
3 jealous, zeal, real, maintain, again, liaison

Space bar
4 as is so or be in am if an me go my do by may

Reach to 0 with ; finger

5 ;0; ;0 ;00 ;00; ;0; ;0 ;00 ;00; ;0; ;0 ;00; 0

6 30 packets; 50 jigsaws; 80 litres; 40 pockets

7 90 umbrellas; 70 friends; 20 hooks; 60 quoits

8 Some 30 or 40 men ate 80 cakes and 90 apples.

9 Did the 70 men catch 50 or 60 fish in 4 days?

Reach to 1 with A finger

10 a1a a1 a11 a11a a1a a1 a11 1aa1 a1a a1 a11a 1

11 1 axe; 11 aims; 111 athletes; 11 nouns; 1 yak

12 Did the 111 runners win 11 medals in 11 days?

13 Knit 11 rows rib, then 11 rows garter stitch.

14 Call 3986 students to studio 107 at 12.45 pm.

Build numeric skills on sentences

15 Alex leaves today on train 9, car 2, seat 10.

16 In 4 bike races 8 prizes were won by 3 women.

17 Jacinta bought 5 pens, 7 pencils and 6 books.

18 The law was passed on 24 August 1976 at 8 pm.

19 Do you attend the class on Monday at 5.30 pm?

Build numeric skills on a paragraph

20 Nigel and Frances drove through 12 countries, 98 villages, 67 towns and 30 cities this year while on their 45-day holiday. Their old car took them the 2875 kilometres over some rough terrain, virtually without incident. Frances spent 1043 pounds and Nigel, 1006 during this exciting, well organised, European adventure.

Speed test: page 42.
Follow the end of session procedure.

Agenda

An agenda is a list of topics or business to be discussed at a meeting. The topics are numbered in the order in which they will be discussed.

An agenda is sometimes combined with the notice as one document.

Chairperson's agenda

You may be asked to prepare a chairperson's agenda, a special version of the agenda with space either below each topic or at the right-hand side to enable the chairperson to make notes.

Refresher

LL: 55 • SS • DS between drills

All alpha keys
1 The polar explorers were amazed at the magnificent view of the penguins jumping quickly back into the icy seas.

First and second fingers
2 Give Jeffrey Hunt the right kind of credit in December.

Symbols/figures
3 100 kW is 136 hp; 200 r/s = 12 000 rpm; 100 nm = 10 kg.

Aim for speed
4 Write your name and phone number in the space provided.

Job 10.2.1

Prepare an exact copy of this agenda.

Plain A4 portrait • SS • centre vertically/horizontally

Against item 1 the names of all persons who attended the meeting will be recorded in the minutes.

Against item 2 the names of all persons who were invited to attend but sent their apologies will be recorded in the minutes.

CENTENARY YACHT ASSOCIATION

TENTH ANNUAL GENERAL MEETING to be held at 7.30 pm on Thursday 6 August 1993 at the Parkville Yacht Club, 118-126 Beach Road, Mount Eliza

A G E N D A

1 Attendance

2 Apologies

3 Minutes of last AGM (15 August 1992)

4 Business arising from previous meeting

5 Treasurer's report

6 Appointment of auditor

7 President's report

8 Fleet report

9 Measurer's report

10 Election of office bearers

11 General business

F N Radford
Honorary Secretary

15 July 1993

Numeric keypad

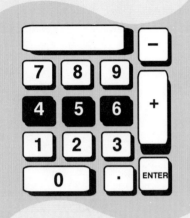

Some computer keyboards have an additional set of numeric keys to the right of the alpha-numeric keyboard.

This separate keypad can be used when large amounts of data are to be entered. It enables numbers to be entered quickly, and is operated in a similar fashion to an adding machine.

It is not recommended that you move on to the keypad as soon as you have learnt the main keyboard, but at a later stage in your course.

- If the keypad on your machine is not the same as the one shown above, make a copy of your own keypad.
- The *home keys* are the **4**, **5** and **6** keys. Use the index finger for **4**, middle finger for **5** and third finger for **6**. Use the right thumb to key the space bar between groups of figures.
- Practise the reach to each new key from the home keys until you are familiar with its location.
- Copy each line at least twice. Strike the *enter key* at the end of each line with the little finger.

Proofread your work and mark any errors.

Follow the end of session procedure.

Learn 4 5 6 (home row)

```
1  44  55  66  44  55  66  44  55  66  44  55  66  4455
2  45  54  45  54  56  65  56  65  46  64  46  64  5566
3  444  555  666  444  555  666  444  555  666  6546
4  456  654  456  654  546  645  445  556  665  4564
5  4444  5555  6666  4455  5566  6644  4564  46546
6  5456  5445  4565  6556  6465  4656  6446  56654
7  4  5  6  44  45  46  55  56  54  66  65  64  456  654
8  546  564  665  554  4454  4455  5566  6644  5465
```

Reach to 7 and 1 with 4 finger

```
9  47  47  474  474  74  74  747  747  4774  4477  74
10 41  41  414  414  14  14  141  141  4114  4411  14
11 7  47  1  41  17  74  71  14  147  741  114  117  71
12 717  771  414  471  4147  4171  4741  4717  1174
```

Review 1 4 5 6 7

```
13 47  41  57  51  67  61  16  76  15  75  14  74  7416
14 475  415  574  514  476  416  674  614  165  7654
```

Reach to 8 and 2 with 5 finger

```
15 58  58  585  585  85  85  858  858  5885  5588  85
16 52  52  525  525  25  25  252  252  5225  5522  25
17 8  58  2  52  28  85  82  25  258  852  225  228  82
18 828  882  525  582  5258  5282  5852  5828  2285
```

Review 1 2 4 5 6 7 8

```
19 58  52  68  62  48  42  26  86  24  84  25  85  8524
20 584  524  485  425  586  526  685  625  265  8645
```

Reach to 9 and 3 with 6 finger

```
21 69  69  696  696  96  96  969  969  6996  6699  96
22 63  63  636  636  36  36  363  363  6336  6633  36
23 9  69  3  63  39  96  93  36  369  963  336  339  93
24 939  993  636  693  6369  6393  6963  6939  3396
```

Review 1 2 3 4 5 6 7 8 9

```
25 14  25  36  45  56  64  74  85  96  31  69  97  8525
26 157  246  369  854  125  436  724  159  365  1254
```

Reach to . with 6 finger   Reach to 0 with right thumb

```
27 6.  6.  6.6  6.6  .6  .6  .6.  .6.  6..6  66..  .6
28 40  50  60  404  505  606  6004  5060  4050  4056
29 .  6.  0  405  0.  4.4  5.0  60.0  209  108  3.075
30 0.1  0.2  0.3  0.4  0.5  6.0  7.0  8.0  9.0  10.0
```

Review 0 1 2 3 4 5 6 7 8 9

```
31 10  20  30  400  500  600  708  809  901  0.1  9.0
32 1.2  3.4  5.6  7.8  0.9  9306  8025  7104  45.60
```

Module 10 Meetings and travel

Performance goals

At the end of Module 10 you should be able to format and key the following documents:

- notice of meeting
- agenda
- minutes
- itinerary.

Notice of meeting

The first document prepared for a meeting is usually the notice. It may be accompanied by an agenda The notice and agenda may even be a single document. If it is not sent with the notice, the agenda is prepared and circulated at a later date.

Notices vary considerably in format. For small, informal meetings, a simple memorandum is all that is required. For more formal meetings (for example the annual general meeting of a large public company), documents may be typeset and printed.

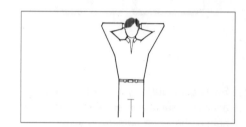

Job 10.1.1

Prepare an exact copy of this notice.

Plain A5 landscape • SS • centre vertically/horizontally

The rules of most bodies state that written notice of a formal meeting must be given to all persons entitled to attend a specified number of days before the meeting date.

```
CENTENARY YACHT ASSOCIATION  R2

NOTICE OF ANNUAL GENERAL MEETING  R2

The Tenth Annual General Meeting of the Association
                will be held at  R2

         THE PARKVILLE YACHT CLUB
            118-126 BEACH ROAD
              MOUNT ELIZA  R2

        on THURSDAY 6 AUGUST 1993  R2

             at 7.30 pm  R2

     The Agenda accompanies this Notice  R4



F N Radford
Honorary Secretary  R2

15 July 1993  R2
```

Parentheses
Solidus
Pound sign
Dollar sign

Technique

- Strike each key with a quick, sharp stroke of the fingertip.
- Keep your wrists low but clear of the keyboard.
- Strike the space bar with a quick, inward movement of the right thumb.
- Keep your eyes on the copy.

Parentheses

Parentheses are also called *brackets*. There is no space between a parenthesis and the word immediately next to it.

Solidus

The *solidus* is also referred to as a *slash, stroke* or *oblique stroke*. It is used

- to express fractions:
  3/4 9/10
- to indicate alternatives:
  she/he and/or
- in some abbreviations, such as:
  a/c.
- to express 'per':
  80 km/h
  No space is left on either side of a solidus.

Speed test: page 42.
Follow the end of session procedure.

LL: 45 • SS

Refresher: warm up on lines 1–6

1 'Please order Gee's Media Guide,' said Clare.
  q
2 Jacques equips us with queer squash racquets.
  r
3 Rumour is that Rupert ran a rather rare race.
  s
4 Samson's super sister Susan sails seven seas.
  Figures
5 See pp 450-67 in Part 8 of Using Lotus 1-2-3.

Key (and) with LEFT SHIFT and L and ; fingers

6 l(l l(l((l((l ;); ;) ;)) ;)); (9) (0) (909)
7 (1) (2) (3) (4) (5) (6) (7) (8) (i) (ii) (iv)
8 Exported: (a) meat (b) wool (c) coal (d) other

Reach to / with ; finger

9 ;/; ;/ ;// ;//; 2/3 3/4 4/5 5/6 6/7 7/8 1/9/0
10 c/d b/d c/f b/f a/c c/o c/s b/l a/s u/s u/l/c
11 She/he must check her/his application yes/no.

Key £ with RIGHT SHIFT and D finger

12 d£d d£ d££ d££d £3 £32 £45 £10 £20 £300 £4000
13 We paid invoices for £33, £81, £122 and £250.
14 She wrote cheques for £2.99, £5.45 and £9.89.

Key $ with RIGHT SHIFT and F finger

15 f$f f$ f$$ f$$f $A $NZ US$ $10 $20 $30 US$400
16 We banked cheques for $68.20, $79.35, $84.50.
17 Invoices for $9, $140 and $35.64 were raised.

Build skill on a paragraph

18 The United Kingdom intended to convert to the metric system but so far this has only partly been implemented. The British people have held on to much of the imperial system of measurement and still talk of miles, while the rest of Europe always use the metric term kilometres. Some of the items are sold in shops by metric weight whilst others are sold by the imperial system. Perhaps, in time, the United Kingdom will be fully metric.

Job 9.4.2

Design and key a suitable form, using the full facility of your system.

- When this form is complete, key in the following: Name of tour – Alton Towers, date of departure – Saturday week, full payment cost – £15, student identification no. – 431. Complete the rest of the form with your own personal details.

CUNNINGHAM COLLEGE

STUDENT ACTIVITIES SERVICE

BOOKING FORM

NAME OF ACTIVITY/TOUR_____

DEPARTURE DATE or DATE OF ACTIVITY_____

Enclosed is a cheque/postal order made payable to STUDENT ACTIVITY SERVICES for £___ in part/full *payment for the above activity/tour (delete whichever is not applicable).
* Some activities/tours will require only part payment and others full payment.

Name _____   _____
        (Surname)   (Given name/s)

Address_____

_____ Postcode _____

Student identification no_____ Date of birth _____

Telephone no (Home)_____ (Work) _____

Signed_____ Date _____

_____

OFFICE USE ONLY

Payment banked_____ Booking no _____

Balance outstanding_____ Amount received _____

Balance received_____ Cheque/postal order /cash _____

Information sent_____ Date received _____

Booking finalised_____ Received by _____

Ampersand Asterisk 'At' sign Per cent sign

The ampersand (&)

The ampersand is the sign for 'and'. It is mainly used

- in company and partnership names:
  Black & White Pty Ltd
- for joint authors:
  Jones & Rees
- for married couples:
  Mr & Mrs E O'Connor

The asterisk (*)

The asterisk is used

- in reports and published material to indicate a source reference
- as a multiplication sign in computer programs
- in displayed work.

Where the asterisk is used to mark a source reference, there should be no space between it and the word to which it refers. When the word is followed by a punctuation mark, the asterisk goes straight after the punctuation mark.

The 'at' sign (@)

The 'at' sign is used to express sums of money and quantities of goods in documents such as invoices, eg:

3 dozen eggs @ o2 per dozen

The per cent sign (%)

The per cent sign may be used in tables and text. No space is left between the figure and the per cent sign.

Variation among keyboards

Your keyboard may have some of these symbols in different positions from the ones shown here.

Speed test: page 42.
Follow the end of session procedure.

LL: 45 • SS

Refresher: warm up on lines 1–6

1 Ann was fined £60 for travelling over 70 mph.
2 One friend was only fined £50 (fifty pounds).
3 *l*
  Lovely Lola and languid Liz lazed listlessly.
4 *m*
  Mamie's memo of 23 May demands my compliance.
5 *n*
  No one Nancy knows needs nine nylon nighties.
6 *p*
  Philip's plump puppy Pepe was pretty playful.

Key & with LEFT SHIFT and J finger

7 j&j j& j&& j&&j & Co & Partners & Associates.
8 Mr & Mrs X Lim; Ash & Co Ltd; Lea & Tan (eds)
9 C/o Ray & Co, Flat 7/9, Cnr Elm & Oak Streets

Key *

10 k*k k* k** k**k form* type* duty* true* ice.*
11 A*B means A times B; MUSIC *** SONGS *** ROCK
12 A single asterisk (*); a double asterisk (**)

Key @ with RIGHT SHIFT and S finger

13 ;@s ;@ ;@@ ;@@; 3 @ £4 2 @ £6 5 @ £17 9 @ £28
14 Order 99 @ 16p, 88 @ 27p, 5 @ 64p and 4 @ £7.
15 We can supply 200 disks @ £14 and 1000 @ £70.

Key % with RIGHT SHIFT and F finger

16 f%f f% f%% f%%f English 61% Maths 59% Art 80%
17 In maths 5% means 5/100 – and 8% means 8/100.
18 Supply 2 @ £7.60 less 33 1/3% trade discount.

Build skill on a paragraph

19 On 1 June we supplied 30 bales @ £48.25, less
   5% trade discount, to Saul & Tom's store. On
   3 July we delivered 69 bales to Link & Co Ltd
   @ £65.70, less 5% discount. The 15% discount
   to which you refer has never applied to trade
   orders of less than £10 000. Sales tax @ 10%
   also applied as neither Saul & Tom, nor their
   associate, Link & Co, has ever quoted a sales
   tax exemption certificate number.*

Form design

These principles apply to form design:
- Select paaper of an appropriate size (usually A4 or A5 to allow you to format the work in a manner that is visually pleasing. The form should fit a standard size envelope.
- Provide adequate space for all details to be inserted

Refresher

LL: 55 • SS • DS between drills

All alpha keys
1 Without question it was the obvious lack of oxygen that caused many people to doze off during her major speech.

Symbols/figures
2 Contact him on (09) 926 3748 between 8 am and 10.45 pm.

v/b
3 Bev's very valuable vegetables were invariably visible.

Aim for speed
4 Now is a good time to clear the file of unwanted paper.

Job 9.4.1

Prepare an exact copy of this form.

Plain A5 portrait

SLOUGH DRAMA SOCIETY

presents

A N T O N Y   A N D   C L E O P A T R A

12 March to 10 April 1993

ORDER FORM

Mail to: Box Office Manager
          Slough Drama Society
          GPO Box 780
          SLOUGH SL3 6PP

Please send me _____ tickets at £25 =

                _____ tickets at £35 = _____

                Total   £ _____

(a) I enclose a cheque for this amount.

or

(b) Please debit my Bankcard, Mastercard,
    American Express or Visa Card number:

    _____ Expiry date _____

Date preferred _____ Day/evening _____

Name (Mr/Ms/Mrs/Miss) _____

Address_____

_____ Postcode_____

Telephone (day) _____ (evening)_____

Signature _____

          (only required if using credit card)

Mathematical symbols

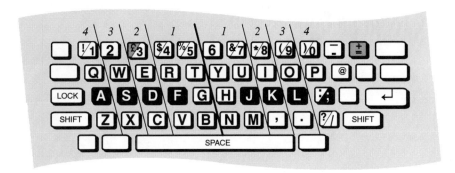

LL: 45 • SS

The minus sign

Use the hyphen with a space on either side.

The division sign

The division sign may not be included on the standard keyboard, but it can be keyed on an electronic typewriter as follows.

- Key a hyphen.
- Backspace once and key a colon.

On a computer, you will need to key a hyphen, print out a hard copy and add the two dots by hand.

Spacing of mathematical symbols

Always key a space on either side of the plus, minus, multiplication, division and equation signs.

Speed test: page 42.
Follow the end of session procedure.

Refresher: warm up on lines 1–7

&/@/$/%
1 Order 30 lamps from Finn & Co @ £4, less 25%.

2 Key in this new line: 030 PRINT (A*B/C/D)*A.

g
3 Easy-going George and gorgeous Greg are agog.

h
4 Has he phoned Hal Hawke this month? No fear!

j
5 Justice Jim Jod just enjoys enjoining juries.

k
6 Ken Ocker keeps khaki jackets in Kim's kayak.

Aim for speed
7 We need her to help us with the daily filing.

Key + with LEFT SHIFT and ; finger

8 1 + 2, 3 + 4, 5 + 6, 7 + 8, 9 + 10, 9 + 8 + 7

9 100 + 201 + 302 + 403 + 504 + 605 + 706 + 807

Reach to = with ; finger

10 a + b = c, c = b + a, a = c - b, ab + c = -de

11 3 x 3 = 9, 4 x 4 = 16, 5 x 5 = 25, 6 x 6 = 36

12 8 ÷ 4 = 2, 20 ÷ 5 = 4, 24 ÷ 6 = 4, 10 ÷ 2 = 5

Build skill on a paragraph

13 Well done! How does it feel to have used all 26 alphabet keys, all the numeric keys on the 'top row', as well as the common symbol keys, in just 23 units of work? You are on the way to realising your worthy ambition of becoming a first-class keyboard operator. In order to reach that objective, however, you must adopt three basic practices: (1) concentrate first and foremost on correct technique - speed and accuracy both depend on it; (2) make a really good effort to follow the sense of the matter you are copying, so that you will become more than a mere 'copy typist'; (3) proofread your finished work for keying mistakes, as well as for spelling and punctuation errors.

Keying on forms

Refresher

All alpha keys

1 His objective is to extend his stay and qualify as fast as possible for West German citizenship along with Ken.

Symbols/figures

2 Supply 36 x Little Sister (ISBN 0 27 016843 9) @ £7.95.

c/v

3 Victor received vocal advice about every victim's vice.

Aim for speed

4 I hope you will be able to come to my office next week.

Job 9.3.1

Prepare an exact copy of this employemnt application.
Blank stationery is on p.198.

Boxes and ruled or dotted lines

On a typewriter:

- add the inserted data in line with the pre-printed indicators
- allow two spaces after the indicators
- in a box key data centrally between horizontally ruled lines
- use the platen knob/variable line spacer or graduated spacing key to adjust the paper so that the data to be keyed will be just clear of the ruled or dotted line.
- be consistent with the style of type, ie all upper case or all upper and lower case.

Stop codes

When inserting variable data on a standard form, first set up a template with stop codes.

J M KENT & CO
EMPLOYMENT APPLICATION

APPLICATION FOR THE POSITION OF: Senior Administrative Assistant

SURNAME: Yee   GIVEN NAMES: Katherine Anne

ADDRESS: 128 Normann Street, LONDON

POSTCODE: SW12 0YY   TELEPHONE NO: 081 642 5678

DATE OF BIRTH: 1 May 1968

EDUCATION/QUALIFICATIONS

SECONDARY: School Burwood High School   Years 1980-1985

Highest qualification gained HSC

TERTIARY: Institution Meadowbank College   Years 1986

Highest qualification gained Advanced Secretarial Cert

PREVIOUS EMPLOYMENT (put most recent employment first)

Year/s	Employer	Position held
1989 to date	W T Campbell Co Ltd	Admin Assistant
1988-89	Department of Finance	Secretary
1987-88	R M Robertson & Co	Typist/Clerk

DUTIES PERFORMED

Keyboarding (90 wpm), shorthand (90 wpm), filing, receptionist duties, telex operation, photocopying, switchboard operation

REFERENCES

1 Name Rev W Menzies   2 Name Mrs W Miller

Address 45 Kent Road   Address 22 Waratah Street

LONDON SW11 6GZ   LONDON SW4 6PX

Telephone No 081 642 7800   Telephone No 081 655 7430

Signature: _____

Date: 1 July 1993

Speed tests
Units 1.8–1.19 and 1.21–1.23

1 *Units 1.8–1.12:* take two 1-minute timings.
Units 1.13–1.19 and 1.21–1.23: take a 1-minute and a 2-minute timing.

2 Record your better rate for future reference.
3 Proofread your work and circle any errors.

LL: 45 • DS • centre vertically

Unit 1.8 SI: 1.53

	Words
Helen and Nola are standing close together at	9
the station. Jack asked directions for Julie	18
as she struggled to hold a huge crate full of	27
red carnations and gladioli she had selected.	36

1 2 3 4 5 6 7 8 9

Unit 1.9 SI: 1.21

	Words
Most of us like going out to dinner from time	9
to time. It makes a welcome change from that	18
routine of eating within the same four walls.	27
Dining out has just a touch of glamour to it.	36

1 2 3 4 5 6 7 8 9

Unit 1.10 SI: 1.37

	Words
The cricket ball shattered the bedroom window	9
with a crash. The children ran away from the	18
house trying to find somewhere to hide before	27
their elder sister came hurrying out from the	36
garage. They wondered just what she would do.	45

1 2 3 4 5 6 7 8 9

Unit 1.11 SI: 1.5

	Words
Skills in proofreading take a bit of practice	9
to develop. A good command of English and an	18
ability to spell and punctuate are necessary.	27
These can be developed. An eye for detail is	36
handy; a little patience can do just as well.	45

1 2 3 4 5 6 7 8 9

Unit 1.12 SI: 1.41

	Words
The tyres squealed as the borrowed sports car	9
was tugged around the corner by the driver in	18
one last attempt to elude the police. Sirens	27
wailing, they were closing in when he swerved	36
quickly, narrowly missing a little schoolboy.	45

1 2 3 4 5 6 7 8 9

Job 9.2.2

Key invoices for these transactions. Use the product codes listed below.

Product codes

To key the items in Job 9.2.2, you will need to use the following product codes:

764732	Baby Joanna doll
762954	Crissy doll
123028	Walking doll
687382	Fire engine
685432	Police car with siren
689342	Station wagon
255375	10-piece jigsaw set

INVOICE NO 2231

Date: 6 August 1993   Order No: 339

Delivery: via Galaxy Transport

To: WR Carr Co Ltd, 18 wessex Street, PAIGNTON, Devon, TQ3 5RA

FOR: 5 Walking doll @ £25.00 each (total £125.00)
8 station wagon @ £9.50 each (total £76.00)
10 fire engine @ £18.50 each (total £185.00)
Total £386.00
Less 30% trade discount £115.80
Sub-total £270.20
Plus 17½% VAT £47.25
Total price £317.45

INVOICE NO 2232

Date: 6 August 1993 Order No: 56

Delivery: via rail

To: Murray & Robson, 223 Doorak Road, TELFORD, Shropshire, TF2 9TA

FOR: 5 10-piece Jigsaw set @ £10.00 each (total £50.00)
8 Baby Joanna doll @ £10.50 each (total £84.00)
Total £134.00
Less 30% trade discount £40.20
Sub-total £93.80
Plus 17½% VAT £16.41
Total price £110.21

INVOICE NO 2233

Date: 6 August 1993 Order No: 458

Delivery: via Galaxy Transport

To: B Jenkins & Co, 228 Burwood Road SWINDON, SN2 4AS

FOR: 6 Crissy doll @ £12.50 each (total £75.00)
3 Walking doll @ £25.00 each (total £75.00)
10 Police car with siren @ £17.50 each (total £175.00)
Total £325.00
Less 30% trade discount £97.50
Sub-total £227.50
Plus 17½% VAT £39.80
Total price £267.30

Unit 1.13 SI: 1.48

Words

As June draws closer, we start to think about 9
our tax returns and we despair of finding the 18
vouchers and receipts required for everything 27
we wish to claim. Some of us do know exactly 36
where they are, but others search everywhere: 45
in boxes, flowerpots and even queerer places. 54

1 2 3 4 5 6 7 8 9

Unit 1.14 SI: 1.56

Words

Until quite recently, handicapped people were 9
only able to get jobs in sheltered workshops. 18
Now they can expand their horizons by joining 27
the wider workforce. The work is both useful 36
and fulfilling; many are amazed at the degree 45
of independence they can gain in the process. 54

1 2 3 4 5 6 7 8 9

Unit 1.15 SI: 1.48

Words

Veronica and Xenia sprinted across the square 9
trying to stop the runaway horse. Terrified, 18
it raced onto the road amongst the east-bound 27
traffic. Cars screeching to a halt: still it 36
kept on! Passers-by jumped nimbly to safety. 45
Finally it stopped, wheezing, at the gardens. 54

1 2 3 4 5 6 7 8 9

Unit 1.16 SI: 1.41

Words

There are a few kinds of headings that can be 9
used in keyboarding, depending on the overall 18
'look' of the job, and you have learned three 27
styles - underscoring, bolding and also upper 36
case. The technique of centring will soon be 45
explained. It's simple and won't puzzle you. 54

1 2 3 4 5 6 7 8 9

Unit 1.17 SI: 1.56

Words

The children in the family wanted to surprise 9
their mother and prepare dinner for her. Tom 18
decided to check the availability of required 27
ingredients. Jan wrote the list as he called 36
out the missing items: 2 cups of champignons, 45
5 veal fillets, unsalted butter and an onion. 54

1 2 3 4 5 6 7 8 9

Unit *1* ·24 cont *Speed tests*

Invoices

Nowadays even small businesses prepare invoices, credit notes and statements of account on computerised systems, using pre-printed computerised stationery, numbered sequentially. Keyboard operators insert the variable data on screen.

On an efficient system, keying is reduced to a minimum. To prepare an invoice, for example, the operator keys

- the customer's name or code (retrieving the full name and address from memory)
- the method of delivery
- the quantity and product (inventory) code of the item. (Keying the product code causes the description and unit cost to be retrieved from memory; the total item price is automatically computed.)

The date of the document is printed automatically at the head.

An invoice is prepared in duplicate by the supplier of goods or services on credit. It lists the goods or services supplied, their price, the trade discount, Value Added Tax (VAT) and the total amount payable for the transaction. The original (top copy) of the invoice is sent to the buyer.

Nearly all businesses prepare their invoices as part of an integrated, computerised accounting system. As the invoice details are keyed, corresponding entries are made automatically in other parts of the system.

In some small businesses, invoices are prepared on a typewriter.

Refresher

LL: 55 • SS • DS between drills

All alpha keys

1 He knows that we have extended our special offer on top quality freezers and other goods from July to November.

Symbols/figures

2 A ratio of 3:5 = 6:20 = 12:20 = 24:40 = 48:80 = 96:160.

k/l

3 Kelvin lacked knowledge but pluckily blocked the leaks.

Aim for speed

4 Do not set yourself deadlines you know you cannot meet.

Job 9.2.1

Prepare an exact copy of this invoice.

Blank stationery is on p. 197.

TOY SUPPLIERS CO LTD
18 Carlton Street
LONDON W13 8SZ

PO Box 65
LONDON W13 8SZ

Fax (071) 644 5655
Telephone (071) 644 5641

B Jenkins & Co
228 Burwood Road
SWINDON SN2 4AS

Invoice No: 2230

Date: 30 July 1993

Order No: 451

Delivery: Galaxy Transport
Terms: net 30 days

Quantity	Description	Rate	Total
2	764732 Baby Joanna doll	10.50	21.00
10	681124 Tow truck – large	12.50	125.00
6	384651 Pull cart with blocks	15.00	90.00
			236.00
	Less 30% trade discount		70.80
			165.20
	Plus 17$\frac{1}{2}$% VAT		28.91
			£194.11
	To follow:		
5	386652 Edutoy mail box with geometric shapes		

Unit 1.18 SI: 1.51

Words

Thirty university students intended to travel   9
to New Zealand, Fiji and Tonga with a stop in   18
Hawaii to relax on the way home. The flight,   27
scheduled to leave London at noon, eventually   36
departed at 10 that evening. They had worked   45
and saved hard all year for their great trip.   54

1 2 3 4 5 6 7 8 9

Unit 1.19 SI: 1.51

Words

Computers work on the binary numbers of 0 and   9
1. Astonishingly enough, when the characters   18
are entered on a keyboard they are reduced to   27
a series of ones or zeros. Once on disk, all   36
figures from one to infinity will become part   45
of this amazing pattern. It is unbelievable!   54

1 2 3 4 5 6 7 8 9

Unit 1.21 SI: 1.46

Words

How lucky you are nowadays! Before computers   9
and electronic typewriters, the only ways you   18
could delete errors were with a rubber and/or   27
white paint. If you should key a dollar sign   36
instead of an s or question mark by mistake a   45
boring, time-consuming task lay ahead of you.   54

1 2 3 4 5 6 7 8 9

Unit 1.22 SI: 1.41

Words

When the leaves on trees and bushes get their   9
autumn tonings it is a very colourful time in   18
the garden. The saddest part about autumn is   27
the anticipation of those cold, dreary winter   36
months that have to be endured before we once   45
again enjoy the sight of the buds coming out.   54

1 2 3 4 5 6 7 8 9

Unit 1.23 SI: 1.41

Words

Travelling overseas can be complicated if you   9
wish to hire and drive a car. We often don't   18
give much thought to the problems encountered   27
in a strange country when we are planning our   36
itinerary. At home it is second nature to us   45
to jump into the car and drive off somewhere.   54

1 2 3 4 5 6 7 8 9

Unit *1*·24 cont *Speed tests*

ORDER NO 458

DATE: Today's

TO: Toy Suppliers Co Ltd

FOR: 6 Crissy doll @ £12.50 each (total £75.00)

3 Walking doll @ £25.00 each (total £75.00)

10 Police car with siren @ £17.50 each
(total £175.00)

DELIVERY: via Galaxy Transport

ORDER NO 459

DATE: Today's

TO: Stationery Supply Co.
21 Kent Street
PLYMOUTH PL12 4PW

FOR: 20 Reams white bank paper @ £4.50 per ream
(total £90.00)

6 boxes window-faced envelopes,
size DL @ £17.50 per box (total £105.00)

12 A4 ruled pads @ £2.00 per pad
(total £24.00)

DELIVERY: to be collected

ORDER NO 460

DATE: Today's

TO: K Walsh Co Ltd
48 Forestville Road
EXETER EX1 1AR

FOR: 1 kit A @ £56.50
1 Drum @ £180.00
for KD440 Photocopier

DELIVERY: via Courier Services

Module 2   Formatting 1   Basic principles

Performance goals

At the end of Module 2 you should be able to:

- tabulate
- use both blocked and indented styles of paragraphs
- format according to basic principles, including planning and setting margins
- work with automatic return function and justify text
- break words at line endings according to accepted rules and use the hard space function on a word processor.

Tab keys

L ----^----^----^----^----^----^----^----^----^----^----^------ R

Ruler line

Formatting

Formatting is the process of planning the display of a document. Good formatting

- is economical
- follows modern display conventions
- is attractive to the eye.

The tabulator

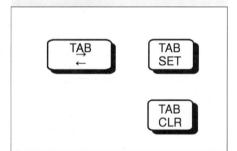

Tab keys

The tabulator enables you to move the printing point or cursor quickly to a pre-set position. It allows you to indent a paragraph or present data in columns.

Using the tabulator

Computers

Most systems feature a *ruler line*. On some systems it is permanently on the screen. On others the operator must call it up. The ruler line will display the default tabs and margins; but you can select your own. The procedure varies with the system. Consult your operator's manual to find out how to set and clear tabs and use the tab key.

Electronic typewriters

Locate these three keys on your typewriter:

- the *tab set key* – to set the tab positions
- the *tab clear key* – to clear the tab positions
- the *tab key* – to move the printing point to the tab position.

1 *To clear tabs:*
   a Single tab stop
      - Position the printing point at the left margin, using the return key.
      - Press the tab key to move the printing point to the tab stop you want cleared.
      - Press the tab clear key.
      - To clear further tab stops, tab to each stop you wish to clear and press the tab clear key.
   b All tab stops
      - Consult your operator's manual.

Note: to check that all tab stops are cleared, position the printing point at the left margin and press the tab key.

2 *To set tabs:*
   - Move the printing point to the desired tab position, using the space bar or backspace key.
   - Press the tab set key.
   - Repeat the operation for all required tab stops.

3 *To key tabulated material:*
   - Strike the tab key with the left or right little finger.
   - Return the finger to the home key.
   - Key the material.

Blocked and indented paragraphs

Blocked paragraphs

This is the most commonly used style of paragraph in business correspondence.

- All lines begin at the left margin.
- Extra line space is left between paragraphs.

Indented paragraphs

Indented paragraphs are not widely used in business correspondence, but the style is still used in some reports and typescripts.

- The first line of an indented paragraph begins five spaces in from the left margin.
- Leave an extra line space between paragraphs keyed in single spacing.
- Always use the tabulator to find the starting point for each paragraph.

Module 9 Business forms

Performance goals

At the end of Module 9 you should be able to

- key data onto pre-printed purchase orders and invoices
- key data onto pre-printed forms
- design and key business forms.

Blank stationery for use with this module can be found on pages 196–8.
This stationery includes:

- a purchase order form
- an invoice
- an application form.

Purchase orders

A purchase order is prepared by the buyer of goods or services and sent to the seller. It records the goods or services required.

Purchase orders are sometimes prepared on a typewriter.

The purchase order is not part of the accounting system.

The operator keys

- the date
- the supplier's name and address
- the method of delivery
- the quantity, product or inventory code, description, unit cost and total for each item.

Job 9.1.1

Prepare an exact copy of this purchase order.

Blank stationery is on p. 196

Address zone for window envelope

Purchase Order No 451

Telephone (0793) 642 7800

LM

Toy Suppliers Co Ltd
18 Carlton Street
LONDON W13 8SZ

B JENKINS & CO
228 Burwood Road
SWINDON SN2 4AS

Telex JENKTOY
Fax (0793) 642 1034

Date: 28 July 1993

Please supply the following goods:

Quantity	Item	Rate	Total
2	Baby Joanna doll	10.50	21.00
10	Tow truck - large	12.50	125.00
6	Pull cart with blocks	15.00	90.00
5	Edutoy mail box with		
	geometric shapes	17.50	a87.50
	Less 30% trade discount		

Delivery: via Galaxy Transport

Frances Wang
Purchasing Officer

Job 2.1.1

1 Key this list of commonly misspelt words. Note how they are spelt.
- If you are using a computer, your teacher will give you the margin and tab settings for your system. Those shown above this job apply to typewriters.
- If you are using a typewriter, set the left margin and tabs shown.

2 Proofread and correct your work.

Tab
↓

LM 29 (10) 37 (12) ↓	*T* 39 (10) 47 (12) ↓	*T* 49 (10) 57 (12) ↓
accept	affect	biased
except	effect	centre
aerial	by-law	wholly

Job 2.1.2

1 Format and key this list of commonly misspelt words.
- Follow the instructions for Job 2.1.1.

2 Proofread and correct your work.

LM 20 (10) 29 (12) ↓	*T* 38 (10) 47 (12) ↓	*T* 53 (10) 62 (12) ↓
absence	bachelor	committee
accidentally	balloon	competent
accommodate	benefited	conscious
accumulate	breathe	consensus
address	calendar	customary
already	catalogue	definite
argument	category	desperate
assess	cemetery	dictionary

Job 2.1.3

1 Format and key this list of commonly misspelt words.
- Follow the instructions for Job 2.1.1.

2 Proofread and correct your work.

Note: these are just some of the words that many people find difficult. You may like to start your own dictionary of 'problem' words.

LM 19 (10) 28 (12) ↓	*T* 37 (10) 46 (12) ↓	*T* 54 (10) 63 (12) ↓
disappoint	library	receive
eligible	maintenance	recommend
embarrass	miniature	satellite
harass	mortgage	separate
incidentally	murmur	successful
install	necessary	supersede
instil	permissible	their
jewellery	personnel	there

4. a certificate of marine insurance (in triplicate)
covering the consignment into the buyer's warehouse for
the full invoice value of the goods plus 5 per cent.

Please let me know if these requirements are not clear
to you.

Yours sincerely,

R. S. Giacoppo,
Assistant Manager.
y.i.
C. N. Taraporevala,
Bank of Calcutta.

4. *a certificate of marine insurance (in triplicate)*
covering the consignment into the buyer's warehouse for
the full invoice value of the goods plus 5 per cent.

Please let me know if these requirements are not clear
to you.

Yours sincerely,

R. S. Giacoppo,
Assistant Manager.

y.i.
C. N. Taraporevala,
Bank of Calcutta.

Job 8.6.2

- Use today's date.
- Correct three spelling errors and one punctuation error.

Letterhead and envelope • LL: you select • SS

The Mgr,
R. M. Sarker & Co. Ltd,
118a Bankin Chatterjee Street,
MADRAS,
INDIA.

ATTN MR R. MAHENDRA

Dear Sir,

Yr order NO. SCL:2078 has been consigned to R. M. Sarker & Co. Ltd on the new m.v. 'Newcastle' wh sailed from Sydney on 18th Dec. The vessel is due in Madras on 5th Jan.

The foll docuements hv bn sent to the Australasian Banking Corp, 114~118 Collins Street, Sydney:

1. bills of lading, in triplicate;
2. certificate of origin;
3. certificate of insurance;
4. our invoice, in triplicate.

The Bunyip, allready one of Australia's best-selling personal computers, is quickly attracting large export sales and, although we have put on more staff to meet the increased demand for our products, there is at present a three month's delay on all models. Pl. keep this in mind when you consider yr next order.

stet

A draft of $60 320 has been presented to the bank and credited to our account.

Yrs ffy,

B. N. Keating (Miss),
Export Mgr,
Bunyip Computers Pty Ltd.

y. i.
Enc. Shipping documents

Proofreading

The 'move left' sign is also used to indicate 'do not indent'.

	Mark in text	Mark in margin	Corrected passage
	You have met this mark before. It means 'do not indent' as well as 'move left'.		You have met this mark before. It means 'do not indent' as well as 'move left'.

Job 2.1.4

1 Study these blocked style paragraphs.
2 Key them.
3 Proofread and correct your work.

A5 landscape • LM: as shown • SS • key line for line • centre vertically

LM (typewriters only)
17 (10)
26 (12)
↓

Return twice ↓

There are two styles of paragraph in everyday use: blocked, like these short examples, and indented. *R2*

All lines in a blocked paragraph begin at the left margin, making it easy to key. *R2*

Return twice between paragraphs.

Job 2.1.5

1 Following the style of Job 2.1.4, key these paragraphs.
2 Proofread and correct your work.

It is not necessary to save this document.

A5 landscape • LM: as shown • SS • key line for line • centre vertically

LM (typewriters only)
16 (10)
25 (12)

↓

Huge amounts of paper are thrown out daily by offices and households. With a little thought, this paper can be collected and used to produce quality stationery.

As people become more/aware *and more* of the dangers of destroying the world's forests, the concept of recycling paper has become a reality.

Job 2.1.6

1 If necessary, clear the tab stops you set for Job 2.1.3.
2 Set a tab stop 5 spaces in from the left margin.
3 Key these paragraphs, indenting the first line of each by using the tabulator.
4 Proofread and correct your work.

A5 landscape • LM: as shown • SS • key line for line • centre vertically

LM (typewriters only)
15 (10)
23 (12)   ↓ *T 5 spaces in*

↓   Indented paragraphs are losing favour in business because they take longer to key. *R2*

The first line of each paragraph in this style is indented five spaces. The tabulator is used to locate the starting point of every paragraph. *R2*

Return twice between paragraphs.

Business letters 12

Semi-blocked style with closed punctuation

In a semi-blocked letter:
- start the date and the complimentary close at the horizontal centre
- indent five spaces at the start of each paragraph.

Semi-blocked letters may be keyed in closed punctuation style.

Refresher

`LL: 55 • SS • DS between drills`

All alpha keys

1 The tropical fish swam around in their heated aquarium. Jack gazed in fixed wonder at the very beautiful sight.

Symbols/figures

2 Invoice 135 m Irish linen @ £34 and 260 m poplin @ £87.

Closed punctuation

3 Mr J. D. Watson, B. Com., Dip. Ed., joined the N.R.M.A.

Aim for speed

4 The theme of her talk will be cash control in the firm.

Job 8.6.1

Study the model and key from the draft, which is continued on the next page.

`Letterhead and envelope • LL: 60 • SS`

Be flexible in formatting. Notice how the text of these enumerated paragraphs has been made to align with the paragraph indents.

The Australasian Banking Corporation

Tasman House 114–118 Collins Street
Sydney NSW 2000
Telephone (02) 777 0844
Fax (02) 777 0873

30th November, 1992.

Miss B. N. Keating,
Export Manager,
Bunyip Computers Pty Ltd,
44 Gloucester Street,
SYDNEY, N.S.W., 2000.

Dear Miss Keating,

CONSIGNMENT TO R. M. SARKER & CO. LTD

The Bank of Madras has opened an irrevocable letter of credit with this bank in your favour on the account of R. M. Sarker & Co. Ltd to the amount of $60 320. The credit is valid until 4 p.m. on 31st December, 1992. Your draft for this sum should be accompanied by the following documents:

1. an invoice, in triplicate, signed by an authorised official of the company and annotated Licence No. AK/3009;

2. a full set of bills of lading, made out to order and blank endorsed, marked: 'Freight paid' and 'Notify R. M. Sarker & Co. Ltd, 118A Bankin Chatterjee Street, Madras, India';

3. a certificate of origin issued by a Chamber of Commerce;

4. a certificate of marine insurance (in triplicate) covering the consignment into the buyer's warehouse for the full invoice value of the goods plus 5 per cent.

Please let me know if these requirements are not clear to you.

Yours sincerely,

R. S. Giacoppo,
Assistant Manager.

y.i.
C. N. Taraporevala,
Bank of Calcutta.

↓ *T at centre*
30th November, 1992.

Miss B. N. Keating,
Export Manager,
Bunyip Computers Pty Ltd,
44 Gloucester Street,
SYDNEY, N.S.W., 2000.

Dear Miss Keating,

CONSIGNMENT TO R. M. SARKER & CO. LTD

↓ *Indent paragraphs 5 spaces*

The Bank of Madras has opened an irrevocable letter of credit with this bank in your favour on the account of R. M. Sarker & Co. Ltd to the amount of $60 320. The credit is valid until 4 p.m. on 31st December, 1992. Your draft for this sum should be accompanied by the following documents:

1.   an invoice, in triplicate, signed by an authorised official of the company and annotated Licence No. AK/3009;

2.   a full set of bills of lading, made out to order and blank endorsed, marked: 'Freight paid' and 'Notify R. M. Sarker & Co. Ltd, 118A Bankin Chatterjee Street, Madras, India';

3.   a certificate of origin issued by a Chamber of Commerce;

Proofreading

The 'move right' sign is also used to indicate an indented first line.

Mark in text	Mark in margin	Corrected passage
You have met this mark before. It means 'indent' as well as 'move right'.	indent	You have met this mark before. It means 'indent' as well as 'move right'.

Job 2.1.7

1 Following the style of Job 2.1.6, key these paragraphs.
2 Proofread and correct your work.

A5 landscape • LM as shown • SS • key line for line • centre vertically

LM
17 (10)
26 (12)
↓

Newsprint cannot be recycled to make quality stationery, though it can be used to produce other grades of paper.

Since this process is labour intensive, paper produced in this way is more expensive than normal paper. Increasing demand will reduce the price.

It may not be long before recycled paper becomes the norm rather than the exception.

Paper manufacturers claim they have wanted to introduce 'quality' recycled paper for years but that until now the public has not been interested.

Speed test (SI 1.4)

1 Take two 2-minute timings.
2 Record your better rate.
3 Proofread and correct your work.

LM: 15 (10) 22 (12) • SS • key line for line

	Words
We have to be more precise when composing a letter than	11
we would be in direct conversation. This is because so	22
much is conveyed by voice and 'body language' when we	33
are talking to somebody face to face. Even when using	44
the telephone, we manage to make our meaning clearer by	55
our tone of voice.	59

1 2 3 4 5 6 7 8 9 10 11

Job 8.5.4

1 Construct complete letters as directed from the skeleton letters below.
   - All letters are from Ruth King, Claims Manager.
2 If your system allowed you to save the standard paragraphs and the complimentary close and signature line in Job 8.5.3, retrieve them from the system. Otherwise key the appropriate paragraphs.

Letter 1

Mr Scott Laws
86 Threadbare Street
LINCOLN   LN2 6DD

Dear Mr Scott

1

2

Letter 2

Mrs B R French
28A Golden Street
GRAYS
Essex RM16 3JE

Dear Mrs French

1

3, 5

Letter 3

Ms June Long
114 Eddystone Street
GLASGOW G15 7LT

Dear Mrs Long

1

4

Letter 4

Miss H Kahn
189 Tacoma Crescent
AYR   KA7 2QZ

Dear Miss Kahn

1

6, 7

Letter 5

Mr R G Winston
84 Jasper Parade
HULL HU1 2AF

Dear Mr Winston

1

6, 8

Planning and setting margins

Planning margins

So far you have set a left margin only and have copied line for line. There has been no need for a right margin.

A general rule for setting margins is to leave 25 mm (1 in) margins all round on plain A4 and 13 mm (1/2 in) margins all round on A5. However, a more balanced appearance between space and text can be achieved by choosing a suitable line length for a particular document and calculating equal left and right margins.

The ability to plan margins quickly and expertly will come with practice. You will gain that practice through following the instructions for margins and line length recommended for the exercises that follow.

Paper sizes and type pitch

Both A4 paper (portrait) and A5 paper (landscape) are 210 mm wide. This represents
- 82 spaces in 10-pitch type
- 100 spaces in 12-pitch type.

Calculating margins

Example 1

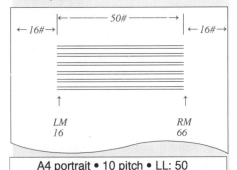

A4 portrait • 10 pitch • LL: 50	
Number of spaces across A4 portrait in 10 pitch	82
Subtract your line length	50
Total amount of white space to right and left of the document	32
Divide this figure by 2 to calculate left margin (32 ÷ 2)	16
Add line length	50
Right margin	66

On a *typewriter* with the left edge of the paper at 0 on the pitch scale, the left margin will therefore be at 16 and the right margin at 66.

On a *computer*, because the left edge of the paper does not correspond with the left edge of the scale shown on the screen, a further calculation must be made. The number of spaces between the left of the computer screen scale and the left edge of the paper must be deducted from the calculated figure. If there are 8 spaces to the left of the scale, for example, the left margin will be $16 - 8 = 8$, and the right margin $66 - 8 = 58$.

Note: On some word processing systems the operator sets the line length and the left margin only. The computer sets the right margin automatically. Some systems only show the actual line length available to enter data. The margins are outside the screen.

Example 2

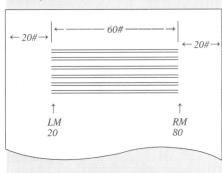

A5 landscape • 12 pitch • LL: 60	
Number of spaces across A5 landscape in 12 pitch	100
Subtract your line length	60
Total amount of white space to right and left of the document	40
Divide this figure by 2 to calculate left margin (40 ÷ 2)	20
Add line length	60
Right margin	80

An adjustment similar to that in the first example must be made for computers.

A5 paper (portrait) is 148 mm wide. This represents
- 59 spaces in 10-pitch type
- 70 spaces in 12-pitch type

To calculate margins for A5 portrait use the same procedure as above substituting the appropriate A5 portrait spaces for the required type pitch.

Setting margins

Find out how to set margins on your system. For typewriters, the general guide on this page may be helpful. You may need to adjust the right margin setting (see 'Pre-set hot zone' on page 48).

Automatic return

Systems with automatic return

All word processing systems and some electronic typewriters have an *automatic return* (also called *wraparound* or *word wrap*) feature. It eliminates the need to strike the return key at the end of a line. When the cursor enters the hot zone (the area immediately before the right margin) and the word being keyed will not fit on the line, or when the space bar on an electronic type-writer is struck, the cursor or carrier moves automatically to the start of the next line. The return key is used only to start a new paragraph or at the end of a line that does not extend to the right margin.

Systems without automatic return

On typewriters without the automatic return function, a beep sounds a set number of spaces before the margin stop. The number of spaces is pre-set on some machines. On others it can be set by the operator. (Consult your operator's manual to find out whether your machine has this feature.) The purpose of the beep is to warn the operator that the carrier is approaching the margin so that the return key can be used to avoid breaking a word.

Your teacher will tell you whether to use the automatic return.

Hot zone

The hot zone is the area immediately preceding the right margin.

Adjustable hot zone

If your system allows you to set the hot zone automatically, set it at 5 spaces. Consult your operator's manual to find out how to do this.

Job 8.5.2

Add this information to the standard letter you keyed in Job 8.5.1, either retrieving the stored form letter or keying the details on the hard copy.

Retrieve standard letter *or* use hard copy from Job 8.5.1

1	6 May 1993
2	Ms E Green, 4 Sturt Street, LONDON WIN 4NJ
3	Ms Green
4	84210/X/04
5	1993
6	£429
7	£10 000
8	1 January 1992
9	£3618
10	1993
11	£429
12	£12 862
13	1 January 2001
14	£17 409
15	£22 064
16	£2491

Job 8.5.3

Key these standard paragraphs, creating a separate document for each one.

- Correct two spelling errors and one spacing error.

Plain A4 portrait • LL: 60

Thankyou for your claim letter.

Enclosed is our official claim form. Please answer all the questions as fully as possible and return the form to this office without delay so that your claim can be processed.

We have received your completed claim form and the claim is being processed.
We have received your claim form. As some of the questions have not been answered the form is being returned to you with this letter for completion. The questions not answered have been marked with *a cross/* ~~an 'X'~~.

Our claims Assesser will telephone you shortly to arrange an appointment for an inspection.

Please check your policy.

You will find that it excludes the first £100 of any claim. As you present claim is below that figure we are unable to accept it.

We are unable to accept your claim as the policy has expired.

Yours sincerely
Ruth King
Claims Manager

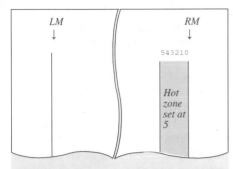

Pre-set hot zone

If the hot zone on your system cannot be adjusted, you can count the number of spaces in the hot zone and, if necessary, adjust the right margin accordingly.

On a typewriter

1 Insert paper in your machine, making sure that the paper edge guide is at 0 on the pitch scale.
2 Set the left and right margins.
3 From the left margin, space along until the beep sounds and then stop.
4 Key 123456 etc until the carrier stops at the right margin.
5 Subtract 5 from the last number you keyed.
6 Press the margin release and reset the margin that number of spaces to the right of the old margin.

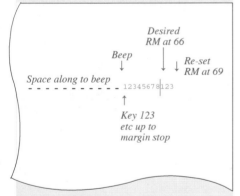

Pre-setting the hot zone

Word division at line endings

Modern practice is to avoid word breaks at line endings as far as possible. Some systems allow you to select word breaks or no word breaks. One or other of them is usually the *default* (the one that applies if you make no selection). In Unit 2.3 you will learn more about word division procedure.

Margin release key

If a long word will not quite fit at the end of a line, use the margin release to key the final one or two characters to the right of the margin.

Justified and unjustified right margin

Your system may allow you to choose either a justified or an unjustified right margin. One or other of them is usually the *default*.

Justified right margin

If the operator has selected 'justified right margin', the system will rearrange the spacing between words (or between words and characters) in each line after it is keyed, so that the line extends to the margin.

An unjustified right margin is also called 'ragged right'.

Unjustified (ragged) right margin

Splitting paragraphs

In most systems, a paragraph can be divided into two simply by moving the cursor to the first character in the new paragraph and pressing the return/enter key. Consult your operator's manual to find out how to use this function in your system.

Before you begin Job 2.2.1:

For word processing systems (and typewriters with automatic return and justified right margin option)
• Select *unjustified right margin* option.
• Select *no word break* option.

For typewriters without automatic return
• Set the hot zone at 5 spaces (if the hot zone is adjustable).
• If the hot zone is not adjustable, follow the instructions under 'Pre-set hot zone' above.

Refresher

Spelling and usage
Note the spelling of the highlighted words.

LL: 55 • SS • key line for line

All alpha keys
1 Jake Weazlore received unexpected gift cheques by mail.
Figures
2 Two men aged 95 and 87 live in Flat 20, 1346 City Road.

LL: 55 • SS • key line for line

3 Janet's business has been superseded by a parallel one.

4 In February this committee deferred the forty licences.

Business letters 11

Standard letters

Documents on template
Letters on certain subjects lend themselves to production in standard form. The content of the letters takes the same form, although some data in each letter are variable. The variable data may be the addressee's name and address only or may include other details.

These variable data may be handwritten or keyed into a hard copy of the standard letter or, more usually nowadays, keyed into a standard form letter (or template) which is then stored. Once the template is set up, the operator keys the variable information or merges it from a secondary or data file.

Standard paragraphs/sentences
In some organisations, letters on a common subject are assembled from a series of standard paragraphs or sentences stored on the system. This saves much keying time. The author instructs the operator to retrieve the paragraphs to be included in a particular letter. Retrieval requires only a couple of keystrokes.

Refresher

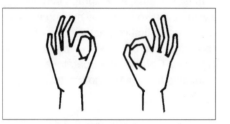

`LL: 55 • SS • DS between drills`

All alpha keys
1 Sky diving is certainly hazardous, but for some the joy
  of free fall is exquisite and worth any expected risks.

Roman numerals/figures
2 Copyright MCMXC UNI Films, 642 Lea Mews, London N5 1LU.

glh
3 Hugh held Hildegarde tightly and gave her a mighty hug.

Aim for speed
4 We shall be glad to advise you on any of these matters.

Job 8.5.1
Study the format of this standard letter and then key it.
Either
- set stop codes at the points marked by the figures if you are using a word processor or an electronic typewriter with at least a page of memory.

or
- use letterhead paper, leaving sufficient space for variable data to be added to your hard copy.

`Letterhead or plain A4 portrait • LL: 55 • SS`

1

2

Dear *3*

POLICY NO: *4*

We are pleased to say that the bonus earned on your
policy during *5* was £ *6.*

The following details explain how the present value of
your policy has been computed.

1 The basic sum assured is £ *7.*
2 Bonuses to *8* were £ *9.*
3 The bonus for *10* is £ *11* .
4 The death benefit is now £ *12.*
5 The estimated cash value of your policy at maturity
  on *13* is £ *14.*

If bonus rates continue at the current level, we
estimate that the sum payable at maturity will be £ *15*
inclusive of a terminal bonus of £ *16* .

Yours faithfully

Sylvia Phelps
Life Assurance Manager

Job 2.2.1

1 In this job your line endings will not correspond with those in the copy. Do not break words at line endings; on a typewriter without automatic return use the margin release key.
2 Proofread and correct your work.
3 If your system allows, name this document FORMAT1 and save it for Job 2.2.3.
4 Print a justified and an unjustified copy if your system allows.

A5 landscape • LL: 60 • SS

↓ LM

FORMATTING *R2*
    ↓ *T*

    Formatting means planning the placement of a document on the page. The principles are the same whether you are using a computer or a typewriter. *R2*

    If you know what your system is capable of and adopt the modern display conventions taught in this book, your finished document will have a professional look and be pleasing to the eye.

Proofreading

Here is the symbol that tells you to transpose a paragraph or group of words.

Mark in text	Mark in margin	Corrected passage
If you want to move a paragraph or phrase to a different place, first draw a circle around it. Transposing paragraphs is easy.	trs	Transposing paragraphs is easy. If you want to move a paragraph or phrase to a different place, first draw a circle around it.

Job 2.2.2

Follow the instructions for Job 2.2.1 but set margins for a 55-space line.

- Key the highlighted words in bold or underscore them.
- It is not necessary to save this document.

A5 landscape • LL: 55 • SS

↓ *LM*

IS YOUR MARGIN JUSTIFIED? *R2*
    ↓ *T*

    Now that computers, and even some electronic typewriters, can give a document an even right margin automatically, documents with all lines finishing at the same point are common. *R2*

Find out what your system can do.

NP   The simplest way to justify is to put extra space between words. Some systems **microjustify**: extra space is inserted between letters as well as words. Text may be **proportionally spaced** too; this means that each character occupies a space related to its size as in printer's typesetting. *R2*

Speed test (SI 1.37)

1 Take two 2-minute timings.
2 Record your better rate.
3 Proofread and correct your work.

LL: 55 *or* decide your own line endings • SS

Word

The 'hot zone' (the area just before the right margin)	1
is common to typewriters and word processors. On a	2
typewriter you hear a beep on entering the hot zone; on	3
a computer a silent message tells the system that the	4
line ending is near and the next word will begin on a	5
new line.	5

1 2 3 4 5 6 7 8 9 10 11

Business letters 10

Circular letter with tear-off slip

A circular may begin with a general salutation, such as 'Dear Householder', 'Dear Customer' or 'Dear Parent'. But with the wide availability of word processors capable of merging names from a database, circular letters are nowadays often personalised. In this instance, they are not so easily distinguished from a personal letter.

No inside address is on the original (master) of the letter.

Circular letters often bear only the month and year as a date or may be headed 'Date as postmark'.

Refresher

LL: 55 • SS • DS between drills

All alpha keys

1 Kate will be just amazed at the quality, style and all-round excellence of this precious jewel among vehicles.

Symbols/figures

2 Insert 13 spaces after '% thiamine' and 'kJ per 250 g'.

d/f

3 Freda defiantly defended Fidelia's fundamental freedom.

Aim for speed

4 The band will soon be joined by a new male lead singer.

Job 8.4.1

Study the model and key from the draft on the right.

Letterhead and envelope • LL: 60 • SS

May 1993

Dear Parents

By arrangement with the school, Swan Guided Shopping Tours gives you the chance to shop for quality goods at low, low prices, have a fun day and help the school. Guided by Swan's hostess

– *you join other parents on a day-long shopping tour, travelling by luxury, air-conditioned coach;*
– *you choose your purchases from well-known manufacturers and wholesalers of electrical goods, clothes, toys, linen, jewellery etc;*
– *the school development fund gets a discount on the bulk purchases made at each shopping stop;*
– *the cost of £20 includes lunch at a well-known restaurant.*

Interested? For more information, return the tear-off slip.

Yours sincerely

Joan Lewis
Secretary, Parents Association

....

To: Ms Joan Lewis, Parents Association, Bainbridge Primary School, Bainbridge Street, BRISTOL, BS4 IPJ

Please send me more information on Swan Shopping Tours.

Surname .... First name/s ....

Address ....

.. Postcode ....

Signature .... Date ....

No inside address – leave enough space for inside address if letter is to be personalised.

Date in full or month and year only.

Bainbridge Primary School
Bainbridge Street
Bristol BS4 IPJ
Telephone 0272 799 2130

May 1993

Dear Parents

By arrangement with the school, Swan Guided Shopping Tours gives you the chance to shop for quality goods at low, low prices, have a fun day and help the school. Guided by Swan's hostess

- you join other parents on a day-long shopping tour, travelling by luxury, air-conditioned coach;
- You choose your purchases from well-known manufacturers and wholesalers of electrical goods, clothes, toys, linen, jewellery etc;
- the school development fund gets a discount on the bulk purchases made at each shopping stop;
- the cost of £20 includes lunch at a well-known restaurant.

Interested? For more information, return the tear-off slip.

Yours sincerely

Joan Lewis
Secretary, Parents Association

To: Ms Joan Lewis, Parents Association, Bainbridge Primary School, Bainbridge Street, BRISTOL, BS4 IPJ

Please send me more information on Swan Shopping Tours.

Surname.................. First name/s................
Address ....
.... Postcode ....
Signature........................... Date..............

Word division

It is not usual practice to break a word at the end of a line. However, it is sometimes necessary
* to achieve a more regular right margin
* to improve the spacing between words (or words and characters) when a justified right margin has been selected.

When a word is divided in this manner, a hyphen is inserted at the end of the line.

When to use word division

Word division can generally be avoided on line lengths of 55 or more character spaces. If you are keying a document with a short line length, however, failure to break a long word may produce a very uneven right margin or, where you have selected right margin justification, excessive spacing between words or between words and letters.

Word division with automatic return

Some systems with automatic return allow you to select
* *hyphenation on* or
* *hyphenation off*.

If you select hyphenation on, the system will suggest line-end word breaks which you may either *accept*, or *cancel* and make your own word breaks. On some systems you have the choice of automatic hyphenation either as you key the document or after you have keyed it. On other systems you may select hyphenation on only after the document is keyed. Find out what your system offers.

Hyphens: hard and soft

Most word processing systems and typewriters with automatic return use two kinds of hyphen.
* *Hard hyphens* are used in words that are always hyphenated; for example:

  father-in-law   twenty-one
* *Soft hyphens* are used only in word breaks at line endings.

After reformatting
* hard hyphens remain
* soft hyphens disappear if they no longer fall at the end of a line.

Find out how to use hard and soft hyphens on your system.

Hard space

Hard (also called *required, protected* or *sticky*) *space* is a feature of most word processing systems. It allows the operator to bind two or more words together so that an undesirable line break can be avoided; for example between the initials of a name, or in a date or address:

R D McGregor
23 May 1901
62 The Avenue

Find out how to use the hard space on your system.

Rules for word division

The complex rules for word division are set out on this page and the next, but do not attempt to memorise them. The best way to learn them is to refer back to this page as you key Jobs 2.3.1 and 2.3.2.

There are several good word division dictionaries. Our reference is *Collins Gem Dictionary of Spelling & Word Division*. Not all authorities agree on the division of some words, but their basic criteria are the same.

Recommendations for word division

Divide	Right	Wrong
1 between sounded syllables	dic-tion chil-dren	dict-ion child-ren
2 between consonants	quan-tity prac-tise	quant-ity pract-ise
3 between vowels in separate syllables	cre-ator	crea-tor
4 between double consonants unless they are part of the same root	sup-pose suf-fuse	supp-ose suff-use
but	pass-ing	pas-sing
5 compound words (but only between the component parts)	down-fall pass-port	dow-nfall pas-sport
6 words already hyphenated (but only at the hyphen)	pre-eminent non-negotiable	pre-emin-ent non-neg-otiable

continued

Job 8.3.2 cont

b During the period we were forced to company-operate two units where we were seriously understaffed. I am pleased to be able to report that arrangements have now been made to (satisfactorily) cover these units.

3 Cooperative income is below expectations, and we now believe our budget estimate may have been optimistic. Current expectations are that cooperative income for the year will be £425 456, which is barely ahead of last year.

4 Press and TV/radio advertising ~~has~~ expenditure been cut-back to help offset the reduced level of cooperative income. Advertising expenditure is made up of a number of elements. (see Table 2 attached.)

5 Unit loan income is hard to predict as it depends on the floating level of credit extended to units. We expect to be able to provide a more accurate forecast next quarter.

We have done well to be in this position at half year. All the signs are that, with the most difficult part of the trading year behind us; we shall comfortably reach our target at year end, although we can expect to be behind budget in some key areas. On the whole we should ~~be pleased~~ with company performance in a difficult year.   not be displeased

6 Export sales are continuing to grow very strongly now that we have established firm trading links with Western Europe and Japan. It is disappointing that we have not yet been able to break into the lucrative North American market, but the attendance of some of our senior marketing executives at forthcoming trade fairs in Atlanta, San Francisco, Chicago and Toronto is bound to open up export possibilities for us.

yi
att 2

Divide		*Right*	*Wrong*
7	after a prefix or before a suffix.	pro-claim wait-ing	proc-laim wai-ting
	Words whose meaning is changed according to their pronunciation are an exception:	pre-sent (verb = give) pres-ent (noun = gift)	

Do not divide

8	words of one syllable	strength	
9	at a point where only two letters would be carried to the next line	greatly hearten strainer	
10	after the first letter of a word	against	
11	proper nouns	December Atkinson	
12	courtesy titles or qualifications	Mr Wade B Jones FRACS	
13	figures or sums of money	48 732 o198.45	
14	abbreviations or contractions.	couldn't RSPCA	

Try to avoid dividing

- dates (and only after the month, if division is unavoidable)   15 December 1990

- words of six or fewer letters   locate

- the last word on a page

- on successive lines.

Refresher

LL: 55 • SS • key line for line

Alternate hands
1 She and Henry may turn down the antique Irish ornament.

Asterisk
2 An asterisk (*) can indicate a footnote or explanation.

Spelling and usage

Note the spelling of the highlighted words.

LL: 55 • SS • key line for line

3 Cocoa coconut and caster sugar adorned the cantaloupe

4 Awful antarctic weather causes anxiety among explorers.

Job 8.3.1 cont

Use the same style of heading for continuation pages in memoranda as for letters (see Unit 8.2, page 146).

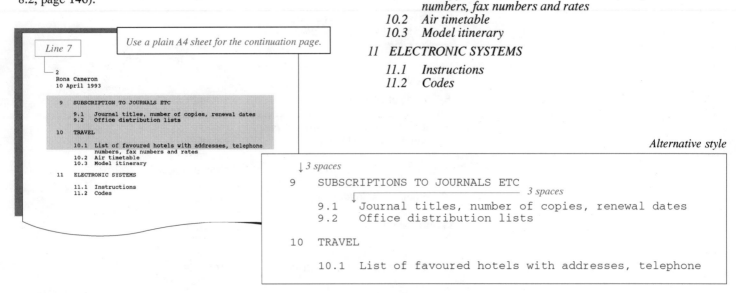

Use a plain A4 sheet for the continuation page.

Line 7

```
2
Rona Cameron
10 April 1993

9    SUBSCRIPTION TO JOURNALS ETC

     9.1   Journal titles, number of copies, renewal dates
     9.2   Office distribution lists

10   TRAVEL

     10.1  List of favoured hotels with addresses, telephone
           numbers, fax numbers and rates
     10.2  Air timetable
     10.3  Model itinerary

11   ELECTRONIC SYSTEMS

     11.1  Instructions
     11.2  Codes
```

Use margin release key.↓

9 SUBSCRIPTIONS TO JOURNALS ETC

9.1 *Journal titles, number of copies, renewal dates*
9.2 *Office distribution lists*

10 TRAVEL

10.1 *List of favoured hotels with addresses, telephone numbers, fax numbers and rates*
10.2 *Air timetable*
10.3 *Model itinerary*

11 ELECTRONIC SYSTEMS

11.1 *Instructions*
11.2 *Codes*

Alternative style

```
↓ 3 spaces
9    SUBSCRIPTIONS TO JOURNALS ETC
                                  ——————————— 3 spaces
     9.1   Journal titles, number of copies, renewal dates
     9.2   Office distribution lists

10   TRAVEL

     10.1  List of favoured hotels with addresses, telephone
```

Job 8.3.2

Key this report in the form of a memorandum, following the formatting guidelines for Job 8.3.1.

- The draft is continued on the next page.
- Use a plain A4 sheet for the continuation page.
- Correct two spelling errors and two punctuation errors.

Simple reports are presented in the form of a memorandum as in Job 8.3.2.

Memorandum paper • LL: 60

To: W T Leighton, Executive Director
From: G K James, General Manager
Today's date,
Subject: Report for the Half Year

I submit the attached printout, which shows trading results for the half year compared with the budget and last years figures.

Overall performance resulted in an operating profit of £89 987, which I believe demonstrates a successful containment of costs, despite unusual pressures.

1 Production weeks were 14 per cent below budget, mainly due to production delays in New South Wales and Queensland. In spite of this, production per unit was stronger than predicted, as demonstrated in Table I attached.

2 Most costs are more or less in line with the budget, but the following matters deserve mention.

   a Computor costs are very much higher than budgeted, and we are now bearing the full cost of all software development and support, in addition to the lease charges levied by the Information Services Division.

Job 2.3.1

Review tabulating on page 43.

1 Key the first line as shown.

2 Key each remaining word twice, the second time hyphenating where you would divide it at a line ending. If you decide a word should not be divided, do not hyphenate it.
  - Do not key the figures. They refer to the recommendations on pages 50-1.

3 Proofread and correct your work.

A4 portrait • DS • centre vertically

On a computer, the margin and tab settings shown will need adjustment (see page 47)

LM *12 (10)* *21 (12)* ↓	T *26 (10)* *35 (12)* ↓	T *41 (10)* *50 (12)* ↓	T *58 (10)* *67 (12)* ↓
mixture	mix-ture	holding	hold-ing

1 knowledge
2 customer
3 amiable
4 telling
5 copyright
6 self-help
7 prepare
8 stretched
9 plainly
10 amongst
11 Coventry
12 A Roberts BA
13 £539 848
14 shouldn't

Job 2.3.2

Follow the instructions for Job 2.3.1.

A4 portrait • DS • centre vertically

LM *12 (10)* *20 (12)* ↓	T *29 (10)* *37 (12)* ↓	T *47 (10)* *55 (12)* ↓	T *63 (10)* *71 (12)* ↓

landscape
foreword
slashed
deny
deserve
symptom
nutrition

scarcely
creator
passing
creature
justice
gradient
custody

Job 2.3.3

1 Review the advice on word division in this unit.

2 Key this paragraph, following the basic principles of word division.
  - If your system allows, insert a hard space at this symbol ∇.

3 Proofread and correct your work.

A5 landscape • LL: 60 • SS • justify

Our annual reunion dinner will be held at 7 o'clock on 17∇September at the usual place. Our speaker will be a Mr∇Solomon Templar∇BA. I can't say I've heard of him; perhaps he was in the ~~next~~ year fol-*low* lowing ours. Time certainly does fly! Every year I meet more new people at these college reunions, and they seem to get younger each time. We ~~were~~ *graduated/* ~~there~~ in 1985. I'm glad we all keep in touch. But we haven't heard from Barbara lately; has anyone?

Speed test (SI 1.42)

1 Take two 2-minute timings.

2 Record your better rate.

3 Proofread and correct your work.

LL: 55 *or* decide your own line endings • SS

	Words
Most English dictionaries do not give word breaks.	10
They show a syllable stress mark, but this has nothing	21
to do with word division. It shows which syllable is	32
stressed in speech. There are, however, special word	43
division dictionaries that give you guidelines on where	54
to break words.	57

1 2 3 4 5 6 7 8 9 10 11

Memoranda 3

Decimal enumeration

To do the work in this unit you should know the technique for decimal enumeration (Unit 5.7, page 112).

Continuation pages

Use plain paper of matching size and quality for continuation pages.

Refresher

LL: 55 • SS • DS between drills

All alpha keys

1 At university Mike excels in sciences, his best subject being without question zoology, followed by physiology.

Symbols/figures

2 We have their order for 135 cedar lattices 2.4 x 0.9 m.

a/s

3 This sad salmon sandwich was on sale several Saturdays.

Aim for speed

4 Please let me have your views with those of your staff.

Job 8.3.1

Study the model and key from the draft on the right.

- The model and draft are continued on the next page.

> On some WP systems it will be necessary to set the left margin a few spaces to the right of the default margin in order to use the margin release for item 10 (see next page).

Memorandum paper: • LL: 60 • SS

EUROPEAN FOOD PROCESSING LTD

MEMORANDUM

TO: Rona Cameron, Administration Director
FROM: Jean Rigby, Senior Administrative Assistant
DATE: 10 April 1992
SUBJECT: OFFICE PROCEDURES

Following my suggestion that desk manuals be kept in a standard form by all administrative assistants in the company, here are my recommendations for the office procedures section:

1 INCOMING MAIL

   1.1 Mail register
   1.2 Mail distribution list

2 CORRESPONDENCE

   2.1 Model letter format
   2.2 Model memorandum format
   2.3 Stationery samples

3 WORD PROCESSING CONVENTIONS

4 POSTAL SCHEDULES

5 COMPANY FORMS

   5.1 Samples of forms
   5.2 Purpose and how to complete them
   5.3 Distribution

6 OFFICE SUPPLIES

   6.1 List of supplies
   6.2 Re-order levels
   6.3 Suppliers' names and addresses

7 RECORDS MANAGEMENT

   7.1 Filing plan
   7.2 Indexing and coding rules
   7.3 Names of persons authorised to dispose of files

8 OFFICE EQUIPMENT

   8.1 Inventories with serial numbers and purchase dates
   8.2 Repair services
   8.3 Depreciation schedule
   8.4 Leasing agreements

To: Rona Cameron, Administration Director
From: Jean Rigby, Senior Administrative Assistant
Date: 10 April 1993
Subject: OFFICE PROCEDURES   R3

Following my suggestion that desk manuals be kept in a standard form by all administrative assistants in the company, here are my recommendations for the office procedures section: R2

1 INCOMING MAIL

   1.1 ↓ Mail register
   1.2 Mail distribution list

Key 3 spaces so that item 10.1 will align correctly.

2 CORRESPONDENCE

   2.1 Model letter format
   2.2 Model memorandum format
   2.3 Stationery samples

3 WORD PROCESSING CONVENTIONS

4 POSTAL SCHEDULES

5 COMPANY FORMS

   5.1 Samples of forms
   5.2 Purpose and how to complete them
   5.3 Distribution

6 OFFICE SUPPLIES

   6.1 List of supplies
   6.2 Re-order levels
   6.3 Suppliers' names and addresses

7 RECORDS MANAGEMENT

   7.1 Filing plan
   7.2 Indexing and coding rules
   7.3 Names of persons authorised to dispose of files

8 OFFICE EQUIPMENT

   8.1 Inventories with serial numbers and purchase dates
   8.2 Repair services
   8.3 Depreciation schedule
   8.4 Leasing agreements

Centring between margins

Automatic centring

Your computer or electronic typewriter can automatically centre a line between the left and right margins. Consult your operator's manual to find out how to use this function on your system. It is also possible to centre manually, if you have a typewriter with no automatic centring facility.

Centring manually

Follow these instructions to centre manually.
- Make sure the left edge of the paper is on 0.
- Either set your margins or move the margin stops to the far left and right.
- Clear all tab stops.
- Set a tab at the centre point.
- Tab to that point.
- Backspace once for every two characters or spaces in the line to be centred.
- Key the line.

Refresher

LL: 55 • SS • key line for line

All alpha keys
1 Dymphna Wafluck travels to Zhaoqing, Xi'an and Beijing.
Maths symbols
2 163 + 970 - 754 = 379; 29 + 8 + 7 + 6 + 5 - 14 - 3 = 38

Spelling and usage

Note the spelling of the highlighted words.

LL: 55 • SS • key line for line

3 The extremely influential councillor seemed an amateur

4 Exhausted athletes were embarrassed by such efficiency

Job 2.4.1

1 Study this example.
2 Key it, centring each line horizontally.
3 Proofread and correct your work.

A5 landscape • DS • key line for line • centre vertically

Centring horizontally

means placing a heading

or display line in a central position

between the left and right margins.

Job 2.4.2

1 Key this document, centring each line horizontally.
2 Proofread and correct your work.

A5 landscape • DS • key line for line • centre vertically

You will find that
horizontal centring
is easy on
an electronic typewriter
or
computer

Proofreading

This is how to indicate that a word or line is to be centred on the page.

Mark in text	Mark in margin	Corrected passage
⌐PROGRESS REPORT⌐ Week ending 18 November	centre	PROGRESS REPORT Week ending 18 November

Business letters 9

Sub-enumeration

To do the work in this unit you should know the technique for sub-enumeration (Unit 5.6, page 110).

Continuation page

If a letter will not fit on one page, use plain paper of the same colour, size and quality for the continuation page or pages. Many organisations use pre-printed continuation pages.

Each continuation page must be numbered and have a heading so that, if it becomes detached, it will be readily identified.

It is unnecessary to number the first page of a two-page letter. The absence of a signature shows that a continuation page follows.

Refresher

LL: 55 • SS • DS between drills

All alpha keys

1 Elizabeth Dropher will examine objectively the question of whether the koala too is on the verge of extinction.

Symbols/figures

2 Please offer £78 500 for the 3 acre block (lot no 127).

r/t

3 Robert's smart dart struck the treasure trove trinkets.

Aim for speed

4 When can they ship the orders for brass rods and clips?

Job 8.2.1

Study the model and key from the draft on the right. Use the underscore if you do not have bold.

Plain A4 portrait • LL: 62 • SS

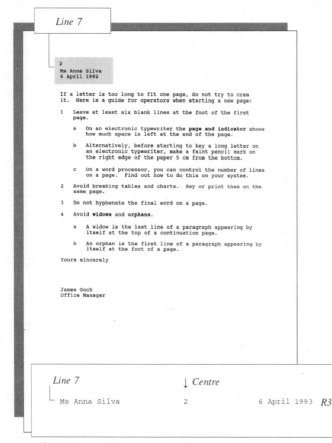

Line 7

Alternative style

2
Ms Anna Silva
6 April 1993   R3

If a letter is too long to fit one page, do not try to cram it. Here is a guide for operators when starting a new page: R2

1   *Leave at least six blank lines at the foot of the first page.*   R2

    a   *On an electronic typewriter the **page end indicator** shows how much space is left at the end of the page.*   R2

    b   *Alternatively, before starting to key a long letter on an electronic typewriter, make a faint pencil mark on the right edge of the paper 5 cm from the bottom.*

    c   *On a word processor, you can control the number of lines on a page. Find out how to do this on your system.*

2   *Avoid breaking tables and charts. Key or print them on the same page.*

3   *Do not hyphenate the final word on a page.*

4   *Avoid **widows** and **orphans**.*

    a   *A widow is the last line of a paragraph appearing by itself at the top of a continuation page.*

    b   *An orphan is the first line of a paragraph appearing by itself at the foot of a page.*

Yours sincerely

James Goch
Office Manager

Job 2.4.3

1 Key these lines.
2 Proofread and correct your work.

Before you take the plunge
consider
NOISE
from
swimming
and
spa pools

centre

Job 2.4.4

1 Key this document, centring each line horizontally.
2 Proofread and correct your work.

Genuine
Antique Mirrors
Britain's Greatest Selection
MORELAND ANTIQUES
432 Elizabeth Street Mitcham

Job 2.4.5

1 Key this document, centring each line horizontally.
2 Proofread and correct your work.

CAST IRON WORK
bring it to use for
REPAIRS
ABRASIVE CLEANING
REPRODUCTION
ASCOT IRON WORK
29 Waverley Road Kew

Speed test (SI 1.5)

1 Take two 2-minute timings.
2 Record your better rate.
3 Proofread and correct your work.

	Words
All office noise should be kept to a level where staff	11
can work without stress or distraction. Keeping noisy	22
machinery away from general work areas and using sound-	33
absorbent material in floors, walls and ceilings are	43
two ways of doing this. However, most of us would not	54
like to work in total silence.	60

1   2   3   4   5   6   7   8   9   10   11

Job 8.1.2

Key this letter, following the formatting guidelines for Job 8.1.1.

- Correct two misspelt words, one punctuation error, one error in capitalisation and one error of style.

Ref SC/32/6

Mrs Eileen O'Hara
Manager
Clifftop Hotel
Eastern Highway
BOURNEMOUTH   BH2 6PU

Use today's date

Dear Mrs O'Hara

bold   ANNUAL SALES CONFERENCE

I was pleased to recieve the brochure describing your conference facilities.

Distinguish between *its* and *it's*.

The company is planning to hold it's annual sales conference from 1 to 7 July 1992, both dates inclusive, and I would like you to provide a quotation based on the following information:

1   The participants will number 58. of these, 20 will need single rooms and the remaining 38 shared accommodation. Both single and double rooms should have private bathrooms.

2   Breakfast, lunch and dinner as well as morning and afternoon tea, are required for all participants. Please supply sample menus.

3   Off-street car parking for 18 vehicles is required.

Numbers up to nine are usually spelt out.

sales/e/   4   Three conference rooms will be needed, one for each division. One room must comfortably accomodate the full compliment of 58 participants as it will be used for plenary sessions. The remaining 2 rooms need accommodate only 20 persons each.

I look forward to having your quotation.

Yours sincerely

Desmond Wang
Assistant Marketing Manager

c Julia Small

Module 3   Punctuation and style

Performance goals

At the end of **Module 3** you should be able to

- punctuate any material that you key so that its meaning is clear
- follow the rules of figure typing and decide when to express numbers in words
- key units of measurement and their symbols and know how to use roman numerals
- treat abbreviations and contractions correctly
- make correct decisions about where to apply upper case
- address individuals according to the accepted conventions.

Punctuation 1

Full stop

A full stop is used

- at the end of a sentence which is not a question or exclamation:

  Please settle our account.
- as a decimal point:

  19.08
- in expressions of time (with 'am' and 'pm'):

  9.30 am   2.45 pm
- after an abbreviation:

  A.B.C.*

Two spaces *or* one space may be keyed after a full stop at the end of a sentence. It is important, however, that the *same number* of spaces is left every time. Two spaces, the style adopted by this book, is the most commonly used.

---

*Its use here is optional – see description of open punctuation on page 82. This use of a full stop in an abbreviation is called 'closed punctuation'. It is important to be consistent in using either open or closed punctuation.

A full stop should not be used after a contraction (a shortened form of a word that ends with the last letter of the word itself):

Dept   *not*   Dept.

Ellipsis

An ellipsis is used

- to mark where words have been omitted in quoted matter:

  . . . shall not . . . be lent . . . or otherwise circulated
- to achieve special effects:

  I'll huff . . . and I'll puff . . .

Key one space before, after and between the three dots.

Leader dots – see page 120

Question mark

A question mark is used

- at the end of a direct question:

  When will you be ready?

Space twice after a question mark when it ends a sentence.

- to indicate doubt:

  It occurred in July (?) last year.

A request in the form of a question is not followed by a question mark:

Would you let me know soon.

Do not use a question mark at the end of a sentence that contains an indirect question:

I wonder whether she bought it.

Exclamation mark

An exclamation mark is used for emphasis or to indicate a feeling of surprise, indignation or emotion:

Hear hear!
How clever of you!

Space twice after an exclamation mark.

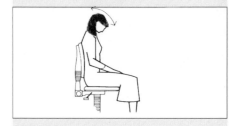

Job 3.1.1

1 Proofread this document and mark in any missing full stops, question marks and exclamation marks. Also mark capital letters.
2 Key a correct copy.

A5 landscape • LL: 65 • SS • centre vertically

When you arrive at Heathrow give me a call from the airport I will pick you up   *R2*

Not one of the orders arrived on time do you know why they were all so late   *R2*

What has happened to Stephen please let me know when you hear from him   *R2*

I hear Kelly won first prize in the design competition what a triumph for one so young

Module 8   Business correspondence 2

Performance goals

At the end of Module 8 you should be able to
- incorporate in business letters and memoranda the appropriate display techniques you have learned
- format business letters and memoranda of more than one page
- format circular letters
- format standard letters
- format and key semi-blocked letters with closed punctuation.

Business letters 8

Numeric enumeration

To do the work in this unit you should know the technique for numeric enumeration (Unit 5.5, page 108).

Job 8.1.1

Study the model and key from the draft on the right.

Letterhead and envelope • LL: 62 • SS

DEO/89/5

2 April 1992

Miss R P Tockek
3/45 Queen Avenue
LONDON SW4 6PX

Dear Robyn

Following your recent interview, I have pleasure in offering you the position of Data Entry Operator commencing on Monday 21 April 1992 at a salary of £146 per week.

The offer is subject to the following terms and conditions:

1   You must provide satisfactory references and documentary proof of academic qualifications.

2   Satisfactory completion of three months' probation is necessary before your appointment to the permanent staff.

3   The Commercial Clerks Award applies to this position.

4   One week's notice of termination of service is required.

Please telephone me by Monday 14 April to confirm whether you accept the appointment.

Yours sincerely

Helena Novak
Personnel Officer

enc

EUROPEAN FOOD PROCESSING LTD

114 Centre Road LONDON SW1V 1RS Telephone (03) 878 1001 Fax (03) 878 9944

In reply please quote:

DEO/89/5

2 April 1992

Miss R P Tockek
3/45 Queen Avenue
LONDON SW4 6PX

Dear Robyn

Following your recent interview, I have pleasure in offering you the position of Data Entry Operator commencing on Monday 21 April 1992 at a salary of £146 per week.

The offer is subject to the following terms and conditions:

1 You must provide satisfactory references and documentary proof of academic qualifications.

2 Satisfactory completion of three month's probation is necessary before you appointment to the permanent staff.

3 The Commercial Clerks Award applies to this position.

4 One week's notice of termination of service is required.

Please telephone me by Monday 14 April to confirm whether you accept the appointment.

Yours sincerely

Helena Novak
Personnel Officer

enc

Job 3.1.2

Follow the instructions for Job 3.1.1.

A5 landscape • LL: 60 • SS • centre vertically

Centre → NEW PACK LEADER

Mrs Nadia Rakic has just been appointed leader of the 2nd Junction Cove Brownie Pack I know you will want to join me in extending her a very warm welcome Mrs Rakic

leader/ is a highly experienced ~~person~~ with lots of exciting ideas How lucky we are to have her join us Will you be able to come along on Tuesday evening to meet her

Job 3.1.3

Follow the instructions for Job 3.1.1.

A5 landscape • LL: 60 • SS • centre vertically

Centre → COMFORT AND STYLE

Are you one of those really fashion-conscious people when it comes to footwear Do you rate comfort highly too If the answer to both questions is yes, join the rush to Brown Brothers Shoe Stores before their fabulous stocktaking sale ends There's a branch near you We're open until 8 pm on Fridays What an opportunity to combine comfort and style with economy

Speed test (SI 1.41)

1 Take two 2-minute timings.
2 Record your better rate.
3 Proofread and correct your work.

LL: 55 *or* decide your own line endings • SS

	Words
Punctuation is to some extent a matter of taste, but	10
there are rules to be followed. One of them is that a	21
sentence must end with a full stop, a question mark or	32
an exclamation mark. That is not too difficult; but	42
many people cannot quite decide where one sentence	52
should end and another begin.	58

1 2 3 4 5 6 7 8 9 10 11

Job 7.15.2

Display this table attractively.

Plain A5 landscape • centre vertically/horizontally

PHOTOCOPIER COMPARISON CHART

	First Copy (seconds)	Copies/minutes	Maximum Size (original)	Maximum Size (copy)	Warm-up Period
Praed Zerox	11.0	55	A3	A3	4.00 min
Merlin	8.0	15	A3	A3	0.45 min
Simms	11.0	8	A4	A4	0.33 min
Kadz	7.5 ~~75~~	20	A3	A3	3.00 min
Sonica X510	7.8	10	B4	B4	0.95 min

Job 7.15.3

Use your skill to display this table attractively.

Plain A4 portrait • centre vertically/horizontally

A GUIDE TO BENEFITS FROM ~~MOST COMMON~~ POPULAR SPORTS

What They Can Achieve
(~~Twenty-one~~ 21 is a Perfect Score)

Health indicator	Running	Biking/Cycling	Swimming	Squash/Handball	Tennis	Walking	Golf	Bowling
Cardiovascular Fitness	21	19	21	19	16	13	8	5
Muscular Strength	17	16	14	(16)	14	11	9	5
Flexability	9	9	15	(15)	14	7	8	7
Balance	17	18	12	17	16	8	6	5
Weight Control	21	20	15	19	16	13	6	5
Digestion	13	12	13	13	12	11	7	7
Sleep	16	15	16	12	11	14	6	6
TOTAL	114	109	106	111	99	77	50 ~~52~~	40 ~~41~~

Punctuation 2

The comma, semicolon and colon all indicate a pause within a sentence.

Comma

The comma is used
- to separate words or groups of words in a list or series:

    She was a cool, clear-headed, able and respected leader.

    Note: it is usual not to place a comma before the second-last item in the list and *and*.
- to mark off words or phrases which could be omitted from a sentence without changing its meaning:

    Our new tutor, a very personable man, starts next week.
- to introduce direct speech:

    He said, 'It will rain today'.

- to mark off an introductory group of words from the rest of a sentence:

    During computer installation, follow these steps.

    Always space once after a comma.

Semicolon

The semicolon is used
- to link two related statements in a sentence:

    Don't drink and drive; it causes accidents.
- to separate items in a complex series:

    Those present were Kaye Smith, the accountant; Mark Novak, the warehouse manager; and Ly Le Hoa, the staff representative.
- before *for example, that is, in fact, for instance,* etc:

    He is a taffy; that is, a Welshman.

    A single space always follows a semicolon.

Colon

The colon is used
- to introduce an example, a series or a list:

    The course includes these subjects: keyboarding, accounting and economics.
- to introduce a statement that enlarges on what went before:

    Our research shows a definite trend: more people are using credit cards.
- to introduce a quotation:

    He ended his speech with the words: 'Thank you for your recognition'.

    Key one space after a colon.

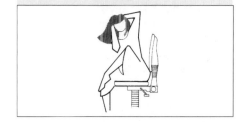

Refresher

LL: 55 • SS • key line for line

Alternate hands

1 If and when they do their work right, the firm may pay.

Semicolon/colon/comma

2 Help me please; buy these: silks, needles and scissors.

Spelling and usage

Note the spelling of the high-lighted words.

LL: 55 • SS • key line for line

3 Terry accidentally achieved excellent personal results.

4 Agreeable, competent secretaries are especially needed.

Job 3.2.1

1 Proofread this document and mark in the missing commas, semicolons and colons.
2 Key a corrected copy.

A5 landscape • LL: 60 • SS • centre vertically

There are no deductions for child care child minding baby sitting or pre-school expenses.

Please order the following for stock 8 reams white bond 2 boxes C6 envelopes and 3 boxes G64 clips.

He has proved a difficult employee for example he repeatedly arrives late.

Tables with vertical column headings

A vertical column heading is used when the heading would not fit across the sheet if positioned horizontally.

Vertical headings are possible only on a typewriter or a sophisticated word processing system. On a typewriter, the vertical headings are inserted after the table has been keyed and the vertical lines have been drawn.

1 Calculate the vertical heading:
   a Count the number of characters in the longest heading and add two characters to allow for a space before and after the longest heading.

> **Guideline for Job 7.15.1**
> Video Players
> = 13 characters + 2 spaces = 15

   b For 10 pitch, multiply this figure by 3 and divide by 5:
      $15 \times 3 = 45 \div 5 = 9$
   c For 12 pitch, divide the figure in (a) above by 2:
      $15 \div 2 = 7$
2 The figure you have calculated is the number of line spaces between the first two horizontal lines.

3 Calculate the vertical placement of the whole document.
4 Calculate the horizontal placement.
5 Key the document, excluding the vertical headings.
6 Insert the vertical lines.
7 Remove the paper and turn the bottom to your left so that the vertical lines become horizontal. Reinsert the paper into the machine in this position.
8 Key the vertical headings centrally between the rules. Ensure that they are correctly aligned. Each heading begins one clear space after the rule at the left.

Refresher

All alpha keys
1 Ask to see this exciting new video camera equipped with zoom lens; then judge its basic qualities for yourself.

Symbols/figures
2 Sales tax (20%) is applied as well as the 35% discount.

h/j
3 Horrid juvenile behaviour has jeopardised this project.

Aim for speed
4 They will take care to meet the needs of these clients.

Job 7.15.1

Prepare an exact copy of this table.

> *10 pitch:*
> Return 10 times between the first two horizontal rules.
> *12 pitch:*
> Return 8 times.

Plain A5 landscape • SS • centre vertically/horizontally

EQUIPMENT SALES

Week Ending 6 October

Salesperson	Televisions	Video Players	CD Players	Amplifiers	Twin Speakers	Radios	
							R2
K James	4	2	1	-	6	2	R1
A Cameron	8	1	2	1	1	8	
L Weston	6	3	4	2	2	5	
D Ferguson	7	2	3	2	3	8	
L Yee	4	9	4	1	3	7	R1

Job 3.2.2

Follow the instructions for
Job 3.2.1.

A5 landscape • LL: 65 • SS • centre vertically

NEW CHIEF EXECUTIVE *Centre*

The Production Manager who is liked by all the
staff has been promoted to Chief Executive. We
have always found him courteous friendly and
sympathetic to any problems the staff may have.
This is why all employees irrespective of their
status in the organisation are delighted at the
news of his success.

Job 3.2.3

Follow the instructions for
Job 3.2.1.

A5 landscape • LL: 55 • SS • centre vertically

Centre → CANCELLED REGULATIONS

The meeting passed all the motions unanimously that is all the members present supported them.

As a result please note that the following schedules have been deleted schedules 10a 23c 38f 45a and 69b. Does this come as a surprise?

This was quite unlike past changes to the constitution which have been very difficult to get through.

Speed test (SI 1.45)

1 Take two 2-minute timings.
2 Record your better rate.
3 Proofread and correct your
  work.

LL: 55 *or* decide your own line endings • SS

	Words
Colons and semicolons have fallen into disfavour,	10
though colons continue to be used to introduce lists.	21
This may be because most of us don't know how to use	32
them. The simple comma remains popular and we badly	43
need it. Remember, though, that you can have too much	54
of a good thing; don't overuse the comma.	62

1   2   3   4   5   6   7   8   9   10   11

Job 7.14.2

Format and key this table correctly.

Plain A5 landscape • SS • centre vertically/horizontally

SUPERANNUATION BENEFITS

Prospective Benefit	Suggested Contribution Each Year			
	10 Years	15 Years	20 Years	25 Years
£ 20 000	1 075	504	261	141
30 000	1 608	756	391	215
40 000	2 145	1 008	522	285
50 000	2 718	1 260	652	352
75 000	4 018	1 891	978	530

Job 7.14.3

Use your skill to format and key this complex table.

Plain A4 portrait • SS • centre vertically/horizontally

EMPLOYMENT CATEGORIES

Category	Age (Years)				
	15-19	20-24	25-44	45+	Total
Managerial and Administrative	379	980	1 694	277	3 330
Professional	3 198	6 909	9 295	1 320	20 722
Artistic, Literary	1 361	2 427	3 248	520	7 556
Clerical, sales, Service	84 566	62 158	73 762	17 554	238 040
Primary Production	2 719	2 337	1 889	243	7 189
Manufacturing and Construction	2 742	3 803	8 329	2 434	17 308
Transport	733	1 225	2 712	797	5 467
Basic Manual	2 811	3 808	6 046	1 525	14 190
Not classified	129	59	75	20	283
TOTAL	98 638	83 706	107 050	24 691	314 085

Punctuation 3

Apostrophe

The apostrophe is used

- to indicate the omission of a letter:
  don't   I'd
- to show possession:
  one month's interest
  three years' sales
  women's issues
  Notice the position of the apostrophe in each example.
- to form plurals of letters, figures etc:
  mind your p's and q's
  your 5's look like 6's

but do not use an apostrophe when expressing decades:
  1920s

Underscoring

Underscoring is used for

- titles of books, long poems and pamphlets:
  <u>Picnic at Hanging Rock</u>
  <u>Paradise Lost</u>
- titles of magazines, newspapers and other periodicals:
  the <u>Advertiser</u>   <u>Cosmopolitan</u>
- titles of plays, ballets, musical comedies, operas and films:
  <u>King Lear</u>   <u>Cats</u>   <u>Star Wars</u>
- specific non-musical titles of major musical compositions:
  Sculthorpe's <u>Sun Music</u>
  but   Mozart's Sixth Symphony

- titles of works of art:
  Van Gogh's <u>Sunflowers</u>
- names of ships, trains or other craft:
  HMS <u>Gloucester</u>
  the <u>Sunlander</u>
  <u>Voyager 1</u>
- scientific names of animals and plants:
  the cane toad, <u>Bufo marinus</u>
  lilly pilly, <u>Acmena smithii</u>
  Note that the first word of a scientific name is capitalised.

  Underscoring is also used for foreign words, if they have not yet been integrated into the English language:
  <u>glasnost</u>   *but*   trio
  <u>Autobahn</u>   *but*   souvlaki

  In typesetting, italics or bold takes the place of underscoring.

Quotation marks

Use quotation marks (inverted commas)

- to enclose the actual words of a speaker or writer:
  Tim said, 'We close at 5 pm'.
- to highlight a word or phrase:
  Mark the file 'Confidential'.
- to identify the title of a chapter in a book or a magazine article:
  chapter 6, 'Punctuation', in the AGPS <u>Style Manual</u>
- to identify the titles of short poems, songs, tunes, essays and lectures:
  'The Raven' by Poe
  Grainger's 'Country Gardens'
- for the titles of radio and television programs:
  'The Sullivans'

Neither quotation marks nor underscoring is used for

- model names, brand names, names of buildings or names of institutions:
  Holden Kingswood
  the National Gallery
- dialogue when it appears in the form of a script or in 'question and answer' form:
  Q: Where were you born?
  A: I was born in Beirut.

If quoted material extends over more than one paragraph, the open quotation is used at the beginning of each paragraph, but the closed quotation appears only at the end of the last paragraph.

Single quotation marks are generally preferred, though double quotation marks are equally correct. Be consistent in your use of quotation marks.

I saw a file marked 'Confidential'.
'Whose is that?' I asked. I didn't think it should lie in the 'in' tray overnight.

Where it is necessary to put quoted material inside quoted material, use double quotes within single quotes (or single within double):

June said, 'We sang "Happy Birthday" and he cut the cake'.

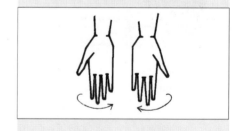

Refresher

LL: 55 • SS • key line for line

All alpha keys

1 Q Jofkemy expects driving conditions will be hazardous.

Single quotation marks/double quotation marks/apostrophe

2 'I live in "Rose Cottage",' said Clarissa to Jo's aunt.

Spelling and usage

Note the spelling of the highlighted words.

LL: 55 • SS • key line for line

3 Conscious of criticism, this government recommended it.

4 Office automation knowledge is desirable for personnel

Tables with sub-divided column headings

To key a table with sub-divided headings:
1 Calculate the vertical placement.
2 Calculate the horizontal placement using the method described on page 123. Disregard the top heading/s.

3 Set margins and tab stops.
4 Key a horizontal rule, extending it beyond the left and right margins half the number of spaces between columns (ie extend it by two spaces in Job 7.14.1). Return twice.
5 Centre braced heading/s over subsidiary headings. Return once.
6 Tab across to the first subsidiary column (column 2 in Job 7.14.1 and backspace half the number of spaces between columns.
7 Key a horizontal rule, extending it beyond the right margin half the number of spaces between columns (ie extend by two spaces in Job 7.14.1).
8 Key the subsidiary headings. Return once.

9 Key the horizontal rule, extending it two spaces to the left and right of the margins.
10 Centre the heading in column 1 between the upper and lower horizontal rules as follows:
   a Subtract the number of lines in the heading from the number of line spaces available.
   b Divide the result by two for the number of lines to be left above the heading.
   c Start keying the heading on the following line.
11 Key the rest of the table.

Refresher

All alpha keys
1 We believe this strike may quickly be extended to every major port and freight terminal throughout New Zealand.

Symbols/figures
2 Saturday's 'News' had a circulation of 38 564 on 1 May.

j/k
3 Ask Jock to jettison the joint dock project in Jakarta.

Aim for speed
4 These fine homes are for sale at prices you can afford.

Job 7.14.1
Key an accurate copy of this table.

Plain A5 landscape • SS • centre vertically/horizontally • 4 spaces between columns

AVERAGE SEASONAL TEMPERATURES *R2*

Capital City	January		July *R1*	
	Maximum	Minimum	Maximum	Minimum
Athens	12	6	32	22
Berlin	2	-3	23	13
London	7	2	23	13
Paris	6	0	24	13
Rome	12	4	31	18
Stockholm	-1	-5	21	13

6 lines

Col 1   Col 2   Col 3   Col 4   Col 5

Job 3.3.1

1 Proofread this document and mark in the missing quotation marks and apostrophes.
2 Key a corrected copy.

A5 landscape • LL: 55 • SS • centre vertically

↓ T

THE DROVERS DOG *Centre*

Bill Hayden, noted for his dry wit, once said: A drovers dog could win the next election. As a result, the term drovers dog took on a new meaning for Australians.

What prominent personality did Mr Hayden have in mind when he used the expression drovers dog?

Job 3.3.2

Follow the instructions for Job 3.3.1, marking in any missing apostrophes, quotation marks or underscoring.

A5 landscape • LL: 60 • SS • centre vertically

↓ T

MAKING A SPEECH *Centre*

If youre ever asked to make a speech and dont know how to start, its not a bad idea to begin with a quotation. youll need to choose one that has some relevance to your chosen topic, of course.

⊙#*cap*

Sources for quotation are The Oxford Dictionary of Quotations and Brewers's Dictionary of Phrase and Fable. If the quotation you find is funny, controversial or just light-hearted that is even better; it will relax the audience and gain their attention before you start.

Job 3.3.3

Follow the instructions for Job 3.3.1, marking in any missing apostrophes, quotation marks or underscoring.

A5 landscape • LL: 55 • SS • centre vertically

EQUAL OPPORTUNITY   Centre

Linda Smiths Company was set up three years ago to advise businesses on EO (Equal Opportunity). Interviewed yesterday by The Advertiser, Ms Smith said: Firms have to recognise now that it is unlawful to treat someone less favourably than another person is or would be treated on the grounds of sex, racial group, or disability.

Speed test (SI 1.6)

1 Take two 2-minute timings.
2 Record your better rate.
3 Proofread and correct your work.

LL: 55 *or* decide your own line endings • SS

	Words
The repeated use of quotation marks on a page looks	10
unsightly. For this reason, in a publication with	20
frequent or lengthy quotations, it is normal practice	31
to typeset them in a smaller size, indent them from the	42
rest of the text, or do both. This emphasises the	52
quoted matter and makes the page more attractive.	62

1 | 2 | 3 | 4 | 5 | 6 | 7 | 8 | 9 | 10 | 11

Job 7.13.2

Display this table attractively.

Plain A5 landscape • SS • centre vertically/horizontally

NEW NAMES FOR OLD PLACES

less #

New	Old	New	Old
Ethiopia	Abyssinia	Ghana	Gold Coast
Botswana	Bechuana *lc* land	Chicago	Fort ~~Darebon~~ *Dearbon*
Sri Lanka	Ceylon	New York	New Amsterdam
Istanbul	Constantinople	Oslo	Christina
Tokyo	Edo	Iran	Persia
Leningrad	St/ Petersburg	Thailand	Siam

Job 7.13.3

Remember to align the bottom line of a two-line heading with a single-line heading.

Plain A5 landscape • SS • centre vertically/horizontally

HOW LONG *IT TOOK/* BEFORE INVENTIONS WERE USED

Product	Year of Idea	Year of Introduction	~~Interval~~ (Years)
Antibiotics	1910	1940	30
Ballpoint pen	1938	1945	~~17~~ 7/
Frozen foods	1908	1923	15
Helicopter *lc*	1904	1941	37
Instant Coffee	1934	~~1556~~ 1956/	22
Nylon	1927	1939	12
Photography	1782	1838	56
Television	1884	1947	63
VCR	1950	1956	6
Zipper	1883	1913	30

Job 7.13.4

Remember to align the bottom line of a two-line heading with a single-line heading.

Plain A5 landscape • SS • centre vertically/horizontally

THE FIRST MEN IN SPACE *u/score*

Astronaut/ Cosmonaut	Country	Spacecraft	Month & Year *sp out*
Yuri Gagarin	USSR	Vostok I	April/ 1961
Alan Shepard	U. S/. A	Freedom 7 *cap*	May 1961
Virgil Grissom	U. S/. A	Liberty Bell 7	July 1961
Gherman Titov	USSR	Vostok II	August 1961
John Glen	USA	Friendship 7	February 1962
Malcolm Carpenter	USA	~~Aurara~~ 7 Aurora	May 1962
Andrian Nikolayev	USSR	Vostok III	August 1962
Pavel Popovich	USSR	Vostok IV	August 1962
Walter Schirra	USA	Sigma 7	October 1962

Punctuation 4

Hyphen

Review 'Hyphens: hard and soft' on page 50.

The hyphen is used

- to join nouns of equal standing:
  captain-coach (ie captain as well as coach)
- in compounds used before the nouns they qualify:

	Compound	Noun
a	well-kept	secret
an	ill-informed	person
an	up-to-date	book
a	ten-year-old	car

but note that where a compound does not precede a noun hyphenation is not necessary:

	Noun		Compound
The	secret	was	well kept
The	person	was	ill informed
The	book	was	up to date

- in colour combinations:
  The decor was grey-blue
- to join numbers, and in fractions:
  She is thirty-three four-fifths
- to separate identical consecutive letters in order to make a word more legible:
  re-educate
- to distinguish words:
  re-cover (cover again)
  recover (regain)
- to avoid ambiguity. Compare:
  three day-old chicks
  three-day-old chicks

Dash

Review keying the dash on page 29.
The dash is used

- to mark off a statement of minor importance:
  The long flight to Singapore – it took 12 hours – gave me a chance to read several books.
- to break a sentence after a complex subject or object:
  The new manager improved staff relations and communication, raised morale, reduced waste and increased profits – all in three months.
- to represent *to* in spans of figures:
  1992–1994
  (with no space either side of the dash).

Parentheses

Parentheses (brackets) are used

- to mark off words that are subsidiary to the rest of the sentence:
  I (and Don) will be at the airport.
  A deposit of o100 (one hundred pounds) is payable.
- to enclose numbers or letters at the start of a paragraph or within a sentence:
  (1) (a) (i)

Punctuation with parentheses

The following examples show where to place the parentheses in relation to the full stop or other closing mark when the parentheses occur at the end of a sentence.

(This is your last chance to change the schedule.)
Follow the boot-up procedure (described on page 86).

Square brackets

Use square brackets

- to enclose words or phrases inserted by someone other than the author:
  When I arrived *Jim Kane* [my italics] was there.

Solidus

The solidus (also called the 'slash' or 'stroke') should be used

- to indicate alternatives:
  yes/no and/or red/green
- for certain abbreviations and symbols:
  a/c km/h
- to denote a fraction:
  1/16 1/4

The solidus should not be used instead of other punctuation marks:
1992–93 *not* 1992/93
London–Paris flight
not London/Paris flight

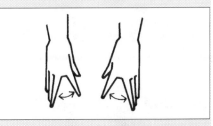

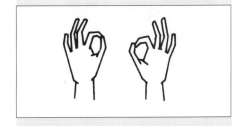

Refresher

LL: 55 • SS • key line for line

Alternate hands

1 Their amendment is a dismal problem for Boris Mayfield.

Solidus/parentheses

2 Section 3 (on page 9) consists of true/false questions.

LL: 55 • SS • key line for line

Spelling and usage

Note the spelling of the highlighted words.

3 It is necessary to negotiate all permanent proceedings.

4 Separate opinions were received on the severe sentence.

 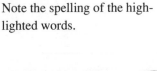

Ruled tables with closed sides

Boxed tables may be presented with vertical rules at left and right.

Follow the technique you used in Unit 10.1 but extend the horizontal rules beyond the left and right margins by half the number of spaces between the columns.

Then use the vertical rule function (or, if your system does not have this function, follow one of the options described in Unit 7.12).

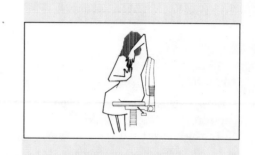

Refresher

LL: 55 • SS • DS between drills

All alpha keys
1 Kim's glitzy, jetset lifestyle and unique excesses have been exposed for fans all over the world to read about.

Symbols/figures
2 The index fell to 1638.5 here after losing 27.4 points.

m/comma
3 Order cream, jam, milk, lemon, ham, mint and mushrooms.

Aim for speed
4 Copy these three disks and keep them in a secure place.

Job 7.13.1

1 Prepare an exact copy of this table.
2 Extend the horizontal rules three spaces beyond the left and right margins.

Plain A5 landscape • SS • centre vertically/horizontally • 6 spaces between columns

LONGEST RIVERS OF THE WORLD *R2*

LM
↓

River	Country/Continent	Length (km) *R1*
Nile	Africa	6670
Amazon	South America	6437
Mississippi-Missouri	USA	5970
Ob-Irtysch	USSR	5569
Chang Jiang	China	5472
Huang He	China	4828
Zaire	Africa	4374
Amur	Asia	4345
Lena	USSR	4314
Mackenzie-Peace	Canada	4241 *R1*

R2

T
↓

Job 3.4.1

1 Proofread this document and mark in the missing hyphens, dashes and parentheses.
2 Key a corrected copy.

A5 landscape • LL: 60 • SS • centre vertically

Centre ALL FEMALE TEAM AHEAD

An all female team, led by 44 year old Glenis Foster, has a first rate chance of winning the London Edinburgh relay race. The map see page 3 shows the route the competitors will take. The assistance of the public is sought, especially people within the inner city area close to the finish.

When the ten strong team reaches Shields probably on Friday morning it will have covered three quarters of the route.

Job 3.4.2

1 Follow the instructions for Job 3.4.1.
2 Key a corrected copy.

A5 landscape • LL: 60 • SS • centre vertically

A ONCE IN A LIFETIME CHANCE

This ☐ well appointed house in a favoured close to the City spot see the map overleaf for the exact location has a delightful open plan living area and is chock a block with top quality fittings. Ring Ted Tregaskis his number is at the head of this letter for an appointment to inspect this not to be missed investment opportunity.

Speed test (SI 1.55)

1 Take two 2-minute timings.
2 Record your better rate.
3 Proofread and correct your work.

LL: 55 *or* decide your own line endings • SS

Words

The rules for the use of the hyphen are not rigid; like 11
other aspects of language, they are gradually changing. 22
Twenty years ago, for example, the forms 'to-day' and 33
'to-morrow' were in common use. Now they are only 43
written as 'today' and 'tomorrow'. It is now becoming 54
common to see 'cooperate' instead of 'co-operate'. 64

1 2 3 4 5 6 7 8 9 10 11

Job 7.12.2

Display this table attractively.

Plain A5 landscape • SS • centre vertically/horizontally

FIRST NOBLE (trs) PRIZE WINNERS

1901

Winner	Country	Category
Wilhelm Roentgen	Germany	Physics
Jacobus Van't Hoff	Netherlands	Chemistry
Emil von Behring	Germany	Physiology
Scully-Prudhomme	France	Literature
Jean Henry Dunant	Switzerland	Peace
Frederick Passy	France	~~Peace~~ stet

i / d (margin notes)

Job 7.12.3

Make full use of your system to display this table.

Plain A5 landscape • SS • centre vertically/horizontally

Stove [Stove] Round-up. ← u/scored caps

Purchase before 31 October

A N D S A V E ← spaced caps

	Full Price £	Special Price £	Save £
Chef Concept 250	617	567	50
Fiesta GUB 152	669	619	60
Modern Made 510GUY	682	622	60
Magichef GMC4/t	879	819	50

Maid /

Job 7.12.4

Use your skill to display this table attractively.

Plain A5 landscape • SS • centre vertically/horizontally

LARGEST ISLANDS OF THE WORLD centre

Island	Ocean or Sea	Area (km^2)
Greenland	Arctic	1 343 998
Papua New Guinea	West Pacific	514 737
Borneo	Indian	467 415
Madagascar	Indian	364 917
Baffin Island	Arctic	295 934
Sumatra	Indian	293 923
Great Britain *	Northern Atlantic	142 879
Honshu, Japan	NW Pacific sp out	138 856

Note: Australia, Antarctica, Afro-Eurasia and the Americas are considered by geographers to be continental land-masses.

* Comprises England, Scotland and Wales

Style 1

Figures or words?

As a general rule express numbers in figures rather than in words. Confine the use of words

- to numbers at the start of a sentence:

  Twenty years ago, he started this business.

- to distinguish between two sets of numbers:

  Order sixteen 38 cm rulers.

- to isolated references to fractions in text:

  The firm dismissed two-thirds of its staff.

- to numbers up to nine not used with dates, times, sums of money, ages, percentages or measurements:

  She made eight attempts to pass the test.

Thousands marker

Key a space between groups of three digits as a thousands marker:

27 904

An exception to this rule applies when you key monetary amounts on cheques or other documents which may be open to falsification. See Unit 3.6 under *Currency* (page 65).

In figures with only four digits the space may be omitted in text:

7904

Note, however, that a figure containing four digits appearing in a tabulation should be keyed with a space so that all figures in the column align:

27 816
7 904
35 808

Review *Hard space* on page 50.

Decimal point

Use the full stop as a decimal point. In text, key a zero before the decimal point if the figure is less than 1:

0.682 397

Note: the thousands separator is also used between groups of three figures to the right of the decimal point.

BC and AD

Use this style:

380 BC *but* AD 1992

Figure spans

Except for dates and street numbers, when keying spans of figures limit the number of digits to those necessary for comprehension:

pages 1420–1

but for 'teens' repeat the tens digit:

pages 1416–18

Dates

Follow this style:

- 1992–93 *or* 1992–1993
  not 1992–3

- 3 June 1990
  not June 3, 1990

Street numbers

Key street numbers in full:

983–984 Power Street
not 983–4 Power Street

Per cent

Use either of these styles but be consistent:

5 per cent *or* 5%
not 5 percent

Refresher

LL: 55 • SS • key line for line

All alpha keys

1 The quick brown foxes jump high over the big lazy dogs.

Hyphen/dash

2 Their get-away vehicle - a two-toned Ford - was stolen.

Spelling and usage

Note the spelling of the highlighted words.

LL: 55 • SS • key line for line

3 It was really quiet when the shooting tragedy occurred.

4 For convenience and consistency follow their procedure.

Job 3.5.1

1 Proofread this document.
2 Key a corrected copy, adopting the recommended style for numbers.

A5 landscape • LL: 60 • SS • centre vertically

↓ *T*

Centre → CLASS REUNION

8 of us from the 1986 class - 2/3 of the students - have planned a reunion dinner on June the 3rd at the Palace Hotel, 385-6 The Esplanade, starting at seven 30 pm. We had 3 or 4 venues in mind but finally settled for The Palace.

Can you come? If so, don't expect an early night!

Ruled tables with open sides

Tables with horizontal and vertical rules (boxed tables) are commonly left 'open' at the sides; ie there are no vertical rules at the left and right of the table.

1 Review the technique for presenting tables with horizontal rules (Unit 7.11, page 135).
2 Calculate the vertical placement of the table. Remember that, as the horizontal rules occupy no space, they are disregarded when calculating vertical placement.

3 Calculate the horizontal placement and set margins and tab stops.
4 Some word processing software and electronic systems have a function to allow you to produce vertical rules. Check whether your system has this function.

Systems with no vertical rule function

- Vertical rules are placed at the central point between columns.
- Mark the centre point lightly in pencil.
- Then use one of the following methods:
  1 Insert the rules with a fine black pen after the table has been removed from the typewriter or printer.

2 On a typewriter:
  a Use a fine black pen and the line ruling aperture to rule the vertical line while the paper is still in the machine.
  b Key the rules after inserting the table in the machine sideways.

Note: Vertical rules must be at right angles to, and join exactly with, horizontal rules. On a word processor, the quality of the finished work may depend on the printer used.

Footnotes: Tabular work often has footnotes to explain some reference to details in the table. The reference sign in the table is typed immediately after the item to which it refers. In the footnote one space is left after the sign.

Refresher

LL: 55 • SS • DS between drills

All alpha keys
1 An earthquake in Brazil injured sixty people and caused extensive damage in the far western parts of the state.

Symbols/figures
2 30 mm, 68.3 cm, 79.2 m, 45.2 km, 3.6 ha, 8.4 mL, 17 kg.

n/m
3 Norman is among the many nimble men and women in Wales.

Aim for speed
4 The firm has an option on land that lies north of here.

Job 7.12.1

Prepare an exact copy of this table.

Plain A5 landscape • SS • centre vertically/horizontally • 5 spaces between columns

EMPLOYEES APPOINTED FEBRUARY *R2*

Employee	Department	Position
David M Kershaw	Sales	Salesman
Michael R Blackwell	Administration	Clerk
Ruth M Dennison	Administration	Accountant
Katherine Huon	Engineering	Audio Typist

R2

R1

R2

R1

Job 3.5.2

Follow the instructions for Job 3.5.1.

A5 landscape • LL: 50 • SS • centre vertically

↓T

Pages 114-6 of the Annual Report dated eight October draw attention to falling attendances. In the period 1990-3 they fell from a high 42685 to a low of 35269, a decline of 17.37 percent. The corresponding fall over the period 1986-9 was only .98 per cent.

38 members of the Social Club have resigned over the last 2 months.

These 3 years have been very disappointing for supporters and management alike. Discussions are under way to try to recruit 6 new players for the senior side, and 11 have indicated interest in the under-18's team. The fund-raising committee is flat out trying to sell 200 books of tickets at 5 pounds each.

Job 3.5.3

Follow the instructions for Job 3.5.1.

A5 landscape • LL: 60 • SS • centre vertically

JAMES COWPER

18 months ago, on 18/1/91, James Cowper joined the company as a junior accounts clerk at a starting salary of 7000 pounds.

For the first 3 months he was employed at our branch at 116-8 High Street, Burwood, where his conduct and work performance were both of the highest standard. On May 4 of that 1st year *he was transferred* to our Head Office, accepting the more senior position of Assistant Accountant, a promotion which brought the reward of an eight % salary increase. The job was a responsible one : 6 junior clerks reported to him.

Speed test (SI 1.51)

1 Take two 2-minute timings.
2 Record your better rate.
3 Proofread and correct your work.

LL: 55 *or* decide your own line endings • SS

Words

Dates may be expressed entirely in numerals, but if you 10
deal with people from the United States of America it 21
can be very confusing. The British arrange the figures 32
in the order of day, month and year; in the States the 43
month comes first, then the day and year. To them, 54
5.11.90 is 11 May 1990; to us it is 5 November 1990. 64

1   2   3   4   5   6   7   8   9   10   11

Tables with horizontal rules

Procedure

1 Calculate vertical placement.
  Note: The horizontal ruled lines *do not occupy any extra vertical space*, so must be ignored when calculating horizontal placement.
2 Clear all margins and tabs.
3 If using a typewriter, insert the paper into the machine.
4 Calculate horizontal placement and set the left margin, tab stops and right margin.
5 Key the main heading and return twice (to leave two clear lines before the horizontal rule). Use the underscore to key a horizontal rule extending from margin to margin.
6 Return twice (to leave one clear line) and block or centre headings over columns.
7 Return once (to leave one clear line before the horizontal rule) and key a horizontal rule extending from margin to margin.
8 Complete the table. Remember to return only once before the final horizontal rule.

Note:
- Horizontal rules may be extended two spaces to the left and right of the table. If the table has extended rules, use the paragraph indent key to set a temporary left margin for the first column.
- Headings typed between horizontal rules in a ruled table are not underscored.
- Headings may be centred or blocked over columns.

Job 7.11.1

Key an exact copy of this document.

A5 landscape • DS body of table • centre vertically/horizontally

WILLIAM BLACKSHORE CO LTD *R2*   *1*
                                  2
    BRANCH OFFICES *R2*   *3*
                                  4
_____ *R2*   *5*
                                                 6
City   Address   Phone No *R1*   *7*
_____ *R2*   *8*
                                                 9
Southend   48 King William Street   08 229 5643   *10*
                                                   11
Plymouth   40 Elizabeth Street   07 748 2950   *12*
                                                   13
Liverpool   75 Swanston Street   03 212 9806   *14*
                                                   15
Manchester 97 Hunter Street   049 572 6482 *16*
                                                   17
Harlow   64 Hassall Road   02 444 6800 *R1* *18*
_____

Instructions

Job 7.11.2

Format and key this document attractively.

Set temporary left margin

Extend the rules two spaces to the left and right of the table.

NIGHTSPORT GUIDE

_____

Day   Nightclubs   Wine Bars
_____

Friday   Survival   Hunter
Saturday   Joey's   Orchid
Sunday   Charlie's   Stylus
_____

Style 2

Currency

- Exact pound amounts are expressed in either of these forms:
  o5 *or* o5.00
- Amounts in pence only are expressed in either of these forms:
  99p *or* o0.99
- Amounts in pounds and pence are expressed in this form:
  o5.85
- Millions of pounds may be expressed in one of three forms:
  o200 000 000 o200 million
  o200 m
- Avoid the use of spaces in money amounts on cheques and other documents which may be open to falsification. Use one of the following styles:
  o70250 *or* o70,250

Metric measurements

The International System of Units (SI) is the standard system of measurement for most countries.

- When keying the units in full, use lower-case initial letters, except for Celsius.
- Metric symbols are keyed with lower-case initial letters, with the exception of those units named after people and the symbol for litres.

Units named after people:

Unit	Symbol
newton	N
pascal	Pa
ampere	A
hertz	Hz
watt	W
Celsius	C
joule	J

Units not named after people:

Unit	Symbol
metre	m
centimetre	cm
millimetre	mm
kilometre	km
gram	g
kilogram	kg
litre	L
millilitre	mL
tonne	t
kilometres per hour	km/h

- All metric prefixes, apart from *mega* (M), *giga* (G), *tera* (T), *peta* (P) and *exa* (E) have lower-case symbols:
  kilojoule kJ
  megapascal MP
- An *s* is never added to a metric symbol:
  km *not* kms
- Metric symbols are not followed by a full stop except at the end of a sentence:
  kg *not* kg.
  but the full stop is used as a multiplication sign within a compound symbol:
  kg.m/s

- A single space is keyed between the preceding figure and the metric symbol, except where the symbols for degrees (°),* seconds ("), degrees Celsius (°C) and per cent (%) are used:
  24 t *but* 35 °C
- Metric symbols may be shown with superscripts
  m^2 kg/m ^{3}
- Key the unit name rather than the metric symbol when there is no accompanying figure:
  How many metres are there in a kilometre?

Hours, minutes and seconds

Use the following style for hours, minutes and seconds:
  20 hours *or* 20 hrs
  17 minutes *or* 17 min *or* 17'
  10 seconds *or* 10 s *or* 10"

*The degrees symbol may not appear on your keyboard. It is often featured as an option only.

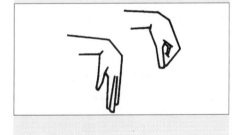

Refresher

LL: 55 • SS • key line for line

Alternate hands
1 If the chaps lend us their bicycle, Roz may go with me.

'At' symbol/dollar sign/cents symbol
2 Marjory bought 6 @ £1.54 and 3 @ 73p from her £20 note.

LL: 55 • SS • key line for line

Spelling and usage
Note the spelling of the highlighted words.

3 Choice of clothes can depend on experience and finance.

4 Acknowledge the beginning of his address with courtesy.

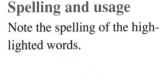 

Money columns with totals

In a money column with a total, the pound sign is placed either at the head of the column or at the foot. It is unnecessary to key it in both places. The following styles are recommended:

```
£                    Pound sign at head (left)

  12.50
 302.05
1480.90              Underscore last figure, R2

1795.45              R1
                     Double underscore
```

```
Pound sign at head   £
(centre)
              12.50
             302.05
            1480.90

            1795.45


  12.50
 302.05
1480.90

£1795.45      Pound sign at left of total
              (do not underscore £)
```

Double underscoring

Some word processing systems allow the operator to double underscore. If your system does not have this facility, a bold underscore can be used instead.

If you are using a typewriter with a variable line spacer:
- Key a single underscore.
- Without using the return key, return the printing point to the beginning of the underscore (ie on the same line).
- Use the variable line spacer to raise the paper very slightly.
- Key a second underscore of the same length.

Job 7.10.1

Key an exact copy of this document.

Remember not to underscore the pound sign.

A5 landscape • SS • centre vertically/horizontally

SALES

October to December

Department	October	November	December	Total
Clothing	15 843	14 768	13 760	44 371
Jewellery	10 109	9 234	12 840	32 183
Furnishing	8 763	8 849	8 450	26 062
Groceries	9 828	9 623	9 764	29 215
Hardware	7 743	6 680	8 580	23 003
Toys	5 890	8 763	14 962	29 615
	£58 176	£57 917	£68 356	£184 449

Job 7.10.2

Format and key this document attractively.

The pound sign is positioned at the head of the column, at the left.

Calculate and key in all totals

```
     £           £           £           £
  65 320     169 516      11 284     117 800
  41 987      10 124      30 373      40 960
   9 611      41 307       8 740      34 261
```

Job 3.6.1

Proofread this document and key a corrected copy, adopting the recommended style for money amounts.

A5 landscape • LL: 60 • SS • centre vertically

↓ T   ⌐TODAY'S STOCK EXCHANGE TRADING ⌐ _Centre_

Shares in the Rash Corporation, which last year invested £4 m in new plant, fell 33p to £4.62 in today's trading on the London Stock Exchange. During the first two months of this year the company has suffered losses of £897000.

The Financial Times Index closed 14 points down at 1 546.

Job 3.6.2

Follow the instructions for Job 3.6.1, adopting the recommended style for symbols.

A5 landscape • LL: 60 • SS • centre vertically

SPORTS NEWS

Sebal Patel, although one of the youngest in the 13/14 age group, paced her 200 metres butterfly victory to perfection when she allowed the opposition to dictate the early pace.

She was placed last at 100 metres, a full two seconds behind the early leader; then gradually closing the gap in the next 50 metres and demonstrating her superior technique and condition, she powered through the field to win by a clear three seconds.

Speed test (SI 1.59)

1 Take two 2-minute timings.
2 Record your better rate.
3 Proofread and correct your work.

LL: 55 _or_ decide your own line endings • SS

	Words
The metric system of measurement, adopted by countries	11
around the world, has yet to be fully accepted by all.	22
Both the United States of America and Great Britain	32
have been slow to give it their support. Miles are	42
still preferred to kilometres in these countries, and	53
litres is still a relatively new term.	63

1   2   3   4   5   6   7   8   9   10   11

Money columns

The pound sign is placed either at the head of a money column or (if there is a total line) at the foot. If the pound sign

is placed at the head of the column, either of the following styles may be used:

Blocked	Centred
£	£
12.50	12.50
302.05	302.05
0.69	0.69

Note that zero is keyed before the decimal point in amounts less than one dollar.

Refresher

All alpha keys

1 The magazine's very next issue will contain two feature articles and just a quick guide to trendy Burlow Manor.

Exclamation/question marks

2 Caution! Are you not aware that speeding is dangerous?

i/o

3 Officials could dispose of society's seniority options.

Aim for speed

4 There is no need to send payment when you book with us.

Job 7.9.1

Key an exact copy of this document.

A5 landscape • SS • centre vertically/horizontally

ANALYSIS OF SALES

January to May

Salesperson	Budget	Actual
	£	£
Ross, Peter	7 500	9 000
Andrades, Mary	6 000	7 200
Archer, Ronald	311 100	9 100
Lee, Michael	7 500	7 212
Bakker, Rosemary	10 400	11 300
Edwards, Douglas	6 800	7 100

Job 7.9.2

Format this document in a uniform style.

A5 landscape • SS • centre vertically/horizontally

CAMBRIDGE PARK MOHAIR FARM

P R I C E   L I S T

Yarn	Size	City Price	Sale Price
		£	£
Wool crepe	5 ply 50 gm	3.40	2.55
Mohair-wool	12 ply 50 g	4.00	2.99
Alpaca-wool	10 ply 50 g	5.30	3.50
Cotton-mohair-wool	8 ply 25 g	4.50	2.75
100% wool	3 ply 25 g	2.00	0.99
Brush mohair	8 ply 50 g	6.00	4.90

lc (City Price, Sale Price) *ed* (Brush mohair)

If your system does not allow you to use the decimal tab and functions together, set a decimal tab after the last character in the second column; the column will align at the right.

Style 3

Abbreviations and contractions are shortened forms of words. They are used to save space and to avoid repetition of a word. You will find a list of some of the most common long-hand abbreviations in the Reference Section on page viii. Use the following accepted forms consistently.

Abbreviations

'To abbreviate' means 'to cut short'. An abbreviation can consist of

- the initial letter of a word:

    g (gram)   m (metre)
    k (kilogram)

- the initial letters of a group of words:

    AGM (Annual General Meeting)
    MP (Member of Parliament)
    eg (*exempli gratia* = for example)
    ie (*id est* = that is)

- the initial letter of a word followed by other letters, but omitting the final letter:

    Jan (January)   etc (*et cetera*)

An abbreviation consisting of a group of initial letters which themselves form a word is called an acronym. It is permissible to use all capitals or an initial capital letter only:

    NATO *or* Nato
    QANTAS *or* Qantas

Contractions

'To contract' means 'to shrink'. A contraction ends with the same letter as the full word:

    Mr (Mister)   Dept (Department)
    Ltd (Limited)

Full stops should not be used with contractions. They may be used with abbreviations:

    cont. (for 'continued')
    but contd *not* contd.

Plurals

Plurals are formed by adding an *s* without an apostrophe:

    MPs   depts   1890s

Refresher

LL: 55 • SS • key line for line

All alpha keys

1 Next Jock Gaze quarrels with my very best friend, Phil.

Ampersand/solidus/per cent symbol

2 H Jones & Partners received a 33-1/3% profit after tax.

Spelling and usage

Note the spelling of the highlighted words.

LL: 55 • SS • key line for line

3 The humorous professor gave a lecture on arctic heroes.

4 The desperate bachelor hurriedly disappeared from view.

Job 3.7.1

1 Key the headings. They may be underscored or bold.
2 Key the first line as in the copy.
3 Then key the rest of the lines, following the style of the first.
   - You may need to refer to a dictionary.

A4 portrait • DS • centre vertically

↓ LM	↓ T
Abbreviation	**Phrase in full**
eg	for example
ie	
etc	
PS	
cv	
viz	
MP	
NB	
BA	
PhD	

Figures in columns

Figures in columns must be keyed in alignment: ie digits under digits, tens under tens, hundreds under hundreds and so on.

Thousands marker

Key a space (or a comma) as a thousands marker. A space is preferable because the comma is used as a decimal point in some European countries.

Decimal points/decimal tab

Decimal points must also align. Most electronic typewriters and word processing systems have an automatic function for decimal tabulation. Consult your operator's manual to find out how to use this function on your system.

The decimal tab (dec tab) key can be used to align whole numbers as well as decimal numbers.

Decimal number	Whole number
93.37	380 642
164.02	29 321
	1 695

Numeric punctuation

On some systems you can select the numeric punctuation of your choice:

1 no comma or space
   12345.00
2 comma every third digit
   12,345.00
3 space every third digit
   12 345.00

Find out if your system has this facility.

Systems without decimal tab

To align numbers at the right, set a tab for the second and any subsequent columns at the point that requires the least forward and backward spacing. Then forwardspace or backspace as necessary.

Job 7.8.1

Key an exact copy of this document.

A5 landscape • DS body of table • centre vertically/horizontally

POULTRY CHART *R2*

> Some systems do not allow you to use the tab and the decimal tab functions in the same document. If this is so, you will need to note the position of the start of each heading rather than set a tab at those points.

Ingredient	Starter (kg in 100 kg) ↓ Dec tab	Grower (kg in 100 kg) ↓ Dec tab	Layer (kg in 100 kg) *R2* ↓ Dec tab
wheat	67.7	69.4	59.5
barley	5.2	10.4	10.8
maize	5.2	10.4	10.8

Job 7.8.2

Format and key this document.

A5 landscape • DS body of table • centre vertically/horizontally

PRODUCTIVITY

Company	Employees	Efficiency rating (%)	Annual output (tonnes)
London	2 350	82.6	249 500
Starr & Co	420	89.4	52 900
Ginter	980	86.2	97 600
Haines	95	94.3	9 800
Siems	740	88.1	89 000

Job 3.7.2

Key list in alphabetical order. You may need to refer to the list on page viii of common longhand abbreviations.

A4 portrait • DS • centre vertically

Contraction	Word in full
a/c	account
bus	
dr	
temp	
necy	
yr	
recom	
flt	

Job 3.7.3

1 This draft includes abbreviations and contractions.
2 Key the document, spelling out the abbreviated or contracted words in full.

A5 landscape • LL: 60 • SS • centre vertically

Ministry of Transport

Our a/c for services rendered to the Ministry of Transport is the only one relating to a govt dept that we have raised this yr. The amt is insignificant when compared with our ttl revenue for the yr. I encl a copy of this a/c, which you will note includes a charge for travelling exps.

Speed test (SI 1.58)

1 Take two 2-minute timings.
2 Record your better rate.
3 Proofread and correct your work.

LL: 55 or decide your own line endings • SS

Words

If a report or document uses any uncommon or special   10
abbreviations and contractions it should include a list 21
that explains what they mean. As well as this, when an 32
abbreviation or contraction is used for the first time, 43
the full word or phrase should be spelt out, followed 54
by the abbreviation or contraction in parentheses.   64

1   2   3   4   5   6   7   8   9   10   11

Multiple-line column headings

Column headings of more than one line are single spaced and can be vertically positioned in a number of ways. In the following exercises the bottom line of each column heading is aligned and underscored.

After setting the left margin and tab stops for the columns:
1 Key the first line of each column heading that has more than one line.
2 Then key the second and any subsequent line or lines.

Refresher

LL: 55 • SS • DS between drills

All alpha keys
1 A team of six New Zealanders has just begun its inquiry into the sinking of a coastal pilot vessel in November.

Symbols/figures
2 'In my article "The Jury" I describe a case', she said.

w/e
3 Wethers and ewes were swept by showers every Wednesday.

Aim for speed
4 A daily work plan could help you to use your time well.

Job 7.7.1

Key an exact copy of this document in blocked style.

A5 landscape • SS • centre vertically/horizontally

FAMOUS OPERAS OF GIUSEPPE VERDI

Underscore bottom line only

Bottom lines align →

Opera	Librettist	Year of premiere	Place of premiere
Macbeth	Piave	1847	Florence
Rigoletto	Piave	1851	Venice
La Traviata	Piave	1853	Venice
Aida	Ghislanzoni	1871	Cairo
Otello	Boito	1887	Milan

Job 7.7.2

Format and key this document, centring the column headings over the columns.

A5 landscape • SS • centre vertically/horizontally

MUSICAL MEMORIES

Christmas Wonderland	Country and Western	World of Melody
The (12) Days of Christmas	Love is No Excuse	Blue Danube
Ave Maria	And I Love You	Clair/e de Lune
The First Noel	Mr Sandman	Elvira Madigan
Sleigh Ride	Sentimental Journey	Londonderry Air
Joy to the World	Blue Ridge Mts	Dream of Olwen

sp out

Style 4

Capital letters

Use capitals sparingly. It is a common fault to use an initial capital when it is not needed. Use initial capitals for

- the names of people and their titles:

  Mr Ian Cole   Dr Angela Poulos
  Dame Joan Sutherland
  Colonel Hill   Senator Day
  Mr Justice Kaufmann

- the names of countries, states, cities, towns and recognised place names:

  Malaysia   Western Australia
  Mackay   South-East Asia
  Simpson Desert

- nationalities and racial descriptions:

  Australian Aboriginal art

- the names of institutions:

  Lloyds Corporation
  Croydon College   the Senate

- proprietary names and trade marks:

  Kodak   Marmite   Vaseline

  but note that some words have come into such common usage that they have ceased to be regarded as proprietary names and are no longer capitalised:

  champagne   macintosh

- days of the week, months, religious days and festivals and public holidays:

  Sunday   May   Christmas Day
  Yom Kippur   Ramadan

- titles of books, plays, poems, films, reports etc:

  The Fatal Shore   The Club
  The Radford Report

- historical events and periods:

  the Boer War   the Depression

- the names of offices, to distinguish them from common nouns with the same spelling:

  the Speaker (of the House of Commons)
  the House (of Commons)
  the Opposition (the parliamentary party or parties opposing the Government)

  Note that the definite article *the* is only capitalised when it is part of a name or title:

  The Hague   *The Group*
  but   the Netherlands   the Pope

Titles and offices

The recommended style is to use initial capitals unless the writer is referring to holders of the office in general:

- The Queen will leave in June.
  but
  There have been many queens of England.

- The Governor of the Bank of England gave a speech.
  but
  The governors of the Bank of England are appointed by the Queen.

- She is Secretary to the Managing Director of Daw Promotions.
  but
  It was her responsibility as secretary to the managing director to notify all heads of departments.

It would not be wrong, however, to use initial capitals for these offices in all cases.

Do not use capitals for

- the seasons:

  spring   winter

- points of the compass, unless they are in abbreviated form or form part of a place name:

  north   south   east   west
  but
  North Ryde   West Irian   NNE

- common nouns:

  - the department
    but   the Department of Employment
  - an act of parliament
    but   the Copyright Act
  - the university
    but   the University of London

- elements of a book, play etc when used specifically:

  part 1   chapter 2   figure 6
  page 3   appendix A
  act IV   scene II

Text in upper case

Words in normal text should not be keyed in upper case if this can be avoided. Upper case should be reserved for headings and those few occasions when a word or words within the text requires extra emphasis:

A sign on the door read PRIVATE.

Refresher

LL: 55 • SS • key line for line

Alternate hands
1 If their country hut burns down they may go to Glenelg.

All upper case
2 The sign read: WARNING - POISONOUS EXPLOSIVES AND GAS.

Spelling and usage

Note the spelling of the highlighted words.

LL: 55 • SS • key line for line

3 Certain exercises usually improve athletic appearances.

4 They agreed to a financial marriage maintenance scheme.

Formatting columns within existing margins (blocked paragraphs)

If a table is included in a letter, report or other document, you must format the columns within the existing margins of the document. For a document in blocked style, follow this procedure.

1 Add together the number of keystrokes in the longest entry in each column.
2 Subtract the total from the line length of the document.
3 Divide the result by the number of gaps between columns (eg if there are three columns, divide by 2). This will give you the number of keystrokes between columns.
4 From the existing left margin, space forward once for every keystroke in the longest entry in column 1 (less one space) and once for every space between columns 1 and 2. Set a tab.
5 Repeat this procedure for any remaining column or columns and set tabs.
6 Test your tab settings by spacing forward the number of keystrokes in the final column to reach the right margin.

Refresher

LL: 55 • SS • DS between drills

All alpha keys
1 Major Dominique Szabo explains that twelve new recruits have been appointed to a fire fighting force in Kilcoy.

Symbols/figures
2 Yesterday I banked cheques for £987 064.52 and £382.79.

i/e
3 Sheila and Daniel Weir tried their eight pieces of pie.

Aim for speed
4 We are at a loss to explain how the plates went astray.

Job 7.6.1

This is an extract from a letter. Key an exact copy of this document.

- Format the columns between the margins.
- Block the column headings (see page 125).

A5 landscape • LL: 53 • SS

↓*LM*
The following is a list of the joint venture partners with whom we have worked over the last five years. *R3*

	↓*T*	↓*T*
Partner	Country	Product *R2*
Lahndorf GmbH	Germany	instruments
Masson SA	France	electronic components
Toray SA	Italy	seat covers
Delta PLC	Britain	radiators
Suka Co	Japan	sun roofs

Job 7.6.2

Format and key this extract from a memorandum. Review centring headings over columns on page 125.

A5 landscape • LL: 60 • SS

We have introduced the following new business studies courses at the college this year:

Code	Title	School
3011-A	Mangaerial Accounting	Business
3080-B	Microeconomics	Business
3081-B	Macroeconomics	Business
4032-A	m/ Business Comunication/s	General studies

Job 3.8.1

1 Mark the letters which should appear in capitals.

2 Key the passage in *upper and lower case*, following the rules for capitalisation.

A5 landscape • LL: 55 • SS • centre vertically

the speaker   (centre)

↓ T

the speaker of the english house of commons acts as a kind of chairperson at a meeting. a member may only speak if he or she has the permission of the speaker - or his or her deputy. the speaker is appointed by the government of the day, usually from the ranks of government members; but if the newly-elected government has a bare majority the speaker may well be appointed from one of the opposition parties.

the house of representatives, australia's equivalent to the house of commons, also appoints a speaker.

Job 3.8.2

Follow the instructions for Job 3.8.1.

A5 landscape • LL: 55 • SS • centre vertically

clovelly national park   Centre caps & u/score

↓ T

three members of staff and 21 students from west brighton college will spend easter camping in the clovelly national park, 18 km east of dubbo in australia. the party which will include 3 exchange students from colleges in the usa, canada and france, will leave sydney by coach on friday 14 may and return the following monday evening.

(2) spat

a committee comprising two staff members and three students have worked hard to make the camp a success.

a further visit to the national park is planned for next autumn.

Speed test (SI 1.5)

1 Take two 2-minute timings.

2 Record your better rate.

3 Proofread and correct your work.

LL: 55 *or* decide your own line endings • SS

	Words
As far as possible, avoid keying words in upper case.	11
Upper case should be kept for headings or, rarely, for	22
extra emphasis in text. Headings may be keyed in	32
spaced capitals, usually either with a single space	42
between letters and three spaces between words or with	53
two spaces between letters and five between words.	63

1 | 2 | 3 | 4 | 5 | 6 | 7 | 8 | 9 | 10 | 11

More complex tables

Where some column headings are narrrower and some wider than the columns below them (as in Job 7.5.1), the headings are treated as a line of the column. Your objective is to

- select the longest line in each column (regardless of whether it is a heading or a column entry)
- centre the column heading over the column (if the column heading is narrower than the widest column entry)
- centre the column under the column heading (if the column heading is wider than the widest column entry).

Follow this procedure:

1 Set the left margin and tab stops. In selecting the longest entry in a column, remember to treat the heading as a line of the column.

2 To key column headings:

a If the column heading is wider than the widest entry in the column, begin keying the heading at the left margin or the appropriate tab stop.

b If the column heading is narrower than the widest entry in the column

- space forward from the margin or appropriate tab stop once for every two keystrokes in the widest entry in the column, ignoring any single character left over
- backspace once for every two keystrokes in the column heading, ignoring any single character left over
- begin keying the heading at that point.

3 To key the first entry in column 1:

a If the column heading is wider than the widest entry in the column,

- space forward from the margin once for every two keystrokes in the column heading, ignoring any single character left over
- backspace once for every two keystrokes in the widest entry in the column, ignoring any single character left over
- reset the margin at this point and key the first entry.

b If the column heading is narrower than the widest entry, begin keying at the margin.

4 To key the first entry in the second or subsequent columns:

a If the column heading is wider than the widest entry in the column,

- tab to the appropriate tab stop and clear it
- space forward once for every two keystrokes in the column heading, ignoring any single character left over
- backspace once for every two keystrokes in the widest entry in the column, ignoring any single character left over
- set a new tab stop at this point and key the first entry.

b If the column heading is narrower than the widest entry, tab to the appropriate tab stop and key the first entry.

Job 7.5.1

Key an exact copy of this document.

- Centre the heading over the column or the column below the heading as appropriate.

> Leave five spaces between the columns.

Job 7.5.2

Format and key this document, centring each heading over the column or the column below the heading as appropriate.

A5 landscape • SS • centre vertically/horizontally

SYMBOLS R3

↓ LM	↓ T	↓ T
Symbol	Definition	Example R2
↓ Reset LM		
*	asterisk	*plus sales tax
&	ampersand	Clark & Jones
@	at, per, each	25 @ $10.50 each
#	number	#16

A5 landscape • SS • centre vertically/horizontally

GIVEN ~~FIRST~~ NAMES

Name	Derivation	Meaning
Amy	French	beloved
Christopher	Greek	Christ bearer
Elizabeth	Hebrew	God-fon-foath
Matthew	Hebrew	gift of Jehovah

Style 5

Roman numerals

Roman numerals can be difficult to read (what is CXII?) and may be confused with arabic figures. (For instance, II can be misread for 11.) For this reason they are not widely used.

Capital roman numerals
Capital roman numerals are used for
- the titles of monarchs, popes and emperors:
  King James II   Pope Pius IX
- numbering the acts and scenes of plays:
  act I scene IV
- the names of ships:
  Gretel II
- the copyright dates of film and television productions:
  Copyright Asta Films MCMLXXIX
- the names of the two world wars:
  World War I   World War II

Small roman numerals

Small roman numerals are used instead of arabic figures to number the preliminary pages of books:
  pages i–ix

Notice that when a span of figures is expressed in the roman form, full numerals are used.

Numbering paragraphs

Capital and small roman numerals may be used to number paragraphs or sub-paragraphs (see page 110), but a decimal point system is preferred (see page 112).

Tabulations

In tabulations roman numerals can be aligned at the right or the left, but alignment must be consistent throughout a task..

How to form roman numerals

1	i	I	21	xx	iXXI
2	ii	II	30	xxx	XXX
3	iii	III	31	xxxi	XXXI
4	iv	IV	40	xl	XL
5	v	V	41	xli	XLI
6	vi	VI	50	l	L
7	vii	VII	51	li	LI
8	viii	VIII	60	lx	LX
9	ix	IX	61	lx	iLXI
10	x	X	70	lxx	LXX
11	xi	XI	71	lxxi	LXXI
12	xii	XII	80	lxxx	LXXX
13	xiii	XIII	81	lxxxi	LXXXI
14	xiv	XIV	90	xc	XC
15	xv	XV	91	xci	XCI
16	xvi	XVI	100	c	C
17	xvii	XVII	200	cc	CC
18	xviii	XVIII	400	cd	CD
19	xix	XIX	500	d	D
20	xx	XX	1000	m	M

Refresher

LL: 55 • SS • key line for line

All alpha keys
1 Jacqui Viewhofer explodes stink bombs in zoology class.

Square brackets
2 Her story begins: 'As a girl [in Java] I kept lizards.'

Spelling and usage
Note the spelling of the high-lighted words.

LL: 55 • SS • key line for line

3 An occasional omission is not noticeable in the budget.

4 The definite arrangements benefited the planning group

Centring columns below column headings

Where in each column of a display the heading is longer than the longest entry in the column, your objective is to
- centre the column headings on the page
- centre the columns below the column headings.

Follow this procedure:
1 Decide on the number of spaces to be left between columns.
2 *If using a computer*, key a trial line and set the left margin and tab stops as described in Unit 7.1 (page 123).

If using a typewriter, backspace from the centre as described on page 123 and set the left margin.
3 From the left margin key the column headings, leaving the required space between columns and setting tab stops at the start of each column heading.
4 Use the forwardspace–backspace method to reset the left margin for the left column entries and tab stops for the remaining columns as follows:
   a From the existing left margin space forward once for every two keystrokes in the first column heading, ignoring any keystroke left over.
   b Now backspace once for every two keystrokes in the column line

with the longest entry. Reset the left margin at this point.

Guideline for Job 7.4.1
To centre column 1 below column heading:

1 Space forward: POSITIVE
2 Backspace: little
3 Reset left margin.

c Tab to the second column, clear the existing tab and repeat the procedure you followed in (a) and (b) to reset the tab for the second column.
d Repeat the procedure for the remaining column.
e Key the column entries.

Refresher

LL: 55 • SS • DS between drills

All alpha keys
1 To qualify for the job you must achieve an extra twelve points in the graduate quiz to take place next Tuesday.

Symbols/figures
2 All 68 copies (valued @ £239.14) were received at 5 pm.

w/e
3 A few powerful new weapons were viewed in West Wenlock.

Aim for speed
4 No job is too small for us to take on during this time.

Job 7.4.1

Key an exact copy of this document.
- Centre the columns below the column headings.

> Leave four spaces between the columns.

A5 landscape • SS • centre vertically/horizontally

COMPARISON OF ADJECTIVES *R3*

LM↓   T↓   T↓

POSITIVE	COMPARATIVE	SUPERLATIVE *R2*
↓Reset LM	↓Reset T	↓Reset T
good	better	best
little	less	least
bad	worse	worst

Job 7.4.2

Format and key this document, centring the columns below the column headings.

A5 landscape • DS • centre vertically/horizontally

COMPARISON OF ~~ADJECTIVES~~ ADVERBS

POSITIVE	COMPARATIVE	SUPERLATIVE
much	more	most
less	less/er	least
well	better	best
late	later	latest

Job 3.9.1

Key this passage.
- Add the heading
  ROMAN NUMERALS
  and centre it.

A5 landscape • LL: 60 • SS • centre vertically

The roman numeral X is used for 10, L for 50, C for 100, D for 500 and M for 1000. The figure 20 is represented by the roman numeral XX, 200 by CC and 2000 by MM.

The figure 9 is represented by IX (ie 10 minus 1), 40 by XL (50 minus 10) and 90 by XC (100 minus 10).

The system is perfectly logical provided you do not try to read the roman numerals as you would arabic figures.

Job 3.9.2

1 Mark small or large roman numerals (as appropriate) in place of the arabic figures.
2 Then key a corrected copy.

A5 landscape • SS • centre vertically • key line for line

Pages 1, 2, 4, 6, 9, 10 and 12 need correction.

Convert these numbers: 14, 17, 19, 51 and 71.

Please read King Richard 2, act 5, scene 3.

Job 3.9.3

1 Mark arabic figures in place of the roman numerals.
2 Then key a corrected copy.

> Copyright symbol (©):
> Unless your system has this symbol, key 'c' and draw the circle freehand.

A5 landscape • LL: 55 • SS • centre vertically

Please refer to pp xxvii–xxviii of the report.

Volume XVIII of the series is unavailable at present.

The copyright line should read as follows:
© Australian Film Association Ltd MCMXCI.

Clause xix of the memorandum of agreement safe-guards the rights of my client.

Speed test (SI 1.59)

1 Take two 2-minute timings.
2 Record your better rate.
3 Proofread and correct your work.

LL: 55 or decide your own line endings • SS

	Words
Roman numerals are not widely used, so we often have	10
trouble with them, especially the ones over twenty. We	21
can be confused by the way some roman numbers, unlike	32
arabic figures, are formed by subtracting a numeral	42
from the one that follows it; also, the handwritten	52
roman two (II) is quite easily mistaken for the arabic	63
eleven (11).	65

1 2 3 4 5 6 7 8 9 10 11

Job 7.3.2

Format and key this document, centring the column headings over the columns.

> Most currencies do not take an initial capital letter.

A5 landscape • DS • centre vertically/horizontally

INTERNATIONAL CURRENCIES

Country	Currency e/
China	yuan
Denmark	Kroner
France	frank c/
Greece	drachma
India	lc Rupee
Japan	yen
Spain	peseta
Germany	Deutschmark

D/S

Job 7.3.3

Format and key this document, centring the column headings over the columns.

A5 portrait • DS • centre vertically/horizontally

BRITISH AND USA

~~BRITISH/US~~ SPELLINGS COMPARED

Ours	Theirs
aluminium	aluminum
catalogue	catalog
centre	center
defence	defense
fulfil	fulfill
jewellery	jewelry
lc Skilful	skillful

Job 7.3.4

Format and key this document, centring the column headings over the columns.

A4 portrait • SS • centre vertically/horizontally

Specific and Generic Terms

Specific	Generic
businessman businesswoman	business people
chairman chairwoman	chair person
draughtsman draughtswoman	draughtsperson
policeman policewoman	police officer
postman postwoman	postal worker

Style 6

Methods of address

It is customary to address a person by his or her title. It may be a courtesy title (*Mr*, *Ms*, *Mrs*, *Miss*), an earned title (such as *Dr* or *Professor*), a conferred title (*Dame* or *Sir*) or a hereditary title (*Lord*, *Lady* etc).

Ms, Mrs and Miss

If a woman has not indicated a preference for *Miss*, *Mrs* or *Ms*, use *Ms* as it applies to both unmarried and married women.

Messrs and Mesdames

Messrs is the plural form of *Mr* and *Mesdames* is the plural of *Mrs* or *Ms*.

Sir, Dame and Lady

The titles *Sir* and *Dame* should be followed by the given name:

> Sir Noel Smith   Dame Sybil Gee

The wife of a man with the title *Sir* is addressed as *Lady* but it is not correct to use her given name with the title:

> Sir Brian and Lady Martin
> Lady Martin

Lady is used with a given name only if you are referring to the daughter of an English earl, marquis or duke:

> Lady Jane Grey

Reverend

The title *Reverend* must be followed by initials or a given name:

> The Reverend James (or J) King

The Right Honourable

A person holding the title of Baron, Baroness, Viscount, Viscountess or Earl is addressed:

> Baron – *The Right Hon Lord*
> Baroness – *The Right Hon Lady*
> Viscount – *The Right Hon The Viscount*
> Viscountess – *The Right Hon The Viscountess*
> Earl – *The Right Hon The Earl of*
> Cabinet Ministers are addressed as:
> *The Right Hon* (followed by their post)

The Honourable

The following positions are addressed as *The Hon*: Barons' sons, Barons' daughters, Viscounts' sons, Viscounts' daughters, and Earls' younger sons. (An Earl's eldest son takes the highest of his father's lesser titles.)

> *The Hon Charles...*

Honours and academic awards

Letters indicating honours and academic awards follow a person's name. It is more usual to include honours than academic awards. If both are given, honours precede academic awards.

University degrees follow the order of conferment. No spaces or full stops should be keyed between the letters of an honour or award, but key one space between consecutive honours and awards:

> Mr E Sparkes BSc MA

The degrees PhD and D Phil (Doctor of Philosophy), DSc (Doctor of Science), DD (Doctor of Divinity), MD (Doctor of Medicine) etc entitle the holder to be styled *Dr*. If the holder has a higher title, such as *Professor* or *Sir*, the higher title is used instead of *Dr*.

> Professor Mary Eaton MA PhD

Medical doctors are entitled to the courtesy title *Dr*:

> Dr Alex Guizzo

Surgeons are addressed in this way:

> Mr Ian Frost FRCS
> Miss/Ms/Mrs Sara White FRCS

Formal methods of address

The most common forms of address are listed below. A fuller list is given in the Reference Section on page xiv.

FORMS OF ADDRESS	SALUTATION
Private individuals	
Mr/Ms/Miss/Mrs/Dr M Smith	Dear Mr/Ms/Miss/Mrs/Dr Smith
Peter Crockford, Esq	Dear Mr Crockford
Mr & Mrs J Ryan	Dear Mr & Mrs Ryan
Mr J & Mrs S Casey	Dear Mr & Mrs Casey
Mr L & Dr B Khee	Dear Mr & Dr Khee
Dr C & Mrs J Arndt	Dear Dr & Mrs Arndt
Drs T & W Webb	Dear Drs Webb
Messrs E & K Cooper	Dear Gentlemen
Mesdames H & G Steiner	Dear Ladies
Ms F & D Morgan	Dear Ladies (*Ms* is both singular and plural)
Misses S & R Romeo	Dear Ladies
Mr G Leek & Mr D Bell	Dear Gentlemen
Ms N Aaron & Ms S Beck	Dear Ladies
Ms T Ward & Mr G Vero	Dear Ms Ward & Mr Vero
Mr P Hicks & Mrs D Ellis	Dear Mr Hicks & Mrs Ellis

A person whose title (but not name) is known

FORMS OF ADDRESS	SALUTATION
The Manager, Secretary etc	Dear Manager/Secretary or Dear Sir or Madam

FORMS OF ADDRESS	SALUTATION
Medical	
Medical practitioner	
Dr Margaret Wells	Dear Dr Wells
Surgeon	
Mr James Simsek FRCS	Dear Mr Simsek
Miss/Ms/Mrs Irene Wells FRCS	Dear Miss/Ms/Mrs Wells
Academic	
Professor	
Professor Mark/Margaret Brown University of ...	Dear Sir/Madam
Business	
Company	
The Manager/Secretary/Accountant etc Smithson & Co Ltd	Dear Sir or Madam *or* Dear Manager/Secretary/Accountant
Organisation/society	
The Secretary/President etc	Dear Sir or Madam *or* Dear Secretary/President

Centring column headings over columns

Where in each column of a display the column heading is shorter than the longest entry in the column, your objective is to

- centre the column entries on the page
- centre the column headings over the columns.

Follow this procedure:

1 Select the longest entry in each column.

2 Decide on the number of spaces to be left between columns.
3 *If using a computer*, key a trial line as described in Unit 7.1 (page 123) and set the left margin and tab stops.
  If using a typewriter, backspace from the centre as described on page 123 to set the left margin and tab stops.
4 Then centre the column headings as follows, using the forwardspace–backspace method:
  a Space forward from the start of the column once for every two keystrokes in *the line with the longest entry*, ignoring any character left over.
  b From that point backspace once for every two keystrokes in *the heading to be centred*, ignoring any character left over.

c Key the heading.
d Repeat the procedure for the right column.
e Return twice.
f Key the first entry in each column, then the second entry, and so on.

Refresher

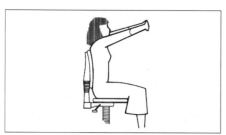

All alpha keys
1 To adjust his game to the very keen breeze, Al required an extra firm grip on the club as well as a steady eye.

Symbols/figures
2 Your invoice J/4128/A did not include our 25% discount.

r/t
3 Partial track trials are now truly in train in Hartley.

Aim for speed
4 Please hand this form to a clerk as soon as you arrive.

Job 7.3.1

Key an exact copy of this document.

Leave eight spaces between the columns.

CAPITAL CITIES *R3*

LM ↓ Country	*T* ↓ Capital *R2*
Switzerland	Bern
Norway	Oslo
Denmark	Copenhagen
Finland	Helsinki
Poland	Warsaw
Canada	Ottawa
Thailand	Bangkok
Indonesia	Jakarta
Turkey	Ankara
Greece	Athens
Egypt	Cairo
Iceland	Reykjavik
Belgium	Brussels
France	Paris
Spain	Madrid

Refresher

Alternate hands
1 He kept an iguana to torment me, but I lent it to Jane.

Underscore
2 <u>Zebras</u> and <u>gazelles</u> graze on grass in <u>Taronga Park Zoo</u>.

Spelling and usage

Note the spelling of the high-lighted words.

3 A chess professional completely eliminated the amateur

4 The foreign intelligence officer is courteous and fair.

Job 3.10.1

Key the form of address and salutation you would use for each of the persons in this list.

- Set tabs as shown for the column headings.
- No 1 has been done for you.
- You will need to refer to the Reference Section (page ix) as well as the first page of this unit.
- If the first line in the 'form of address' column is very long, break the line rather than let it extend into the 'salutation' column (*but* review *Rules for word division* on pages 50–51).

1 The Public Relations Manager of Jones Stores Limited, whose name you do not know
2 Marion Summers FRCS, a surgeon
3 Your local Member of Parliament
4 The Prime Minister
5 The Chief Justice of the High Court of England, The Honourable Hugh Braithwaite

6 Baroness Whitehead
7 The Bishop of Liverpool
8 A member of the Royal Family of your choice
9 The Earl of Bradford
10 Ann Stuart, who has the degrees MA and PhD

```
FORMS OF ADDRESS

Form of address              Salutation

The Public Relations Manager
Jones Stores Limited         Dear Sir or Madam
```

Speed test (SI 1.6)

1 Take two 2-minute timings.
2 Record your better rate.
3 Proofread and correct your work.

```
                                                          Words
At first, Australia used only the British system of        10
honours.  When the Order of Australia was introduced,      21
there were four grades: Dame or Knight, Companion,         31
Officer and Member.  Eleven years later the grade of       41
Dame or Knight was removed, without prejudice to those     52
people who already held this award.  There is also a       62
Medal of the Order.                                        66

     1    2    3    4    5    6    7    8    9   10   11
```

Blocking headings over columns

1 A blocked heading is one that aligns with the left side of the column.

2 A blocked heading is considered to be part of the column in calculating the margins and tab stops. The longest line may therefore be the heading or one of the entries in the column.

3 If there is a main heading, it may be blocked left or centred.

4 Underscoring/bolding of headings may be used provided there are no horizontal rules.

5 At least one blank line should be left between the column heading and the first entry in the column.

6 The column headings should be keyed first, then the first entry in each column, and so on.

Refresher

LL: 55 • SS • DS between drills

All alpha keys

1 A major fire at the Mount Eliza squash club in Leighton was known to cause extensive damage to four play areas.

Symbols/figures

2 Can you spare £150? Excellent! We're indebted to you.

e/r

3 Her earlier versions were therefore really rather rare.

Aim for speed

4 If we agree to your terms will you give us time to pay?

Job 7.2.1

Key an exact copy of this document.

> Leave five spaces between the columns.
> The column headings may be in bold or underscored.

A5 landscape • SS • centre vertically/horizontally

LM
↓

VERB TENSES 1 *R3*

Present Tense	Past Tense	Past Participle *R2*
(I) bring	(I) brought	(I) have brought
(I) buy	(I) bought	(I) have bought
(I) dive	(I) dived	(I) have dived
(I) do	(I) did	(I) have done
(I) see	(I) saw	(I) have seen

Job 7.2.2

Format and key this document, centring the main heading and blocking the column headings.

A5 landscape • SS • centre vertically/horizontally

VERB TENCES 2

Present tense	Past tense	Past participle
(I) catch	(They) caught	(They) have caught
(I) drink	(They) drank	(They) have drunk
(They) eat	(They) ate	(They) have eaten
(They) hang (execute)	(They) hanged	(They) have hanged
(They) lay (deposit)	(They) laid	(They) have laid
(They) lie (recline)	(They) lay	(They) have lain
(They) lie (falsify)	(They) lied	(They) have lied

2# They/ They/

one line space between each entry

Module 4 Business correspondence 1

Performance goals

At the end of Module 4 you should be able to

- format standard and simplified memoranda in the fully blocked style on both plain and headed paper
- format and key business letters in the fully blocked style on both plain and headed paper
- address envelopes, labels and cards for destinations within U.K. and overseas
- make carbon copies if you are using a typewriter
- use confidential, personal, enclosure and copy notations.

Memoranda 1

Memoranda (memos) are sent within an organisation. The same memorandum may be sent to several people.

Memoranda are usually sent through the internal mail system and may be enclosed in unsealed pre-printed envelopes, allowing for multiple use. A confidential memorandum is sent in a sealed envelope.

Memoranda can be faxed to distant locations or sent by electronic mail and printed out by the recipient only if a hard copy is required.

Standard memoranda are prepared on plain paper or pre-printed forms, usually A4 portrait or A5 landscape.

Standard memoranda on plain paper

If memoranda are on plain paper, the words 'INTEROFFICE MEMORAN-DUM' or 'MEMORANDUM' are keyed at the head. The labels 'TO', 'FROM', 'DATE' and 'SUBJECT' appear below, usually in that order.

Except for the subject, which is normally in upper case, the headings themselves are usually keyed in upper and lower case.

The headings and labels may be stored in memory and called up each time a memorandum is prepared.

Formatting tip

Depending on the length of a memor-andum and whether A5 or A4 paper is used, you may vary the spacing as shown in the model on this page.

Features of a blocked memor-andum with open punctuation

The examples of memoranda in Units 4.1 to 4.4 are in *blocked style* with *open punctuation*. In this kind of format

- all lines start at the left margin
- no punctuation is used outside the body of the memorandum
- abbreviations and contractions in the body of the memorandum are keyed without full stops.

Job 4.1.1

Study the model and key from the draft on the right.

Heading labels

INTEROFFICE MEMORANDUM

```
>
    TO:       All new employees
    FROM:     E Winter, Office Manager
    DATE:     1 February 1992
>   SUBJECT:  MEMOS
    There is a wide variety of memo styles in offices today.
    This is our preferred layout.
    The sender's name is not included at the foot of the memo,
    as it already appears above the text.  The signature (or
    initials) of the sender gives the memo its authority.
>
    ew/as
    c G Wynne
```

Text

Reference initials

'Copy to' notation

> In some memoranda it will be necessary to leave extra line spaces here to balance the document on the page.

Plain A5 landscape • LL: 60 • SS • returns as indicated

↓ *LM*

          ↓*Centre*

Line 7   **INTEROFFICE MEMORANDUM**   *R2*

  ↓*T 10 spaces from LM*

TO: *All new employees* *R2*

FROM: *E Winter, Office Manager* *R2*

DATE: *1 February 1992* *R2*

SUBJECT: *MEMOS* *R2*

There is a wide variety of memo styles in offices today. This is our preferred layout. *R2*

The sender's name is not included at the foot of the memo, as it already appears above the text. However, the dictator's and typist's initials may be keyed two line spaces after the last *R4* *line of the message.*

ew/as *R2*
c G Wynne

Compare your finished work with the model.

Job 7.1.2

Format and key this document with equal space between columns.

Words ending in *-able* and *-ible* are often misspelt.

A5 landscape • DS • centre vertically/horizontally

WORDS ENDING IN -ABLE

likable	managable	liable
noticeable	inevitable	applicable
preferable	useable	acceptable
separable	changeable	agreeable

Job 7.1.3

Format and key this document with equal space between columns.

Two words in this exercise have been misspelt. Correct them.

A5 landscape • SS • centre vertically/horizontally

WORDS ENDING IN -IBLE

feasible	plausible	audible
forcible	eligible	acessable
tangible	credible	legible
permissible	edible	deductible
admissible	gullable	defensible

Job 7.1.4

Format and key this document with equal space between columns.

Correct the three misspelt words.

A5 landscape • SS • centre vertically/horizontally

accommodate

DIFFICULT WORDS TO SPELL

adhere	economical	parallel
anonymous	embarrassed	precede
benifited	fulfilment	vaccination
buoyant	grateful	separate
calendar	liason	superintendent
column	mortgage	tariff
definate	occurrence	yield

Job 7.1.5

Format and key this document with equal space between columns.

Correct the two misspelt words.

A5 landscape • SS • centre vertically/horizontally

IE/EI WORDS   u/score

achieve	counterfeit	protein
ancient	deceive	receive
believe	either	seize
field	forfeit	sovereign
lien	foriegn	surfeit
sieve	height	weigh
wield	leisure	wierd

Job 4.1.2

Key this memo on plain paper, following the formatting guidelines for Job 4.1.1.
- Your line endings will be different from those in the copy.
- Correct two misspelt words.

Plain A5 landscape • LL: 60 (10) 70 (12) • SS

INTEROFFICE MEMORANDUM

TO: All Staff, Training Division

FROM: David Scott, Manager, Training Division

DATE: ⟨ Today's

STAFF/   SUBJECT: ⟨TRAINING VIDEOS

Two new staff training videos will be avalable for
viewing in the Theatrette⟨Thursday 31 July and   on/
1/   Friday ⟨ August from 9 am to 10 am and from 2.30 pm
to 3.30 pm.

Please use this oportunity to see the videos more
than once in order to become thoroughly familiar with
them.

DS/FG

c Janet Goeman

Job 4.1.3

Key this memo on plain paper, noting its length.
- Correct three misspelt words.

Plain A4 portrait • LL: 60 (10) 70 (12) • SS

⌐INTEROFFICE MEMORANDUM¬ centre

To: All administrative staff
FROM: CJ Peters, Administrative Services Manager
DATE: Today's
SUBJECT: OFFICE MAILING PROCEDURE

Increasing costs make it neccesary to redefine
our office mailing procedure. In future, all mail
is to be delivered, unsealed, to the receptionist
by 4·30 pm. Our envelopes conform to Post
bold or   Office Preferred sizes in order to take advantage
u/score   of the cheap rates.
stet   Please note that we have installed a new system
for recording all outgoing mail in the Postage Book.
In future the Receptionist will record the date,
name and address of the reciever, any enclosures
and the postage cost. No item will be posted
untill the appropriate entry has been made.

Module 7   Formatting 4   Tabular work

Performance goals

At the end of Module 7 you should be able to

- format columns with headings blocked or centred and with entries and headings of varying lengths
- centre columns below column headings
- format columns within the existing margins of a document in blocked style
- set up columns with headings of more than one line
- align figures and decimal tabs in columns correctly
- set up money columns with dollar signs and totals
- format tables with horizontal rules
- format tables with vertical rules
- format tables with sub-divided column headings
- format tables with vertical column headings.

Formatting columns

In formatting a table, your objective is to set equal left and right margins and to key equal space between columns.

Computers

1 Use the default margins.
2 Clear tab stops.
3 Calculate vertical placement.
4 Key the heading, centring it horizontally.
5 Key a trial line comprising
- the longest entry in column 1 plus the number of spaces you decide to place between columns 1 and 2 (which will be governed by the number of columns and the number of keystrokes in the longest entry in each column)
- the longest entry in column 2 plus the number of spaces between columns 2 and 3 (the same number between columns 1 and 2)
- the longest entry in column 3 and so on.
6 Give the centre command and set the left margin and tab stops at the appropriate points.

7 Delete the trial line.
8 Key the table using the tabs you have set.

Typewriters

Use the *backspace-from-centre* method as follows:
1 Insert the paper with the left edge on zero.
2 Move the margin stops to the ends of the scale.
3 Clear tab stops.
4 Calculate vertical placement.
5 Key the heading, centring it horizontally.

Set left margin:
6 Decide on the number of spaces to be left between columns. This will be governed by the number of columns and the number of keystrokes in the longest entry in each column.
7 Select the longest entry in each column.
8 Move the printing point to the centre of the page and backspace
- once for every two spaces in the longest entry in each column
- once for every two spaces between columns.
Ignore any extra keystroke in the last column.
9 Set the left margin.

Guideline for Job 7.1.1
Backspace from centre to set left margin:

| 1 | 2 | 3 | 4 | 5 | 6 | 7 | 8 | 9 | 10 | 11 | 12 | 13 | 14 | 15 |
Mercury#####Jupiter#####Neptun

Set tab stops:
10 Using the space bar, space across once for every keystroke in the longest entry in column 1 and once for every space between columns 1 and 2. Set a tab stop.
11 Repeat the procedure for the longest entry in column 2 and the number of spaces between columns 2 and 3. Set a tab stop.
12 Do the same for any further columns.
13 Test your calculation by spacing across once for each keystroke in the final column. Check that the right margin is equal to the left margin.

Guideline for Job 7.1.1
Forwardspace and set tabs:
↓T   ↓T
Mercury#####Jupiter#####

Job 7.1.1

Key an exact copy of this document.

Leave five spaces between the columns.
The longest words in each column are highlighted.

A5 landscape • SS • centre vertically/horizontally

	PLANETS *R2*	
↓ LM	5 spaces ↓T	5 spaces ↓T
Mercury	Mars	Uranus
Venus	Jupiter	Neptune
Earth	Saturn	Pluto

Memoranda 2

Standard memoranda on headed paper

Some organisations produce memoranda on paper pre-printed with headings and labels. The headings and labels are 'MEMORANDUM', 'TO', 'FROM', 'DATE' and 'SUBJECT', usually in that order.

The name of the organisation may be printed at the head. In a large organisation with several offices, the office location and telephone and fax numbers may also be included. Such a memorandum is in effect an 'internal letterhead'.

Formatting tip

Depending on the length of a memorandum and whether A5 or A4 paper is used, you may vary the spacing as shown in the model.

Refresher

LL: 55 • SS • DS between drills

All alpha keys

1 Ogilvy McNeil was just quick enough to seize a big lump of springy damper, but had to relinquish it to Maxwell.

Symbols/figures

2 Snapper sells @ £21.90 a box; bream is priced @ £18.75.

Double letter drill

3 Collect Effie Potter's classic, witty, weekly comments.

Aim for speed

4 Your phone call came too late for us to stop the order.

Job 4.2.1

Study the model and key from the draft on the right.

Memorandum paper: • LL: 60 • SS • returns as indicated

↓ T 2 spaces to right of labels

Space down to the first label

To: *All Branch Managers*   *R2*

From: *General Manager*   *R2*

Date: *14 March 1992*   *R2*

Subject: *FORMAL MEMORANDUM*   *R2*

Our new Office Manual contains examples of the various formal memorandum styles used by large organisations such as ours with offices in several locations.   *R2*

We find this style of memorandum easy to use because the heading labels are arranged to avoid the need to calculate a tab stop.   *R4*

Pre-printed headings and labels

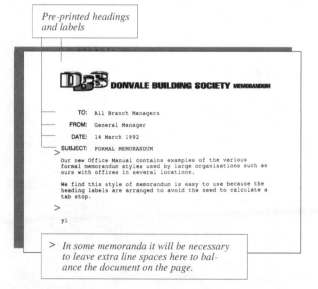

> *In some memoranda it will be necessary to leave extra line spaces here to balance the document on the page.*

Compare your finished work with the model.

Job 6.4.5

Format and key this document.

> Use grouped leader dots (two full stops, three spaces).

> Ensure that the leader dots are aligned vertically.

A5 landscape • SS • centre vertically/horizontally

PETER

R WELLS & COMPANY

Internal Telephone Directory   *bold or u/score*

ine/

ACTON, Paula 396
BLENHEIM, Howard 209
CAMILLERI, Alexander   395
CECIL, John 285
CONN, Oscar 396
COX, Neil   210   *— SMITH/*
CRITTENDEN, Sebastian ~~Lawrence~~   .. 320
DAVIS, Lyn   418
DE FRANCESCHI, ~~Deborah~~ 239
                    Debbie

Job 6.4.6

Format and key this document.

> Use grouped leader dots (three full stops, two spaces).

A5 landscape • SS • centre vertically/horizontally

OTHELLO

by William Shakespeare   *Block right-hand column at left*

C A S T

Duke of Venice.. .. ..Andrew Craig
Othello, a noble ~~Moor~~.. .. ...Kevin Byrnes
Cassio, Othello's lieutenant.....James Cameron
Iago, his ancient.........Stephen Welsh
Roderigo, a Venetian gentleman......Kim Lee
Desdemona, Othello's wife....Katherine Hall
Emilia, Iago's wife.........Jane Saxton
Bianca, mistress to Cassio...Juanita Perez

A play in Five Acts set in Venice and Cyprus

Job 6.4.7

Format and key this document.

> Use leader dots of your choice.

A5 landscape • DS • centre vertically/horizontally

spaced caps u/scored   Executive Magazine

Publisher-in-chief............Karen O'Keefe
Managing Editor..........Mark Sacher *Martin*
Editor.........Claire Desmortes
National Advertising Mgr.....John Thorsby
Art Director.........Virginia Johnston
Production Dir.........Edwin Guest

Unit *6* ·4 cont *Leader dots*

122

Job 4.2.2

Key this memo following the formatting guidelines for Job 4.2.1.

- Your line endings will be different from those in the copy.
- Correct two misspelt words.

Memorandum paper • LL: 60 (10) 70 (12) • SS

```
TO:        All staff

FROM:      Stephen Lee, Personel Manager

DATE:      Today's

SUBJECT:   NEW STAFF MEMBER
```
                                                    rom
I announce the appointment of (**Hans Schultz**), who ⤾

will start work with us on Monday.

(I am sure you will all join me in welcomming Hans
to this company.)

Hans will replace Megan King as trainee draughts-
person. Megan is now fully qualified and will
become part of our special projects team.

SL/TSV

Job 4.2.3

Key this memo on the pre-printed stationery if available.

- Correct two misspelt words and one punctuation error.

Memorandum paper • LL: 55 (10) 65 (12) • SS

To: Les Blair, Paul Moller, Elaine Cox

FROM: Joan Pakavakis

DATE: Today's

SUBJECT: HALF-YEAR EXAMINATIONS

The Winter examination dates this year are as follows: Monday to Thursday, 25-28 November.

Dispite the increase in fees (5%) we are confident that entries will exceed last years' record of 2936 Fees have been set at £10·80 for the Intermediate level and £14·20 for the Finals.

Please confirm – by Monday ~~week~~ at the latest – that the approved examination centre in your area will again be able to accomodate our candidates

Job 6.4.1

Key an exact copy of this document.

- Note that leaders are necessary because the matter in the left column is of varying length.

Use unspaced leader dots.

CALENDAR *R2*

```
Martial Arts and Cultural Exhibition .. 2-5 April
Moscow Circus ........................ 3-26 May
Royal Ballet ......................... 9-20 June
Army Tattoo .......................... 9-10 July
Comedy Festival ...................... 15-30 August
Cats ................................. 1-28 September
```

Job 6.4.2

Format and key this document.

Use one-space leader dots.

Make sure that you align the leader dots vertically.

centre C O N T E N T S ~~LIST~~

```
Preface . . . . . . . . . . . . . . . .   iii
Introduction . . . . . . . . . . . .     1
A history of the retail industry  . . . . .   5
How to get started in retailing  . . 13
Franchising . . . . . . . . . . . .  19
Auction . . . . . . . . . . . . . .  27
Direct selling . . . . . . . . . .   36
Case studies in retailing . . . . .  41
Bibliography . . . . . . . . . . .   58
```

Job 6.4.3

Format and key this document.

Use two-space leader dots.

Building a Spreadsheet

```
Steps to build a spreadsheet......1·1
Executing the program.........1·2
stet The spreadsheet.................1·3
Status lines................1·4
Entering data................1·5
Entering formulas........1·6
Summery..................1·7
Assignments................1·8
```

Job 6.4.4

Format and key this document.

Use three-space leader dots.

Justify the right column.

spaced caps (underscored) **Around Town**

```
Shows. . . . . . . . . . . . . Fiona Aposhun
Gastronomic delights. . . . . . . John Hennessy
Sights for the visitor. . . . . Alan Levy  Allan
Cruises. . . . . . . . . . . Sue Le Gassick
```

Addressing envelopes, labels and cards

Address format

- name of addressee
- name or number of house and name of street
- name of village if in a country district
- post town in capitals
- postcode should have a line to itself – if this is impossible, type it two to six spaces to the right of the last line
- there should be one clear space etween the two halves of the code

Keying the address

1 Key address parallel to the longer side of the envelope, label or card.
2 Start the first line of the address approximately half way down and one-third in from the left edge.
3 Use single line spacing unless there are specific instructions otherwise, or unless the envelope is very large.
4 Block style is the most commonly used, with open or standard punctuation according to what has been used on the letter.
5 Special instructions such as *Personal*, *Confidential* or *For the attention of* should be placed two spaces above the name of the addressee.

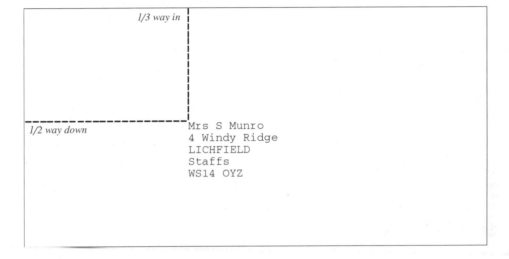

```
                              1/3 way in

   
   
   
   
   1/2 way down
                    Mrs S Munro
                    4 Windy Ridge
                    LICHFIELD
                    Staffs
                    WS14 OYZ
```

```
                    FOR THE ATTENTION OF MR R IRWIN

                    T D White & Co Ltd
                    13 Land Way
                    ARBROATH
                    Angus
                    DD11 2US
```

Leader dots

Leader dots are used in tabulations to lead the eye from entries in one column to related entries in an adjacent column.

Styles

- *unspaced (continuous)*

No space
. . . .

- *spaced*

One space
.   .   .   .
Two spaces
.   .   .   .
Three spaces
.   .   .   .   .   .

- *grouped*

Two full stops, three spaces
..   ..
Three full stops, two spaces
... ...

Unspaced leader dots are the easiest to use because there is no need for any special technique to align them vertically.

The simplest format for leader dots is to block the right-hand column at the left. This allows all the leader dots to finish at the same point.

General rules for leader dots

1 Keep to the same style in any one document.
2 Align the leader dots vertically.
3 Leave at least one space to the left and right of a line of leader dots.
4 For an item of more than one line, key the leader dots on the last line.

Computers

1 Key a trial line comprising
  D the longest line in the left column
  D the minimum number of leader dots and spaces between the columns
  D the longest line in the right column.
2 Set margins and *either*
  D set a tab at the start of the right column (if you are blocking the right column at the left) *or*
  D set a decimal tab one space to the right of the right margin (see page 118) if you are justifying the right column.
3 Delete the trial line.
4 Key the document.

Typewriters

1 From the right margin backspace once for every keystroke in the longest entry in the right column plus one space. *Note this position* on the scale.

Unspaced or spaced leader dots

2 Position the printing point or cursor at the left margin and key the first entry in the left column.
3 Space once and key leader dots up to the *noted position* on the scale. If you are using spaced leaders, note whether the leader dots are on odd or even numbers on the scale.
4 Space once and *either*
  D key the first entry in the right column (if you are blocking the right column at the left) *or*
  D align from the right margin and key the first entry in the right column. If you are justifying the right column, you will need to go back to the *noted position* and key leader dots to one space before the right column entry.
5 Return to the left margin and key the second line. If you are using spaced leader dots, align them vertically with the leader dots in the first line (ie on odd or even numbers on the scale).

6 Repeat steps 2–5 for the remaining lines.

Grouped leader dots

1 From the left margin set tab stops every five spaces until the *noted position* on the scale is reached. The final tab stop is placed in a position to allow you to key a complete group of leaders up to the *noted position*. If more than one space follows the last group of leader dots and you are blocking the right column at the left, set a tab at the *noted position*.
2 Position the printing point or cursor at the left margin and key the first entry in the left column. Then tab across to the next tab stop.
3 Key one set of two or three grouped leader dots. Then tab across to the following tab stop and key a second set of leader dots and so on until the *noted position* is reached.
4 *Either*
  D tab to the *noted position*, space once and key the first entry in the right column (if you are blocking the right column at the left) *or*
  D align from the right margin and key the first entry in the right column. If you are justifying, you may find there is a large gap between the last leader dot and the right column entry. Starting at five spaces after the last tab stop, continue keying the leaders till the printing point or cursor is one space before the right column entry.
5 Return to the left margin and key the second entry.
6 Repeat steps 3–6 for the remaining lines.

Refresher

LL: 55 • SS • DS between drills

All alpha keys
1 Japanese equity in five high-value property areas south of Milton Keynes is due to expire in the coming decade.

Symbols/figures
2 Jones & Bell stock 3-ply board @ £9.75 a square metre.

i/o
3 Caroline's glorious heroism averted serious demolition.

Aim for speed
4 Shares in these firms are worth very little at present.

Refresher

All alpha keys

1 Ask whether mad Ziggy Quintner put a jinx on Fernando's clubs while we were in the town plaza drinking tequila.

Symbols/figures

2 This 3 acre plot sold for £712 568 on 19 November 1984.

Double letter drill

3 All trainee swimmers attend three pool sessions weekly.

Aim for speed

4 Plan your day so that you finish all your work on time.

Job 4.3.1

1 Do not key the punctuation marks.
2 Key the addresses on envelopes or labels.

Envelopes or labels • SS

1 Ms J O'Shea, 29 Dingo Drive, WIGAN, Lancs, WN8 7PD

2 Dr P Von Wisse, 64 Sutherland Street, BANBURY, Oxon, OX2 4DB

3 Captain John Hayes, Secretary, Military History Society, 113-116 Bridge Street, LONDON, W1Y 3XP

4 The Managing Director, Central Paper Mills, 10 Fowler Street, YORK, YO1 1BM

5 The Principal, Heathcote High School, 8 Bellamy Drive, REIGATE, Surrey, RH2 0GP

6 Messrs G & D O'Toole, 118-120 Duke Drive, READING, Berks, RG1 2UX

Job 4.3.2

1 Key the addresses on envelopes, labels or cards.
2 Mark the first envelope: For the attention of Mrs B Barrett and the second Personal.

Envelopes, labels or cards • SS

1 Gooch Enterprises Ltd, 128-130 Leahy Street, HAYES, Middx, TW12 3JN
2 Mr S Harris 12 Cumberland Road, WORKINGTON, Cumbria, CA14 1FA
3 Ms J Davis, Managing Director, Rees Publishing Co, 99 Rosanna Street, LONDON, NW4 1WA
4 Mr L R Hartnell, 30 Baxter Crescent, Chenies, RICKMANSWORTH, Herts, WD3 6PY
5 Ms R Maruel, Flat 6, 64 Vincent Drive, SHILDON, County Durham, DL4 2NE
6 The Broadford Advertising Partnership, 25 Embridge Square, LONDON, W1V 5FZ

Job 6.3.2

Format and key this document, justifying as shown.

A5 portrait • LL: 37 • SS • centre vertically/horizontally

> Rearrange the towns in alphabetical order.

10 spaces ↓

Justify

Penzance	Cornwall
Canterbury	Kent
Preston	Lancs *(Sp out)*
Chelmsford	Essex
Abergavenny	Gwent
Belfast	Northern Ireland
Matlock	Derbyshire
Strathaven	Lanarkshire

Job 6.3.3

Format and key this document, justifying as shown.

A5 landscape • SS • centre vertically/horizontally • spaced caps as shown

> *Barbecue* is a commonly misspelt word.

BETTA AMUSEMENT HIRE

Justify

LL: you select →

Festivals	Parties
Fetes	Carnivals
Picnics	Barbeques c/

spaced caps E V E R Y T H I N G   Y O U   M A Y   R E Q U I R E

Justify

LL: you select →

Giant Slide	Inflatable fun house
Mini Ferris Wheel	Trackless Train
Mini Carousels	Merry-Go-Round

Fairy Floss Centre
Popcorn

LL: you select → Ring Now *(lc)*

848 9613

Overseas addresses

Overseas destinations

Overseas addresses should be keyed with special care.

- It is essential to include the post-code or zip code.
- Make sure that the address shows the country of destination. It is easily overlooked, especially if you are replying to an incoming letter from overseas which does not show the country of origin on the letterhead.

The Reference Section gives examples of address styles for overseas countries.

Refresher

LL: 55 • SS • DS between drills

All alpha keys
1 Jane Villikins has the quaintest way of dozing at Max's boring parties, but this is not exactly good etiquette.
Symbols/figures
2 The price of 16 mm tubing has risen 8% to £28.34 today.
Double letter drill
3 Warren Robb has been accused of harassing office staff.
Aim for speed
4 There are no hard and fast rules about office clothing.

Job 4.4.1

Using C6 envelopes, labels or cards, key one for each of these addresses. You will need to study 'Overseas addresses' in the Reference Section (page x) for the correct styles.

- Include the name of the country on each envelope. If it is not given, you may need to consult a reference book.
- Do not key the punctuation marks.

> The abbreviation for West Virginia is 'WV'.

Blank C6 envelopes • SS

1 IWAYAMA MASAKO, 3-10-8 SANEICHO, CHUO/KU, TOKYO —/

2 HERR WOLFGANG BAEDER, SCHERRSTRASSE 4, D-800 MUNCHEN 19, WEST GERMANY

3 JULES MARCHAND, BRODARD ET ROMAIN SA, 62 AVENUE JEAN MOULIN, F-75006, PARIS

caps 4 F<u>rau</u> A ZIMMERMANN, ZEITWEG 64, CH-8032, ZURICH

5 SIG.RA GINA CIANO, VIA GUASTI 7/, I-50134, FIRENZE, 2/ ITALY

6 MS PETA BURNSIDE, 38 PATARO WAY, SAN FRANCISCO, CA 94104-3250

7 MR PAUL SMART, 63 ELM LANE, ADELAIDE SA 5000

R/ 8 HER/HEINRICH PAREY, SPITALERSTRASSE 212, POSTFACH 106803, D-2000 HAMBURG

9 PIERRE RONSARD, 1409 RUE GARANCIERE, F-75285 PARIS CEDEX 06, FRANCE

10 MR R FOWLER, 198 CHARTERS (RD) WELLINGTON   *sp out*

11 MRS ALISON GAMBLE, 78 WOOD LANE, MELBOURNE VIC 3000

USA/ 12 DR S/ GRIDDLE, ROUTE 6, BOX 49 C, ROMNEY, WEST ○/ VIRGINIA 26757, AMERICA

13 ROLAND DE VIGNY, 2839 BOULEVARDE LAURIER, SAINTE-FOY, QUEBEC, CANADA G1V 2M3

Right margin alignment (justification)

On most electronic typewriters and word processing systems, lines can be automatically aligned at the right margin

(ie *right justified*, *flush right* or *right aligned*). Consult your operator's manual to see whether your system has this function.

If your system does not have this function, follow these steps:
1 Position the printing point one space to the right of the point at which the line is to end.
2 If more than one line is to be justified, set a tab stop at that point.

Systems with a decimal tab function
3 Press the decimal tab key and key the line to be justified.
4 Press return. Repeat steps 3 and 4 for the remaining lines.

Systems without a decimal tab function
3 Backspace once for each character or space in the first line to be justified.
4 Key the line and return.
5 Tab and backspace for the next line.

Refresher

LL: 55 • SS • DS between drills

All alpha keys
1 Seize the next opportunity to prove that you have those high qualities essential to the job of marketing chief.

Symbols/figures
2 We can offer you 10% discount on orders for 25 or more.

r/t
3 Tracy Witrod is certain to entertain the triple troupe.

Aim for speed
4 Sign these blanks and send them to head office at once.

Job 6.3.1

Key an exact copy of this document.

If your system has no automatic function for right margin alignment, follow the steps at the head of this page.

A5 portrait • SS • centre vertically/horizontally

Justify
↓
Administration
Sales
Accounts
Advertising

Two-column display with justified right column

Computers
1 Key a trial line comprising
   D the longest line in the left column
   D the minimum number of spaces between the two columns
   D the longest line in the right column.
2 Centre the trial line and set the margins. Set a decimal tab one space to the right of the right margin.*
3 Delete the trial line.
4 Key the first line of the first column.
5 Tab across to the decimal tab stop, justify the first line in the right column and press return to move your cursor to the next line.
6 Repeat steps 4 and 5.

Typewriters with a decimal tab function
1 Add:
   D the number of keystrokes in the longest line in the left column
   D the number of keystrokes in the longest line in the right column
   D the minimum number of spaces between the two columns.
2 Set a decimal tab one space to the right of the right margin.*
3 Repeat steps 4–6 above.

Typewriters without a decimal tab function
1 Add:
   D the number of keystrokes in the longest line in the left column
   D the number of keystrokes in the longest line in the right column

   D the minimum number of spaces between the two columns.
2 Set the left and right margins so that the document is centred on the page.
3 Key the first line in the left column.
4 Space to the right margin and backspace once for each keystroke in the right column.
5 Key the first line in the right column and press return.
6 Repeat steps 3–5.

*Your system may not allow you to set a tab stop here; if this is so, set your actual right margin two spaces to the right of your intended margin and set the decimal tab stop one space before it.

Business letters 1

Personal business letters

If you have access to a typewriter or computer with word processing software at home, you can key rather than handwrite your personal business letters. It is usual to keep a hard copy (ie a photocopy or carbon copy) on file. If you are using a computer or electronic typewriter with disk storage you can save a copy on disk instead of, or in addition to, the hard copy. Remember to index your disk.

Fully blocked style with open punctuation

In this format

- all lines start at the left margin
- no punctuation is used outside the body of the letter.

This style is commonly used in business correspondence of all types. The advantages of the fully blocked style are that

- it is easy to key
- no unnecessary keystrokes are used, so time is saved.

Features of a personal business letter

1 Author's address
Use single line spacing.

The preferred position for the author's address in a personal business letter is at the top of the letter above the date.

It is possible to have personalised stationery printed with the individual's name and address at the head. If personalised stationery is used, it is unnecessary to key the author's name and address.

2 Date
This is the date on which the letter was keyed. The letter should be posted on that date.

3 Inside address
The letter may be addressed to a named person or the unnamed holder of an office (such as 'The Secretary', or 'The Manager'). The addressee's name and/or title is followed by the full postal address.

4 Salutation
The salutation is on a separate line. Do not punctuate after the salutation. The wording of the address should agree with the inside address.

- If the letter is addressed to a named person, use the name in the salutation; for example, if the letter is addressed to Mr & Mrs B Wright, the salutation would be 'Dear Mr & Mrs Wright'. (When less formality is required, or when the writer knows the addressee well, first names may be used, eg 'Dear Bruce and Julie'.)

  Many women prefer to use the title 'Ms' which, like 'Mr', does not indicate marital status.

  If you do not know the sex of the person to whom you are writing, it is acceptable to omit a title from the salutation and use the given name and surname; eg 'Dear Chris Swift'.

- If the letter is addressed to an unnamed holder of an office, use the salutation 'Dear Sir' or 'Dear Madam'. If the sex of the addressee is unknown, either use 'Dear Sir or Madam' or avoid using 'Dear Sir' altogether. For example, you can use 'Dear Manager'.

  Address the person by name, where possible, and where it is appropriate.

5 Text
The first paragraph of a business letter usually summarises its purpose. Use single line spacing. Double space between paragraphs.

6 Complimentary close
Use 'Yours faithfully' with the salutation 'Dear Sir' or 'Dear Madam'. Use 'Yours sincerely' when a person's name is used in the salutation. 'Yours truly' is common in the USA.

It is an error to capitalise 'faithfully' and 'sincerely'. Only the first word, 'Yours', should be capitalised.

7 Signatory
Use both the first name and the surname of the writer. The printed name ensures that the writer is addressed correctly in the reply. A woman signatory may choose to add 'Ms', 'Mrs' or 'Miss' in brackets after her name to indicate how she wishes to be addressed in any reply.

Selecting line length

A4 paper is commonly used for business letters of all lengths and types, but A5 (portrait) can be used for short letters (up to 75 words [10 pitch] and up to 90 words [12 pitch] in the text of the letter).

Guide to line length for single-page business letters

Approx no of words	Paper size	Line length in text
10 pitch:		
up to 75	A5 (portrait)	40
up to 150	A4	55
151–220	A4	60
12 pitch:		
up to 90	A5 (portrait)	50
up to 180	A4	65
180–260	A4	75

Note: These are only estimates and the actual number of words that will fit a page will vary according to the number of paragraphs and notations (see later units). Continuation pages are used for long letters.

Folding letters

See 'Envelopes' inside the front cover for the correct way to fold letters.

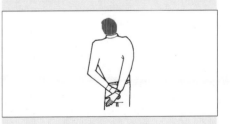

Job 6.2.3

Format and key this document, block centring where indicated.

A5 portrait • SS • centre vertically/horizontally

Note these spellings:
operator processor
but
computer

EXCEL PERSONNEL

Permanent and Temporary Office Staff

We have vacancies <u>now</u> for:

block centre
- Secretary's Secretaries
- Typists
- Receptionists
- Computer operators
- Word processor operators

If you are looking for permanent or temporary work

spaced caps→ C A L L   U S   N O W

0848 11223

Job 6.2.4

Format and key this document, block centring where indicated.

A4 portrait • SS • centre vertically/horizontally • spaced caps as shown

G L A M A - G L A S S centre

<u>Britain's Best Built-in Wardrobes and Shower Screens</u>

Block centre
- Designed and custom-made to your specifications/
- Installed by qualified trades people
- 15 frame colours
- All sliding doors run on nylon-encased rollers
- Shower screens slide with the touch of a finger
- Full range of laminated/safety glass and /

All Work Fully Guaranteed

<u>R I N G   N O W</u>

For a no-obligation free measure and quote

<u>G L A M A - G L A S S</u>

Centre each line
- A British (Co) sp out
- 9 CHATSWOOD
- 104 Willoughby Road trs
- 848 9001

Refresher

All alpha keys

1 How can Davina buy those thick-pile jackets and leather ankle boots tax free every time she goes to Mozambique?

Symbols/figures

2 Lot no 34, measuring 174 x 26 m, is priced at £150 860.

Double letter drill

3 Emma's scatty puppy Belle ripped Ann's Russian Grammar.

Aim for speed

4 The business you work for will be judged by your deeds.

Job 4.5.1

Plain A5 portrait • envelope • LL: 50 • SS • returns as indicated

1 Study the model and key from the draft on the right.
2 Prepare an accompanying envelope and fold the letter correctly according to the directions inside the front cover.

Line 4   3 Shackelton Avenue
Hull
HU1 1AF   *R2*

27 March 1992   *R2*

The Secretary
The German Shepherd Association
14 Kingsley Place
London
SW8 1DX   *R2*

Dear Sir or Madam   *R2*

I wish to ask you for advice about breeders.   *R2*

My family and I have recently migrated from Holland to live in this country. In Amsterdam we were the proud owners of a wonderful German Shepherd bitch but, because of her advanced age and Britain's strict quarantine regulations, we had to leave her behind. We miss our dog very much and would like to adopt another. Could you please put us in touch with a reputable breeder close to Hull who might be able to help us find a suitable puppy.

Yours faithfully   *R5*

Irena Landen (Mrs)

```
1      3 Shackleton Avenue
       Hull
>      HU1 1AF
 2     27 March 1992
>
3      The Secretary
       The German Shepherd Association
       14 Kingsley Place
       London
>      SW8 1DX

4      Dear Sir or Madam

       I wish to ask you for advice about breeders.

       My family and I have recently migrated from Holland
       to live in this country.  In Amsterdam we were the
       proud owners of a wonderful German Shepherd bitch
5      but, because of her advanced age and Britain's
       strict quarantine regulations, we had to leave her
       behind.  We miss our dog very much and would like
>      to adopt another.  Could you please put us in
       touch with a reputable breeder close to Hull who
       might be able to help us find a suitable puppy.

6      Yours faithfully
>
7      Irene Landen (Mrs)
>
```

Use 'Yours sincerely' if addressee's name is in salutation

Compare your finished work with the model.

Block centring

Part of the body of a display may be blocked left and centred.

Consult your operator's manual to find out whether your system can perform this function automatically.

If your system has no automatic function to centre a block of text (ie more than one line), follow this procedure:

Computers

1 Key the longest line in the block, centre it and set a temporary left margin or tab at the starting point.
2 Delete the line.
3 Key the block of text.

Typewriters

1 Position the cursor or carrier at the horizontal centre.
2 Select the longest line to be keyed.
3 Backspace from the centre one space for every two characters or spaces in the longest line.
4 Set the left margin stop (or the paragraph indent) at this point.
5 Key the text to be block centred.

Refresher

LL: 55 • SS • DS between drills

All alpha keys
1 A major order for twelve dozen quilts would exhaust our already diminished stock of this category of bedspread.

Symbols/figures
2 Check that Invoice No 1258 for £17 643 has been posted.

e/r
3 Are there areas where express letters aren't delivered?

Aim for speed
4 Will you please find out if there is any truth in this.

Job 6.2.1

Key an exact copy of this document.

- Block centre the lines as shown.

> If your system does not block centre automatically, backspace from the centre *once* for every *two* keystrokes in the longest line.

A5 portrait • SS • centre vertically/horizontally

Centre→ WORD PROCESSING TERMS *R2*

↓*LM*
Conditional hyphen
Global search and replace
Hot zone
Cursor
Decimal tabulation
Wraparound
Scrolling
Longest line → Temporary margin - margin inset
Bolding
Shadow printing

Job 6.2.2

Format and key this document, block centring where indicated.

> Underscore the heading.

A5 landscape • SS • centre vertically/horizontally

GLENRAY OFFICE FURNITRUE *trs*

Any colour at no extra charge

g Desks (steel and timber)
Ergonomic chairs
Filing cabinets
block centre Card cabinets
Plan cabinets
Lockers
Show-cases
Bookcases

Job 4.5.2

1 Key this letter on plain paper.
  - Your line endings will be different from those in the copy.
  - Correct one misspelt word and one punctuation error.
  - Remember to add today's date.
2 The postcode may be keyed on the same line as the town or county, but in this case six spaces must be left before the code.
3 Prepare an accompanying envelope and fold the letter correctly.

63 Munro Grove
ILFORD Essex   IG6 3JJ

The Manager
British Telecom
St Peters House
St Peters Street
COLCHESTER
ESSEX   CO1 1ET

Dear Sir or Madam

I shall shortly be making an extended overseas business trip and I wish to make sure, that any accounts likely to fall due during my absence are payed before I leave.
For the year I expect to be away my house will be occupied by my son and daughter, both of whom are students. The telephone will therefore be in use, but before I go I would like to settle any arrears and make any advance payment for rent and calls that you may require. I understand you will be able to let me have an estimated account.

My account number is /03 999001 702 3/.

Yours faithfully

Alexander Drake

Job 4.5.3

1 Key this letter on plain paper.
  - The author is Ms J Boulos, 10 Juniper Close, CATERHAM, Surrey, CR3 6SZ
  - Correct two misspelt words and one punctuation error.
2 Prepare an accompanying envelope and fold the letter correctly.

Mr D. Anderson
Anderson TV Antennas
43 Deganny Road
SUTTON
Surrey SMT 4ZZ

Dear Mr Anderson

I am very sorry to say that the new aerial you fitted two weeks ago has proved unsatisfactory.

The picture was excellent for about three days after installation, but it then began to deteriorate rapidly. I have tried in vain to reach you several times by phone to tell you this. There has been no reply to several messages I have left on your telephone answering system.

Please call me as soon as possible on 777 8899; any time during the day or evening to make an appointment to inspect the TV and aerial.

Yours sincerely

Job 6.1.3

Format and key this document
with spaced capitals as shown.

A5 landscape • SS • centre vertically/horizontally

AVVENTURA TRAVEL — (spaced caps)

Before you go anywhere

¶ ASK FOR OUR PACKAGED TOURS

UK
City breaks
Worldwide

WE KNOW TRAVEL — (spaced caps)

trs 15B Belize Road
RICHMOND SURREY TW9 4DZ
081 521 6658

Job 6.1.4

Format and key this document
with spaced capitals as shown.

A5 landscape • SS • centre vertically/horizontally

SHORT MICROCOMPUTER COURSES

H E P B O U R N   C O M P U T E R   C E N T R E

Introduction to Lotus 1-2-3
trs Intorduction to dBase IV
Introduction to DOS
Advanced Lotus 1-2-3 -/-/
Advanced dBase IV
Advanced DOS

614 Vermont Road Croydon

Job 6.1.5

Format and key this document
with spaced capitals as shown.

A5 portrait • DS • centre vertically/horizontally

Select suitable styles for displayed
capitals.

Accommodation is a commonly
misspelt word.

A U C T I O N

Saturday 2 September
at 3 pm 5h

B A R N E S   C O T T A G E

Briar wood Lane Worcester
Superb 2 acre property
Accommodation includes 4 bedrooms

CECIL HUNT ESTATE AGENTS
0905 52475

Business letters 2

Simple business letters

Letters are an essential part of the operation of a business. If they are well formatted and expressed and contain accurate information, they will give clients or customers a good impression of the organisation.

The style used in the model on page 86 is fully blocked with open punctuation.

Presenting letters for signature

- Place completed correspondence in an easily identified folder.
- Attach all enclosures.
- Place each letter under the flap of its corresponding envelope, with the address and envelope facing out, as shown in the illustration on this page.

Features of a simple business letter

1 Heading

Letters sent by a business or other organisation are almost invariably produced on pre-printed letterhead paper. The letterhead includes the name of the organisation in display type, the full street address, any private bag or post office box number, and telephone, telex and fax numbers. It may also include the names of directors or partners.

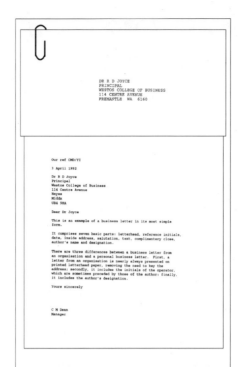

Letter and envelope presented for signature

Some letterheads bear the organisation's logo (distinctive emblem).

2 Reference initials
These may comprise the author's initials followed by the operator's, or the operator's initials alone.

3 Date
Use this style:
   3 April 1992

4 Inside address
Letters should, if at all possible, be addressed to a named person. The person's title and/or department should be included next, followed by the full postal address. If the author does not know the addressee's name, a title

such as 'The Secretary' or 'The Manager' should be used. Use single line spacing. If you are taking the inside address from a data base which is set up in upper case, it is an acceptable alternative for it to be in upper case rather than capitals and lower case.

5 Salutation
Follow the style for personal business letters in Unit 4.5 (page 82). If the author and addressee are on 'first name terms', the addressee's given name may be used.

6 Text
The opening paragraph should briefly state the purpose of the letter. Use single line spacing. Double space between paragraphs.

7 Complimentary close
Follow the same style as personal business letters.

8 Signature line
The signature line includes not only the author's name but his or her title or description. Use single line spacing.

In the absence of the author, the secretary signs the letter (with the author's permission) in the style shown in the model on page 86.

Mail merge

Mail merge is a program that enables the operator to print out multiple copies of a document. It also allows variable information, such as addresses, to be added to a standard letter before printing. If you have this capacity on your system, consult your operator's manual to find out how to use it.

Refresher

LL: 55 • SS • DS between drills

All alpha keys
1   Briefly, the Kiwi quiz experts do not descend to sleazy tricks but simply try not to jump to hasty conclusions.

Symbols/figures
2   I can provide 160 x 235 cm 3-ply board @ £8.40 a metre.

Double letter drill
3   Will canny Matt Plummer seek Harry Gibbons' assistance?

Aim for speed
4   We allow the person who made the call to hang up first.

Module 6 Formatting 3 Spaced capitals
Block centring
Right margin alignment   Leader dots

Performance goals

At the end of Module 6 you should be able to

- spread centre and block centre display material
- align text at the right margin
- use leader dots effectively.

Spaced capitals

Spaced capitals are used to emphasise words or lines in a displayed format. Extra space is keyed between letters and between words. It is usual to centre displayed capitals horizontally. To centre spaced capitals, follow the technique you have been using for centring but key

- *one* space between letters and *three* spaces between words.

Review:

- centring between margins (page 53)
- vertical centring (page 15).

Job 6.1.1

Key an exact copy of this document.

- Use spaced capitals as shown.

A5 landscape • TS • centre vertically/horizontally

1 space between letters
↓   ↓ *3 spaces between words*

T H E   S N O W Y   M O U N T A I N S

T H E   L A K E   D I S T R I C T

T H E   T H A M E S

Job 6.1.2

Format and key this document with spaced capitals as shown.

A5 landscape • SS • centre vertically/horizontally

E A S T V I E W   E L E C T R O N I C S

RADOI AND TV SERVICE

centre each line horizontally

Prompt Same Day Service

NO JOB TOO SMALL

Call us for all your radio and TV repairs
081 443 6051

Job 4.6.1

1 Study the model and key from the draft.
2 Prepare an accompanying envelope and fold the letter correctly.

Our ref CMD/YI

3 April 1992 R2

Dr R D Joyce
Principal
Westos College of Business
114 Centre Avenue
Hayes
Middx
RB4 9RA R2

Dear Dr Joyce R2

This is an example of a business letter in its most simple form. R2

It comprises seven basic parts: letterhead, reference initials, date, inside address, salutation, text, complimentary close, author's name and designation. R2

There are three differences between a business letter from an organisation and a personal business letter. First, a letter from an organisation is nearly always presented on printed letterhead paper, removing the need to key the address; secondly, it includes the initials of the operator, which are sometimes preceded by those of the author; finally, it includes the author's designation. R2

Yours sincerely R5

C M Dean
Manager

> Compare your finished work with the model.

These numbers correspond with the paragraph numbers under Features of a simple business letter *on page 85.*

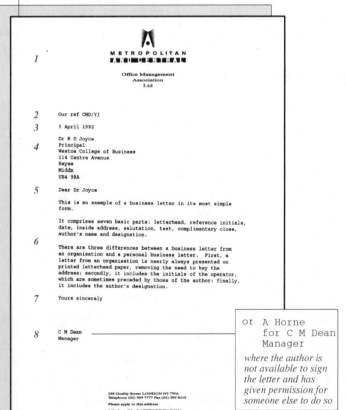

1

METROPOLITAN
Office Management
Association
Ltd

2   Our ref CMD/YI

3   3 April 1992

4   Dr R D Joyce
     Principal
     Westos College of Business
     114 Centre Avenue
     Hayes
     Middx
     UB4 9RA

5   Dear Dr Joyce

     This is an example of a business letter in its most simple
     form.

     It comprises seven basic parts: letterhead, reference initials,
     date, inside address, salutation, text, complimentary close,
     author's name and designation.

6   There are three differences between a business letter from
     an organisation and a personal business letter. First, a
     letter from an organisation is nearly always presented on
     printed letterhead paper, removing the need to key the
     address; secondly, it includes the initials of the operator,
     which are sometimes preceded by those of the author; finally,
     it includes the author's designation.

7   Yours sincerely

8   C M Dean
     Manager

238 Quality Street LONDON N9 7WA
Telephone (02) 999 7777 Fax (02) 999 8219
Please apply to this address
8 Burbage Way DARTFORD DAZ 8XA

```
or A Horne
   for C M Dean
   Manager
```
where the author is not available to sign the letter and has given permission for someone else to do so

Job 5.7.2

Key this document, following the formatting guidelines for Job 5.7.1.

- Correct three spelling errors and one error of style.

PREPARING AN ITINERY

After all travel reservations have been made and hotel bookings are completed, a detailed itinerary should be prepared which should show details of:

1   Flights

    1.1   Airline and flight numbers
    1.2   Name and address of hotel
    1.3   Departure and arrival times
    1.4   Amount of airport tax payable
    1.5   Details of person meeting traveller (where applicable)

2   HOTEL ACCOMODATION

    2.1
    2.2   Telephone and telex numbers
    2.3   Reservation confirmation number
    2.4   Alternative hotel (for emergencies)

3   APPOINTMENTS *ARRANGED*

    3.1   Contact name;
    3.2   Company and adress
    3.3   Telephone and telex numbers
    3.4   List of topics for discussion

Job 5.7.3

Key this document.

- Correct three spelling errors and one punctuation error.

GRAPHICS

1   Business documents ~~often~~ commonly contain graphics. They make it easier for the reader to interpret information, and nowadays they can be produced quickly and in a sophisticated form on a computer.

    1.1   *Line graphics* show trends over a period; in sales or expenses, for example.

    1.2   *Bar graphs* are often employed to show comparitive information; for example, this years' sales can be compared with the previous year's.

    1.3   *Pie charts* are used to show the proportions of component parts to the whole.

2   The following notes will help you to prepare the graphics for a report.

    2.1   All graphs should be numbered in sequence and bear a title.

    2.2   Graphs are placed as near as possible to the point at which they are first referred to in the text.

    2.3   Sufficent space should be left above and below the graph.

Job 4.6.2

1 Key this letter on pre-printed stationery if available.
- Your line endings will be different from those in the copy.
- Correct one misspelt word and one punctuation error and reference **KOH/YI**.
- Remember to add today's date at the head of the letter.
2 Prepare an accompanying envelope and fold the letter correctly.

Ms Laurel Gibbs
Shipping Manager
Hornsby Industries PLC
501 East Street
MITCHAM
Surrey   CR4 4RS

Dear Ms Gibbs

Following the government's recent economic statement and the passage of the Customs Tariff Bill through parliament, changes in duty will apply from ~~1 July~~. *the first of next month*

The act will remove the 2 per cent duty that now applies to tarrif concession orders and a number of general tariff rates. These items will be free ~~of~~ *stet* duty.

As soon as ~~Once~~ more information is available I will write to you again. In the meantime, please let me know, whether you have any questions about this move.

Yours sincerely

C Perry for

Kevin O'Hara
Southern Area Manager

Job 4.6.3

1 Key this letter on pre-printed stationery if available.
- Correct two misspelt words.
2 Prepare an accompanying envelope and fold the letter correctly.

Mr S R Bourke OBE
Managing Director
Hoehne (Hoehne) Office Design PLC
14 Redfly Walk
MANCHESTER   M14 3QU

Dear Simon,

Since your telephone call last week, I have been giving serious thought to the idea of setting up a joint management training scheme for our two companys.

I would like to take the proposal a stage further by arranging a meeting between ourselves and our training managers. Are you and Tim free next Wednesday at 10am? Graeme and I could visit you, but you would be very wellcome at our newly-furnished boardroom which, as you know, I am very anxious to show off. Let me know if this suits you.

Your sincerely

James Dacosta
Managing Director

Decimal enumeration

Decimal enumeration is an efficient method and is widely used in formal documents.

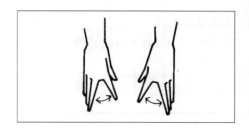

Refresher

All alpha keys
1 A judge is the best-equipped person to win next month's election in Sutton; he will attract half the town vote.

e/r
2 Later she remembered reading three more chapters there.

Caps/underscore
3 <u>HAZCHEM</u>: this sign is used to show hazardous chemicals.

Aim for speed
4 We fully expect these seven courses to begin next year.

Job 5.7.1

Study the model and key from the draft.

A5 portrait • LL: 41 • SS • centre vertically/horizontally

2 spaces
↓

1   **BASIC REFERENCE BOOKS**   *R2*

  ↓ *2 spaces*
  1.1   *Dictionaries*   *R2*

    ↓ *2 spaces*
    1.1.1   *Accounting dictionaries*
    1.1.2   *Dictionaries of quotations*
    1.1.3   *Marketing dictionaries*

  1.2   *Directories*

    1.2.1   *Australia*
    1.2.2   *United Kingdom*
    1.2.3   *United States of America*

2   *INSURANCE AND ASSURANCE*

  2.1   *Insurance*

    2.1.1   *Classes of insurance*
    2.1.2   *Insurance terms*
    2.1.3   *Fire insurance*
    2.1.4   *Marine insurance*

  2.2   *Assurance*

    2.2.1   *Life assurance*

```
1  BASIC REFERENCE BOOKS

   1.1  Dictionaries

        1.1.1  Accounting dictionaries
        1.1.2  Dictionaries of quotations
        1.1.3  Marketing dictionaries

   1.2  Directories

        1.2.1  Australia
        1.2.2  United Kingdom
        1.2.3  United States of America

2  INSURANCE AND ASSURANCE

   2.1  Insurance

        2.1.1  Classes of insurance
        2.1.2  Insurance terms
        2.1.3  Fire insurance
        2.1.4  Marine insurance

   2.2  Assurance

        2.2.1  Life assurance
```

Business letters 3

A subject heading in a business letter serves the same purpose as a heading in a memorandum.

- It draws the reader's attention to the subject of the letter.
- It is an aid to filing.

  There is no need to begin the subject line with the word 'Subject' or 'Re'.

Refresher

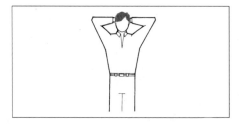

LL: 55 • SS • DS between drills

All alpha keys

1 The judge was amazed to see Ivan qualify for extra back pay when Jock Vern, who was equally deserving, did not.

Hyphen key

2 A well-to-do woman made a never-to-be-forgotten speech.

Double letter drill

3 Aaron Rigg will soon accrue three full weeks' fees too.

Aim for speed

4 Two large firms made an offer for the first floor flat.

Job 4.7.1

1 Study the model and key from the draft.
2 Prepare an accompanying envelope and fold the letter correctly.

Letterhead and envelope • LL: 60 • SS • returns as indicated

Blue Water Pools Ltd
746 Blue Gum Avenue COBHAM KT11 1LA
Telephone: (08) 777 8170 Fax: (08) 777 8171

Our ref MW/YI

14 October 1992

Mr & Mrs L M Milner
34 Buccaneer Drive
BRIXHAM
Devon
TQ5 8BX

Dear Mr & Mrs Milner

WINTER SEMINAR

An invitation is extended to you and your friends to join us at out annual Winter Seminar.

This educational evening will provide you will invaluable tips on 'bedding' your pool down over the colder months to save you expense later on. We view our pool school as an extension of the initial instructions given to new pool owners, and hope that all those with new pools will attend.

The evening will be informal, supper is provided and, of course, it's FREE. We ask that you reply by 1 November, and look forward to seeing you on Friday 6 November at 7.30 pm.

Yours sincerely

Max Water
Managing Director

Frequently used components such as the complimentary close and signature line can be stored on electronic systems to save keying time.

Our ref MW/YI   R2

14 October 1992   R2

Mr & Mrs L M Milner
34 Buccaneer Drive
BRIXHAM
Devon
TQ5 8BX   R2

Dear Mr & Mrs Milner   R2

WINTER SEMINAR   R2

An invitation is extended to you and your friends to join us at our annual Winter Seminar.

This educational evening will provide you with invaluable tips on 'bedding' your pool down over the colder months to save you expense later on. We view our pool school as an extension of the initial instructions given to new pool owners, and hope that all those with new pools will attend.

The evening will be informal, supper is provided and, of course, it's FREE. We ask that you reply by 1 November and look forward to seeing you on Friday 6 November at 7.30 pm.

Yours sincerely   R5

Max Water
Managing Director

Job 5.6.2

Follow the instructions for Job 5.6.1, using this alternative style to key the first part of the same list.

A5 landscape • LL: 55 • SS • centre vertically/horizontally

TIPS ON CARAVANNING   *R3*

2 spaces ↓

1 Before you set out, adopt the following procedure.   *R2*

2 spaces ↓

   a Make sure your caravan complies with safety regulations and check these parts for wear and damage: *R2*

2 spaces ↓

      i brakes
     ii chassis and coupling
   iii gas bottle holder and regulator
   iv jockey wheel and parking jack
    v roof and roof hatch
   vi springs and wheel bearings
 vii water supply system.

Inset document (student work):

TIPS ON CARAVANNING

Before you set out, adopt the following procedure.

a Make sure your caravan complies with safety regulations and check these parts for wear and damage:

    i brakes
   ii chassis and coupling
 iii gas bottle holder and regulator
 iv jockey wheel and parking jack
  v roof and roof hatch
 vi springs and wheel
vii water supply system.

Job 5.6.3

Key this document, following the formatting guidelines for Job 5.6.1.

- Correct two spelling errors.

A4 portrait • LL: 40 • SS • centre vertically/horizontally

TS [USE OF THE TELEPHONE] centre

1 THE SOUND OF YOUR VOICE /DS
  (a) Distance from the mouthpiece
  (b) Clarity
    (i) Pronunciation
    (ii) Volume of sound
    (iii) Rate of speech
  (c) Manner and tone
2 PLACING A CALL <DS
  (a) Find*ing* the number <DS
    (i) Telephone lists
    (ii) Telephone directories
  (b) Getting the connection
    (i) Correct dialing
    (ii) Getting the person you wanted
3 RECIEVING THE CALL <DS
  (a) Promptness in answering <DS
  (b) Preferred form of greeting
  (c) Getting the person called
    (i) Correct procedure
    (ii) Taking messages <DS
4 TELEPHONE CONVERSATIONS
  (a) Need for conciseness <DS
  (b) Importance *of* courtesy
  (c) Closing the call

Job 4.7.2

1 Key this letter on pre-printed stationery if available.
   - Your line endings will be different from those in the copy.
   - Correct one punctuation error and one spacing error.
   - Remember to add today's date at the head of the letter.

2 Prepare an accompanying envelope and fold the letter correctly.

Letterhead and envelope • LL: 60 (10) 70 (12) • SS

Our ref MW/YI

Mr W B Del Sasso
87 Grand Ridge
BANSTEAD
Surrey   SM7 1FB

Dear Mr del Sasso   *cap*

FREE COMPUTERISED ANALYSIS - FREE HOUSE CALLS

Now is the time to prepare your pool for summer.

NP [We care about your pool so we'll come to you!

We will visit your pool, take a water sample and analyse it back at our lab. If chemicals are required, we will deliver them too! All that and no delivery costs and no hidden charges. That saves you valuable time and money.

Ring Cathy now to arrange for our represent*at*ive to call. This offer is available for seven day's only.

Yours sincerely

Max Water
Managing Director

Job 4.7.3

1 Key this letter on pre-printed stationery if available.
   - Correct one misspelt word, two punctuation errors and one error in capitalisation.

2 Prepare an accompanying envelope and fold the letter correctly.

Letterhead and envelope • LL: 60 (10) 70 (12) • SS

The Town Clerk
Shire of Eltham
Shire Offices
Main Road
ELTHAM EN1 2SD

Dear Sir or Madam

PLOT 26, ORMEAU PLACE, ELTHAM

I refer to your letter informing us of the decision,

trs (to) not allow the owner of this property to purchase the carriageway easement alongside the land.

I understood from discussions with Ms Edmunds of the Town Planning Department that the Council's consent would be a formality. As I explained on the telephone, the owner of the land, Mr Groppi, wishes to subdivide his property, and unless he is able to purchase the carriageway the easement access will not be gained at the rear of the property.

Please clarify the Council's decision on this matter?

Yours faithfully
William Chester

Sub-enumeration

If there is more than one level of enumeration, follow the style shown in Job 5.6.1. This style uses arabic figures, then alphabetic characters (alphabetic enumeration), followed by small roman numerals, in that order.

If more than three levels of enumeration are required, use decimal enumeration (see page 112).

Refresher

All alpha keys

1 Mazdas and Suzukis performed quite well in this month's Victory Grand Prix at Hampton's recently built raceway.

e/i

2 Viewing movies is a prime leisure activity in Leighton.

Symbols/figures

3 Your order for 36 shelves (G-421) @ £9.50 is cancelled.

Aim for speed

4 We share your concern about high prices of some stocks.

Job 5.6.1

Study the model and key from the draft.

A4 portrait • LL: 55 • SS • centre vertically/horizontally

Alternative style for computers

3 spaces
↓
```
(1)    brakes
(ii)   chassis and coupling
(iii)  gas bottle holder and regulator
(iv)   jockey wheel and parking jack
(v)    roof and roof hatch
(vi)   springs and wheel bearings
(vii)  water supply system.
```
↑
1 space

```
TIPS ON CARAVANNING

1 Before you set out, adopt the following procedure.

  (a) Make sure your caravan complies with safety
      regulations and check these parts for wear and
      damage:

        (i)   brakes
        (ii)  chassis and coupling
        (iii) gas bottle holder and regulator
        (iv)  jockey wheel and parking jack
        (v)   roof and roof hatch
        (vi)  springs and wheel bearings
        (vii) water supply system.

  (b) When packing your caravan you should

        (i)   place heavy equipment in lower cupboards
              and lighter materials in overhead
              cupboards

        (ii)  pack very heavy and bulky items on the
              floor at the front of the van

        (iii) use plastic containers with screwtop lids
              (but not for petrol).

2 During your trip, take note of the following points.

  (a) When parking the caravan for the night consider
      the slope of the ground, the prevailing winds,
      shade and privacy.

  (b) You can use a plastic garbage bin as a makeshift
      washing machine.  Half fill it with water, add
      detergent, put in clothes to be washed and put
      the lid on tightly.  The movement of the water
      in the bin will do the work for you.
```

```
  LM  T
  ↓   ↓
  1   Before you
      ↑      ↓ T
2 spaces  (a) Make s
      ↑
  1 space
```

The brackets around (a) and (i) etc are optional

TIPS ON CARAVANNING   R3

1 *Before you set out, adopt the following procedure.*   R2

  (a) *Make sure your caravan complies with safety regulations and check these parts for wear and damage:*   R2

     (i)   *brakes*
     (ii) *chassis and coupling*
     (iii) *gas bottle holder and regulator*
     (iv) *jockey wheel and parking jack*
     (v)   *roof and roof hatch*
     (vi) *springs and wheel bearings*
     (vii) *water supply system.*

  (b) *When packing your caravan you should*

     (i)   *place heavy equipment in lower cupboards and lighter materials in overhead cupboards*

     (ii) *pack very heavy and bulky items on the floor at the front of the van*

     (iii) *use plastic containers with screwtop lids (but not for petrol).*

2 *During your trip, take note of the following points.*

  (a) *When parking the caravan for the night consider the slope of the ground, the prevailing winds, shade and privacy.*

  (b) *You can use a plastic rubbish bin as a makeshift washing machine. Half fill it with water, add detergent, put in clothes to be washed and put the lid on tightly. The movement of the water in the bin will do the work for you.*

Business letters 4

Attention line

It is common for business letters to be addressed to the holder of a senior position in an organisation (eg 'The General Manager' or 'The Secretary') but to be marked for the attention of a named person or the manager of a department or section.

An attention line is normally keyed in upper case with two blank lines above and below it.

Refresher

LL: 55 • SS • DS between drills

All alpha keys

1 Morgan's one objective was to explore the forward zones quickly and quietly and return the next day unobserved.

Symbols/figures

2 Flight 17 to Yass departs at 8:45 and arrives at 12:30.

Double letter drill

3 Sally Tripp's office needs glasses and cheese platters.

Aim for speed

4 The form must be signed by all ten members of the club.

Letterhead and envelope • LL: 60 • SS • returns as indicated

Job 4.8.1

1 Study the model and key from the draft.

2 Prepare an accompanying envelope and fold the letter correctly.

Ref DS/BB   R2

30 November 1992   R2

FOR THE ATTENTION OF MS J COMPTON   R2

The Chief Administrator
Life Assurance Society of Britain
PO Box 88
LONDON
W1Y 3TP

Dear Sir or Madam

In past years your society has been a major sponsor of our association; we hope we can look forward to your continued support in the coming year.

As you know, the association provides business studies teachers with a wide range of services, including provision of resource materials, advice on curriculum development and the setting up of conferences, seminars and workshops. Sponsors are able to promote their services through our association.

May I contact you next week to arrange an appointment to discuss what form of sponsorship your society may wish to take?

Yours faithfully   R5

David Spiros
President

> The salutation is 'Dear Sir or Madam' even though the letter is marked for the attention of Ms Compton. This style is correct because the letter is addressed to the Chief Administrator, who may be a man or a woman.

THE BRITISH BUSINESS TEACHERS ASSOCIATION

30 November 1992

The Chief Administrator
Life Assurance Society of Australia
GPO Box 86
SYDNEY   NSW   2001

ATTENTION MS J COMPTON

Dear Sir or Madam

In past years your society has been a major sponsor of our association; we hope we can look forward to your continued support in the coming year.

As you know, the association provides business studies teachers with a wide range of services, including provision of resource materials, advice on curriculum development and the setting up of conferences, seminars and workshops. Sponsors are able to promote their services through our association.

May I contact you next week to arrange an appointment to discuss what form of sponsorship your society may wish to take?

Yours faithfully

David Spiros
President

ds.yi

Job 5.5.2

Key this document, following the formatting guidelines for Job 5.5.1.

- Correct one spelling error and two errors of style.

On computer systems it has become acceptable to align figures in a list as follows:

```
9    Column manipulation
10   Arithmetical calculation
```

When keying a list of 10 or more items, insert one character space before numbers 1–9

↓

SOME FUNCTIONS OF A WORD PROCESSOR

1   Storage and retreival of documents   ← *Do not key a full stop in an enumerated list of words or phrases*

ing/
2. Print/copy/copies of documents

ing/
3   Edit/a document

4   Allowing document parameters to be ~~changed~~ *altered* stet
    (ie margins, pitch etc)

5   Rearranging blocks of text;

6   Removing text from one document and
    inserting it into another

7   Alphabetical and numerical sorting   *stet*

8   Merging documents

9   (Manipulation of columns)   *trs/ lc/ ℌ/ uc/ ℌ*

10 Arithmetical calculations

11 ~~Perform~~ global search and replacement
    (ie searching through a document and finding
less # (
    and replacing a word each time it occurs)

12 Assembling documents from standard
    paragraphs

13 Inserting variables into standard letters

14 Justifying text

15 Spelling check

17 ~~16~~ Creating headers and footers

18 ~~17~~ Merging with files   *trs*

16 ~~18~~ Automatic pagination

Job 4.8.2

1 Key this letter on pre-printed stationery if available.
 - Your line endings will be different from those in the copy.
 - Correct one misspelt word, one punctuation error and one error in capitalisation.
 - Remember to add today's date at the head.
2 Prepare an accompanying envelope and fold the letter correctly.

Letterhead and envelope • LL: 60 (10) 70 (12) • SS

The Principal
Greenbank High School
Stoneham Street
INVERNESS
IV3 6QX ⟵ ————— *ATTENTION DR ALAN FRANCIS*

Dear Sir or Madam

On behalf of the committee of the British Business Teachers Association; I express sincere thanks to the principle and staff of the school for ~~your~~ help *their*|
with the regional conference last week.

It was generous of you to allow us to hold the conference at the school once again. We are very grateful for the assistance of your staff in the administration of the conference and ~~for~~ the   *stet*
provision of equipment for our workshops.

Yours Faithfully

Betty Carnegie
Conference Organi~~z~~er *s*|

Job 4.8.3

1 Key this letter on pre-printed stationery if available.
 - Correct two misspelt words, one capitalisation error.
 - Remember to add today's date at the head and reference initials at the foot of the letter.
2 Prepare an accompanying envelope and fold the letter correctly.

Letterhead and envelope • LL: 60 (10) 70 (12) • SS

FOR THE ATTENTION OF MRS C MONETTI

The Public Relations Manager
The British Banking Corporation
Tasman House
114-118 Collins Street
LONDON   EC2A 2JY

Dear Sir or Madam

I seek your permission to include in a forthcoming
lc lc *Resource Kit for teachers extracts from too of your publications*

The passages concerned appear on pages 92-6 of ⁹/
Banking Today and pp116-18 of Managing You're Finances.
we would like to reprint this material without alter-ation in a kit which is to be made available to 500 schools free of charge. The source of the original publication will be printed in the acknowledgements page of the kit.

Yours faithfully

Adrian Long
Publications Officer

Numeric enumeration

For reference purposes it is sometimes necessary to enumerate (ie list by number) items in correspondence, reports, contracts or other text. An enumeration may consist of a word, a phrase, a sentence or a paragraph.

The most common method is to use arabic figures (numeric enumeration).

Refresher

LL: 55 • SS • DS between drills

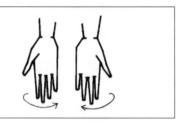

All alpha keys
1 Equally amazing scenes have taken place just where Fred and Rebecca are due to take their exams in middle June.

e/i
2 Greiner & Wein tie their eight-tier policies to cities.

Hyphen
3 ankle-deep in water; blue-green hair; well-kept secret;

Aim for speed
4 Please ask your employer to fill out the enclosed form.

Job 5.5.1

Study the model and key from the draft.

A4 portrait • LL: 50 • SS • centre vertically/horizontally

WP/electronic systems with indent key

LM   Indent key
↓   ↓
1   Keep disks clean
     ↑
   2 spaces

Systems with no indent key

T   LM
↓   ↓
1   Keep disks clean
     ↑
   2 spaces

CARE OF FLOPPY DISKS

1 Keep disks clean and free from dust or other foreign matter. Do not touch the exposed section of a disk with your fingers. Body oil can cause damage.

2 Keep disks away from any magnetic equipment as exposure to magnetism can clear all data from a disk.

3 Do not bend disks.

4 Do not place any object on disks.

5 Always label disks with a felt pen.

6 Be careful to insert disks into disk drives correctly.

7 Do not open the disk drive door while a disk is being used.

8 Do not remove a disk from the disk drive unless you are at the appropriate part of the program. This can cause damage to the master disk.

9 Always make a backup of any disk.

> Key a full stop at the end of a sentence in an enumerated list.

CARE OF FLOPPY DISKS   R3

1 *Keep disks clean and free from dust or other foreign matter. Do not touch the exposed section of a disk with your fingers. Body oil can cause damage.*   R2

2 *Keep disks away from any magnetic equipment as exposure to magnetism can clear all data from a disk.*

3 *Do not bend disks.*

4 *Do not place any object on disks.*

5 *Always label disks with a felt pen.*

6 *Be careful to insert disks into disk drives correctly.*

7 *Do not open the disk drive door while a disk is being used.*

8 *Do not remove a disk from the disk drive unless you are at the appropriate part of the program. This can cause damage to the master disk.*

9 *Always make a backup of any disk.*

Business letters 5

Confidential/personal notation

The words 'confidential' and 'strictly confidential' indicate that the correspondence concerns a matter sensitive to the organisation and should be opened only by the addressee.

The word 'personal' or 'private' indicates that the correspondence concerns an individual (eg relating to salary or administrative matters) and should be opened only by the addressee.

These notations are keyed in upper case, followed by a blank line.

Postscript

A postscript is a short note added to a letter. It may contain information that the writer forgot to include in the text of the letter, but it may also be used to emphasise an important matter.

Electronic typewriters and word processors have made it so easy to include 'afterthoughts' in the text of letters that postscripts have become less common.

A postscript starts a clear line below the reference initials or enclosure notation. It is identified by 'PS' or 'ps' (without punctuation). The author usually initials a postscript.

Refresher

LL: 55 • SS • DS between drills

All alpha keys

1 At the Byzantine exhibition gravy oozed sluggishly down Quincy's expensive lame jacket and made me feel queasy.

Symbols/figures

2 Order 214 m red ribbon @ 99p less 5% discount tomorrow.

Double letter drill

3 All schools will attempt to withhold offers from staff.

Aim for speed

4 Pay this bill before any of the others you are holding.

Job 4.9.1

Study the model and key from the draft.

Letterhead and envelope • LL: 60 • SS

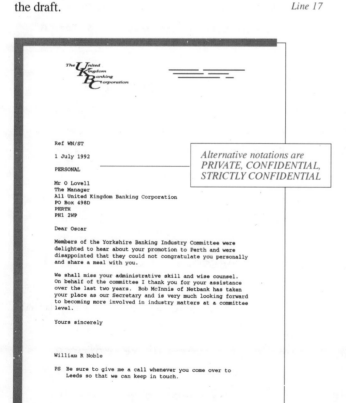

Line 17   *Ref WN/ST*   R4

1 July 1992   R2

PERSONAL   R2

Mr O Lovell
The Manager
All United Kingdom Banking Corporation
PO Box 498D
PERTH
PH1 2WP

Dear Oscar

Members of the Yorkshire Banking Industry Committee were delighted to hear about your promotion to Perth and were disappointed that they could not congratulate you personally and share a meal with you.

We shall miss your administrative skill and wise counsel. On behalf of the committee I thank you for your assistance over the last two years. Bob McInnis of Netbank has taken your place as our Secretary and is very much looking forward to becoming more involved in industry matters at a committee level.

Yours sincerely

William R Noble   R2

PS   Be sure to give me a call whenever you come down to Leeds so that we can keep in touch.

> Alternative notations are
> PRIVATE, CONFIDENTIAL,
> STRICTLY CONFIDENTIAL

Job 5.4.2

Key this document, following the formatting guidelines for Job 5.4.1.

- Correct one spelling error and two errors of style.

D/S KNOW YOUR SPIDER

SYDNEY FUNNELL WEB	15 - 30 millimetres long. Black to very dark brown. Constructs burrow in moist soil under houses, in rockeries, compost heaps etc. Extremely venomous.
BROWN TRAP-DOOR	20-35 mm long. (Dk) brown. Head section patterned with light honey colour. Painful bite; not fatal.
RED BACK	10 mm long. Jet black to dark brown. Top of abdomen usually, but not always, features a red flash. Bite can be fatal.
HUNTSMAN	30-45 mm long. Light grey to all shades of brown. Flat body, very long legs. Painful bite; not fatal.
WHITE-TAILED	15 - 20 mm About 2 cm long. Grey-brown with a u/ conspicuous white mark on tip of long, oval abdomen. Bite can cause permanent tissue damage.

Job 5.4.3

Key this document.

- Correct two spelling errors, one punctuation error and one error of style.

ACTIVE LISTENING   centre & u/score

Listening is a necessary part of the communication process. However well a speaker may communicate a message, there is no communication unless it is taken in by the listener.

ACTIVE LISTENING	Listening is an active skill requiring effort on the part of the person who is receiving the message. It should not be confused with hearing, which is merely a passive physical sensation. (stet)
MENTAL ATITUDE	To be a good listener you must adopt the proper mental attitude. Be attentive to the speaker. Make a positive effort to comprehend the message. Do not switch off.
PARAPHRASE	Mentally summarise the speakers key points. To do this you will need to think about what is being said. This will re-enforce the message in your mind.
CLARIFY:	If the message (isn't) clear to you, ask the speaker to clarify it.

If necessary, review the rules for the use of the apostrophe.

Job 4.9.2

Key this letter, correcting one misspelt word and one punctuation error.

- Remember to add today's date and reference initials.

Job 4.9.3

Key this letter, correcting one spelling error and two errors of style.

Letterhead and envelope • LL: 60 (10) 70 (12) • SS

STRICTLY CONFIDENTIAL

Ms J Nicholls
Managing Director
Lefkas Party Hire
98 Redwood Grove
BRISTOL   BS9 4DG

Dear Ms Nicholls   *LOAN NO 184/94*

I am bound to raise again the matter of your failure to repay the short/term loan of £180.00 which has now been outstanding for more than three month's.

several/ You have made ~~three or four~~ firm promises to settle the debt, yet the entire principal and interest remains outstanding. I have on at least two occassions offered to advise you on how best to overcome your present difficulties, but you have declined my help.

Unless the sum is paid in full within (7) days of this date legal proceedings to recover the debt will begin.

Yours sincerely

Owen Rees
Branch Manager

Letterhead and envelope • LL: 60 (10) 70 (12) • SS

Confidential *caps*

stet Mrs R G Turnbull
Personnel Manager
Sterling Stores Co. Ltd
PO BOX G333
YORK YO1 1BL

Dear M/s Turnbull

I have received your enquiry about Ms Margot Gerritsen. She did work with this company as an accounts clerk from Sept 1988 to December '90 when she resigned to travel around Australia. She worked in my department for the final eight months.

She is a very hard worker, with an eye for detail and an excellent sense of humour. We were sorry to see her go; however, I can certainly recommend Ms Gerritsen for the position you mentioned.

Yours ~~faithfully~~ sincerely/

Phillip Konrado
Credit Manager

Marginal headings at left

Marginal headings are usually placed in the left margin. The first line of the paragraph is on the same line as the heading (or the first line of the heading if it occupies more than one line).

WP/electronic systems

1 Space forward from the left margin once for every keystroke in the longest line in the headings plus at least three spaces.

2 Set a temporary left margin at this point, as described on page 100.
3 Use the margin release to key the first heading at the left margin.
The procedure may differ if the heading occupies more than one line; consult your operator's manual.

Typewriters with no automatic function for temporary margins

1 Set a tab at the point at which the headings are to begin.
2 Space forward once for every keystroke in the longest line in the headings plus at least three spaces.
3 Set the left margin and a tab stop at this point.

4 Use the margin release key to return to the extreme left.
5 Tab to the point at which the heading is to start and key the first heading (or the first line of the heading if it occupies more than one line).
6 Tab to the left margin and key the first line of text.
7 If there is a second line in the heading, use the margin release key with the return key and then tab to the starting point for the second line of the heading.
8 If the heading occupies only one line, press return to reach the starting point for the second line of text.

Refresher

LL: 55 • SS • DS between drills

All alpha keys

1 To qualify for a job in Zambia you will need experience in teaching vocational skills in a college of the arts.

r/t

2 Trabert's trucks started this trivial transport strike.

Symbols/figures

3 The speed limit is 70 mph (60 mph in some other towns).

Aim for speed

4 I am sure he will want to come in to inspect our range.

Job 5.4.1

Study the model and key from the draft.

A4 portrait • LL: 60 • SS • centre vertically/horizontally

WP/electronic systems

LM   3 spaces   Temp LM
↓   ↓ ↓

CONVEYANCE   The transfer

REAL ESTATE TERMS

AGENT   A person authorised to act on behalf of another in the sale, purchase, letting or management of property.

CAVEAT   A warning to intending buyers that a third person (the person who lodged the caveat) has some right or interest in the property.

CHATTELS   Property other than real estate. Movable possessions which may be included in a sale; eg carpets, blinds.

CONVEYANCE   The transfer of ownership of property from the vendor's name to the buyer's name.

DEED   A document recording an agreement, obligation or conveyance of property as required by law.

EASEMENT   The right that someone is given to use land belonging to another. It is not a transfer of the land and is usually for right of way, access, flow of water, etc.

Typewriters

T   3 spaces   LM and T
↓   ↓ ↓

CONVEYANCE   The transfer

ESTATE AGENT TERMS   *R3*

AGENT — A person authorised to act on behalf of another in the sale, purchase, letting or management of property. *R2*

CAVEAT — A warning to intending buyers that a third person (the person who lodged the caveat) has some right or interest in the property.

CHATTELS — Property other than real estate. Movable possessions which may be included in a sale; eg carpets, blinds.

CONVEYANCE — The transfer of ownership of property from the vendor's name to the buyer's name.

DEED — A document recording an agreement, obligation or conveyance of property as required by law.

EASEMENT — The right that someone is given to use land belonging to another. It is not a transfer of the land and is usually for right of way, access, flow of water, etc.

Business letters 6

Enclosure notation

The text of a letter usually mentions any enclosures or attachments. In addition they are indicated by the notation 'enc' or 'encs' at the foot of the letter.

When there is more than one enclosure or attachment, the number may be stated, eg 'enc 3'. An enclosure may be named, eg 'enc deed', especially if it is small or valuable.

Enclosures should be listed in the same order as they are referred to in the text of the letter.

Note the number and size of enclosures before preparing the envelope.

Refresher

LL: 55 • SS • DS between drills

All alpha keys
1 Hecate's growly bark just froze Petula Xavier where she stood, but Zilla Monks calmed her with her quiet voice.

Symbols/figures
2 Nunn & Pope Ltd's order no H6/92 is valued at £870 954.

Double letter drills
3 Abbie too will struggle to apply better written skills.

Aim for speed
4 Have they moved their head office west of the city yet?

Job 4.10.1

Study the model and key from the draft.

Letterhead, envelope and label • LL: 60 • SS

Line 19 **10 July 1992**

```
10 July 1992

Mrs D McWilliam
44 Henshaw Road
MORDEN    SM4 65F

Dear Mrs McWilliam

Enclosed are full details of the net asset position of your
nursery at 30 June, the date the nursery was sold on your
behalf.  Supporting papers to enable you to verify these
calculations are being posted to you separately.

We propose to hold our signing authority on your bank
account for another ninety (90) days to ensure all invoices
are received.

At the end of this period we expect to send you a letter for
your bank stating that we have no further interest in your
account.

Yours sincerely


Simon Spenser

enc net asset statement
```

Mrs D McWilliam
44 Henshaw Road
MORDEN   SM4 6FP

Dear Mrs McWilliam

Enclosed are full details of the net asset position of your nursery at 30 June, the date the nursery was sold on your behalf. Supporting papers to enable you to verify these calculations are being posted to you separately.

We propose to hold our signing authority on your bank account for another ninety (90) days to ensure all invoices are received.

At the end of this period we expect to send you a letter for your bank stating that we have no further interest in your account.

Yours sincerely

Simon Spenser

enc net asset statement

Job 5.3.2

Key this document, following the formatting guidelines for Job 5.3.1.

- Correct two spelling errors, one punctuation error and one error of style.

A5 landscape • LL: 60 • SS • centre vertically/horizontally

QUITTING SMOKING

THE BENEFITS   *No extra space*

3 WITHIN TWO HOURS nicotine will have left your blood-stream, although bye-products may remain in the system for about 2 days.

WITHIN 24 HOURS carbon monoxide will be excreted from your body. Your lungs will work more efficently.

⊙ NP WITHIN THREE WEEKS you will be able to excercise with less discomfort; within three months the cleaning *caps* mechanism in your lungs will operate normally.

AFTER FIVE YEARS the risk of sudden death from heart attack will be almost the same as that of non-smoker's.

Job 5.3.3

Key this document.

- Correct three spelling errors and one punctuation error.

> If necessary, review the rules for the use of the question mark (page 55).

A4 portrait • LL: 55 • SS • centre vertically/horizontally

EFFECTIVE WRITING

The ability to write effectively is a vital office skill. What are the elements of effective writing.

Clarity / To write clearly you must first know what you want to communicate, why you want to communicate it and who the recipient is. You must then present your message in a logical form. Correct grammar, spelling and punctuation will help to make your message clear.

Conciseness ~~Give~~ *State* your message breifly in simple language. Avoid long words and (stilted) *stilted* sentences.

Accuracy Ensure that all the information you give is accurate. Attention to detail will save both you and the recipiant time and (trouble) *trouble* and will reflect well on the organisation for which you work.

Completeness Supply all the relevent information that the recipient will need to understand the message fully.

Courtesy However tempted you ~~may~~ *might* be, there is no place for discourtesy in a business letter.

Job 4.10.2

Key this letter, correcting three misspelt words.

- Remember to add today's date and reference initials.
- A Deposit Release Authority is to be enclosed with the letter.

Letterhead, envelope and label • LL: 60 (10) 70 (12) • SS

Sir James Vienet
85 Loret Street
HOUNSLOW   TW4 5QD

Dear Sir James

PURCHASE OF 7/15 EAST TERRACE, CROYDON

trs We have received the enclosed section 27 Deposit Release Authority. Would you please sign the document alongside the pencilled crosses and return *l/* it to me at once to enable the vendor to obtain release of her deposit money prior to settlement.

I am sending you seperately the Instrument of Transfer for execution by you as indicated. [As   *NP* soon as you recieve it you should sign the document in the presence of an independant witness and return it to me.

Yours sincerely

Margaret Farrow

Job 4.10.3

Key this letter, correcting three misspelt words and one punctuation error.

Letterhead and envelope • LL: 60 (10) 70 (12) • SS

MS Golzen
900 Symons Lane
LONDON NW4 1WA

Dear Ms Golzen

trs For the purposes of insurance your liability, for any property you may wish to purchase arises from the date of the contract or from the date of satisfaction of any prior condition in the contract. It is adviseable to discuss your insurance needs with your bank or building society before making any arrangement.

In response to your request, I enclose a leaflet with info on strata tiles.

Yours sincerly

Edward Kruse
enc

Side headings Paragraph headings

Side (shoulder) headings

Side headings rank after the main heading in importance.

Paragraph headings

Paragraph headings rank after side headings in importance.

- Leave two spaces after the heading.
- It is unnecessary to key a full stop.
- If the paragraph heading forms part of the first sentence in the para-graph, leave one space only (as in Job 5.3.2).

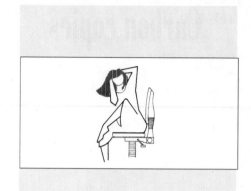

Refresher

LL: 55 • SS • DS between drills

All alpha keys
1 Hazardous liquid and explosive devices must not be kept within the buildings for the months of July and August.

w/e
2 We went to Lew's wedding in West Pewsey in wet weather.

Symbols/figures
3 Order 3 L Superseal @ £18.60 to cover 28 square metres.

Aim for speed
4 You may take the test here or at our centre in Bristol.

Job 5.3.1

Study the model and key from the draft.

A5 landscape • LL: 60 • SS • centre vertically/horizontally

Main heading

Bold or underscore

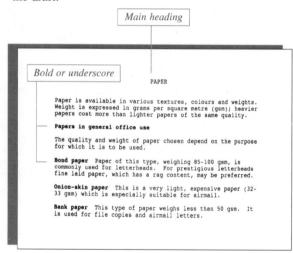

PAPER   R3

Paper is available in various textures, colours and weights. Weight is expressed in grams per square metre (gsm); heavier papers cost more than lighter papers of the same quality.   R2

Papers in general office use   R2

The quality and weight of paper chosen depend on the purpose for which it is to be used.   R2

Space twice

Bond paper *Paper of this type, weighing 85–100 gsm, is commonly used for letterheads. For prestigious letterheads fine laid paper, which has a rag content, may be preferred.*

Onion-skin paper *This is a very light, expensive paper (32–33 gsm) which is especially suitable for airmail.*

Bank paper *This type of paper weighs less than 50 gsm. It is used for file copies and airmail letters.*

Carbon copies

Carbon paper is used to make copies of business documents on typewriters, but it is less widely used nowadays because it is possible to make photo-copies cheaply or to print out copies at high speed on computer printers.

Carbon copies are possible only if the printer used is one that makes an impression. Laser and ink jet printers do not do this.

A carbon pack consists of a top sheet (original) and as many sheets of carbon paper and copy paper as the number of copies required. Read the text of Job 4.11.1 below to find out how to assemble a carbon pack.

Because of the extra thickness of a carbon pack, you will need to adjust your equipment to make a heavier impression. Use your operator's man-ual to find the impression control and adjust it appropriately.

No carbon required (NCR) paper

NCR paper is paper that has been treated on the back so that the impression of a pen or a typewriter print element will mark the paper under it. It can also be supplied with tractor feed for computers. This paper is mainly used for forms such as invoices and courier dockets which require a number of duplicates, but can also be used for correspondence. Again, it is not suitable for use with non-impression printers.

Refresher

Job 4.11.1

1 Carefully read the instructions in this passage for assembling and inserting a carbon pack.
2 Key the passage, following the instructions.
   - If your system allows, use two plain sheets plus one carbon sheet.
   - Centre the heading.
   - Correct one punctuation and three spelling errors.

LL: 55 • SS • DS between drills

All alpha keys
1 Since Jemima is privy to these complex tax laws and not dazzled by slick jargon she is quick to discover fraud.

Symbols/figures
2 On 28 July the price fell 13p to £4.75, a 2.7% decline.

Double letter drill
3 Maggie's foolish, muddled errors happen to annoy staff.

Aim for speed
4 Her aim was to pass the test at her very first attempt.

Plain A4 portrait • LL: 60 (10) 70 (12) • SS • DS between paragraphs

ASSEMBLING AND INSERTING CARBON PACKS

Make sure you have carbon paper of the same size as the paper (original and copy or copys you are using. *ie/*

On the desk in front of you place the sheet of paper on which you wish to make a copy.

Place a single sheet of carbon paper, with the carbon side down, on top of the copy sheet. If more than one copy is needed repeat the process as many times as necessary.

Place the top sheet (the original) face up on top of the carbon paper.

Holding the pack losely, tap it on the desk to aline the paper and carbon paper.

Holding the pack with one hand, use the other hand to turn the platen knob to fed it into the typewriter.

A simple way to keep the pack straight as you feed it into the typewriter is to place the top edge in a folded sheet of paper. Remove the folded paper when the pack is securely in the machine.

Then, taking a firm grip on the pack, insert it into the typewriter.

Job 5.2.2

Key this document, following the formatting guidelines for Job 5.2.1.

- Correct three spelling errors.

> If necessary, consult your dictionary.

A5 landscape • LL: 60 • SS • centre vertically/horizontally

THE MODERN BALLOON

The modern balloon is a simple machine made from a series of rip-stop nylon panels ~~that~~ are joined *which*/ together to make the envelope that traps the hot air. A wicker basket is attached with fire-resistent load wires to carry the passangers and *e*/ the balloon.

The size of most balloons varies between 13.5 and 17.5 metres in diameter with a capacity of 849 to 5660 cubic metres. When inflated/the balloons stretch to a heighth of 27.4 meters. They cost up to o12 000, including ancilliary equipment.

Job 5.2.3

Key this document, setting the tab two spaces to the right of the left margin.

- Correct two punctuation errors and one error of style.

> If necessary, review the rules for the use of commas (page 57).

A5 landscape • LL: 65 • SS • centre vertically/horizontally

HOW IT'S DONE

It takes three people about 30 minutes, to inflate a hot air balloon. Under normal conditions up to 8 people can be carried in the wicker basket.

When the balloon takes off it flies in an air stream, at one with the wind. The pilot manoeuvres the balloon through different altitudes to achieve the direction of flight required. Ballooning takes place between 152.5 and 1/525 metres above ground level and usually a number of different wind directions can be found between these altitudes to give the pilot a reasonable range of directions, the flight is slow and graceful.

Business letters 7

Hard copies

In most offices a hard copy of all outward correspondence is filed. The file copy may be a photocopy, a carbon copy or a copy printed at high speed on a computer printer. (See page 96 for instructions on how to prepare carbon copies.) The use of carbon paper to make copies has become less common in offices, as it cannot be used with laser or ink jet printers.

Electronic filing systems

Copies may be filed electronically instead of, or in addition to, making and filing a hard copy.

Disclosed copy notation

The author of a letter may wish to send a copy to another person. A copy notation – 'c' (copy), 'pc' (photocopy) or 'cc' (carbon copy) – is keyed at the foot of the letter. The simple notation 'c' is recommended.

Copies may be sent to more than one person.

Blind copy notation

A blind copy notation ('bc', or 'bcc') is used when the author does not wish to disclose to the addressee that a copy has been sent to another person. This notation appears on the file copy (as a record of who has received copies) but

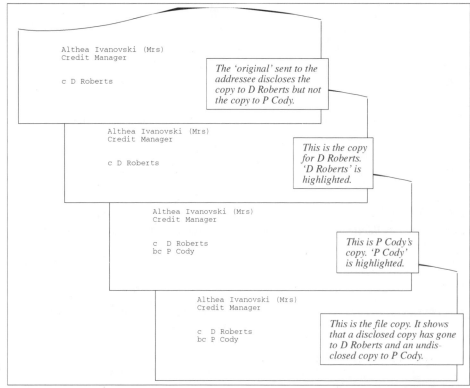

Copy and blind copy notations

not on the original or 'top copy' of the letter that the addressee receives.

A blind copy notation may, if the author prefers, appear on copies sent to persons other than the addressee.

A single letter may have both disclosed copy and blind copy notations.

If carbon paper is used before keying the notation remove the original and any other copies on which the blind copy notation is not to appear.

Highlighting/ticking copy notations

After a letter has been signed it is common practice to tick the notation

with a pencil or mark it with a highlighter pen on the copy that is sent to that person.

Envelopes for copies of letters

It is necessary to prepare an envelope for a copy
- which is addressed to a person outside the organisation
- which is marked 'PERSONAL' or 'CONFIDENTIAL'.

A 'with compliments' slip should be attached to the copy when it is being sent to someone outside the organisation.

Refresher

LL: 55 • SS • DS between drills

All alpha keys

1 Private Suzuki waxed lyrical about Janet's rough draft, which she had executed mainly with a quill pen and ink.

Symbols/figures

2 Carnegie* (a convert to the system!) devised Plan 3/89.

Double letter drill

3 Lennie will offer floods of support to fellow furriers.

Aim for speed

4 These are skills which should stand them in good stead.

Hanging paragraphs

In a hanging paragraph, the second and subsequent lines begin two to five spaces to the right of the first character in the first line. Hanging paragraphs are usually single spaced.

WP/electronic systems

Set a temporary left margin as described on page 100 for the second line of the paragraph.

Typewriters with no automatic function for temporary margins

1 Set the left margin for the second and subsequent lines in each paragraph.
2 Set a tab stop the required number of spaces to the left of the left margin.
3 As you return at the end of the last line in each paragraph, press the margin release key and the return key together.
4 Tab to the start of the extended line.

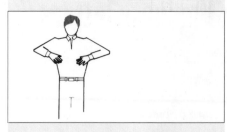

Refresher

All alpha keys
1 Josephine quickly sized up the very first task given to her on her college work experience program, then began.

e/r
2 Her career entered a rather fresh era here in Research.

Symbols/figures
3 The site lies 26 km north of Perth and covers 13 acres.

Aim for speed
4 I have passed your query to our customer service staff.

Job 5.2.1

Study the model and key from the draft on the right.

A5 landscape • LL: 60 • SS • centre vertically/horizontally

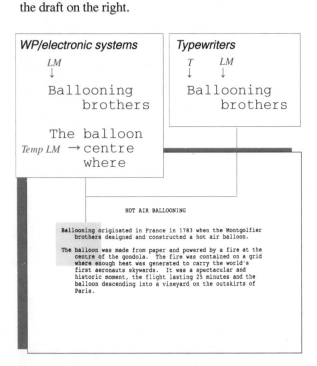

HOT AIR BALLOONING   R3

Ballooning originated in France in 1783 when the Montgolfier brothers designed and constructed a hot air balloon.

The balloon was made from paper and powered by a fire at the centre of the gondola. The fire was contained on a grid where enough heat was generated to carry the world's first aeronauts skywards. It was a spectacular and historic moment, the flight lasting 25 minutes and the balloon descending into a vineyard on the outskirts of Paris.

Job 4.12.1

1 Study the model below and key from the draft. You will also need to consult the model on page 97.
2 Prepare a disclosed copy for D Roberts, an undisclosed copy for P Cody, both employees of Premier Printing, and a hard copy for the file.

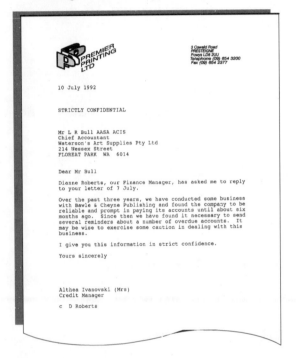

Letterhead and envelope • LL: 60 • SS

Line 18 *10 July 1992*

STRICTLY CONFIDENTIAL

Mr L R Bull ACA
Chief Accountant
Waterson's Art Supplies Ltd
214 Wessex Street
EDINBURGH   EH4 5YX

Dear Mr Bull

Dianne Roberts, our Finance Manager, has asked me to reply to your letter of 7 July.

Over the past three years, we have conducted some business with Bawle & Cheyne Publishing and found the company to be reliable and prompt in paying its accounts until about six months ago. Since then we have found it necessary to send several reminders about a number of overdue accounts. It may be wise to exercise some caution in dealing with this business.

I give you this information in strict confidence.

Yours sincerely

Althea Ivanovski (Mrs)
Credit Manager
⌐——— *Space twice*
c *D Roberts*
bc *P Cody* ← *Undisclosed and file copies only*

Job 4.12.2

1 Key this letter, correcting two misspelt words, one spacing error and one punctuation error.
2 Prepare a disclosed copy for Dan Speed, an employee of Premier Printing.

Letterhead and envelope • LL: 55 (10) 65 (12) • SS

Ms P Wheatley
Principal
Western College of Printing
48 Caroline Drive
TORQUAY   TQ1 2UW

Dear Penny,

I except ~~the~~ invite [action] to speak to your students about future directions in the industry. [your]

It will be a general talk because I realise I'll be adressing a varied group who will in the next couple of years be seeking employment over the whole ~~wide~~ spectrum of the industry. But if you want me to talk to any particular section of your students do let me know. [¶ cap]

I look forward to seeing you at the college at 3pm next Friday.

Yours sincerely

Michael Giang
Managing Director

c Dan Speed

Job 5.1.2

Key this document, following the formatting guidelines for Job 5.1.1.

- If your system has no temporary left margin function, set a tab stop for the block indented paragraph.
- Correct two spelling errors and one punctuation error.

A5 landscape • LL: 60 • SS • centre vertically/horizontally

D/S SEX DISCRIMINATION

The purpose of Britain's Sex Discrimination Act is to make sure that, in areas such as employment, consumer affairs, education and recreation, people are treated equally. The Human Rights Comission defines sex discrimination as follows/

Discrimination means giving preference to one person over another simply because of that person's sex or marital status. It can also occur where a woman is treated unfairly just because she is pregnant.

Many people who discriminate against other's are unaware that they are being unfair. This is because they ## have stereotyped images of catagories of people.

Job 5.1.3

Key this document.

- Correct two punctuation errors.

A4 portrait • LL: 60 • SS • centre vertically/horizontally

EXPLORING THE AMAZON   centre

In 1983 Jacques-Yves Cousteau and a team of divers, scientists and photographers completed an exploration of the worlds' mightiest river system, the Amazon. He noted in his journal:

A turbid brown 'sea' of silt-laden river extends to the horizon, mingling by graduations with the blue Atlantic. We are at least a six-hour sail from Cabo Norte, the nearest lip of the Brazilian coast. so immense is the outpouring of this great river that its effects can be detected 300 kilometres from the coast.

The Amazon is 6500 km long and is also the widest river in the world. It contains nearly one-fifth of all the fresh water in the world. Large ocean-going ship's can sail 3700 kilometres upstream to the port of Iquitos, Iquitos/ Peru.

Job 4.12.3

1 Key this letter, correcting two misspelt words, one capitalisation error and one punctuation error.
2 Prepare an undisclosed copy for Jill Rogers.

Mr Phillip Mace
23 Wellings Street,
CREWE CW1 4GZ

Dear Phillip

Thank you for your letter seeking employment with the company.

I was very impressed by your CV Your achievements at college and during your relatively brief career to date are outstanding and I would like you to call and see our Personell Manager, Jill Rogers.

The company is expanding and we are constantly on the lookout for young people with drive, enthusiasm and technical qualifications. Unfortunately, Ms Rogers is on holiday, but I am sure she would like to interview you. Please phone her at this office early next month to make an appointment.

Do pass on my best wishes to your Grandfather. We were not only colleagues at work for many years, but good friends. I have happy memories of our times together.

Yours sincerely

Howard Foot
General Manager

bc Jill Rogers

Module 5 Formatting 2 Paragraph and headings

Performance goals

At the end of Module 5 you should be able to
- key block indented and hanging paragraphs
- use side headings and marginal headings
- enumerate and sub-enumerate items in lists using arabic, roman and decimal styles.

Block indented paragraphs

Block indented paragraphs may be used to distinguish quoted matter that would occupy three or more lines of normal text. Block indented paragraphs may also be used to emphasise text of particular significance within a document.

Block indented paragraphs are usually indented on the left only, but may also be indented an equal number of spaces from the right margin.

The first line of a block indented paragraph is not indented, even if the document as a whole has indented paragraphs.

WP/electronic systems

Temporary left margin
On most WP systems and some electronic typewriters you can set a temporary left margin which indents consecutive lines of text or a paragraph.
1 Set left and right margins in the usual way.
2 Use the specified function keys to create a temporary left margin. At the end of each indented line the cursor or carrier will return automatically to the indented position.
3 Cancel the indent function by pressing return at the end of the paragraph.

Temporary left and right margins
On some systems you can set temporary left and right margins

simultaneously. The indentions from the left and right margins are an equal number of spaces.

Typewriters with no automatic function for temporary margins

If the block indented paragraph will occupy no more than five lines:
Set a tab stop the required number of spaces to the right of the left margin.

If the block indented paragraph will occupy more than five lines:
1 Reset the left margin at the indention point.
2 Set a tab stop at the old left margin.
3 Reset the margin at the tab point when you have keyed the block indented paragraph.

Job 5.1.1
Study the model and key from the draft on the right.

A5 landscape • LL: 60 • SS • centre vertically/horizontally

```
                TEMPORARY MARGINS

The temporary left margin function on a word processing
system saves time for the operator.  The steps vary between
different systems but, broadly, this is how it works.

    Instead of having to use the tab key at the start of
    each line, you press the function key or keys only at
    the start of the first line to be indented.  You now
    have a temporary left margin.  As you reach the end of
    each line the text will wrap around to the temporary
    left margin.  Pressing RETURN cancels the indent.

Some systems also have a temporary margin function which
sets equal left and right margins simultaneously.
```

The temporary left margin function on a word processing system saves time for the operator. The steps vary between different systems but, broadly, this is how it works. [R3]

Instead of having to use the tab key at the start of each line, you press the function key or keys only at the start of the first line to be indented. You now have a temporary left margin. As you reach the end of each line the text will wrap around to the temporary left margin. Pressing RETURN cancels the indent. [R2]
Set temporary LM or T stop 5 spaces in

Some systems also have a temporary margin function which sets equal left and right margins simultaneously. [R2]